Aligning Incentives, Information, and Choice

How to Optimize Health and Human Capital Performance

Wendy D. Lynch, PhD and Harold H. Gardner, MD

Health as Human Capital Foundation
Cheyenne, Wyoming
www.hhcfoundation.org

Wendy D. Lynch is Research Director of the Health as Human Capital Foundation (HHCF) and Vice President of Strategic Development at Human Capital Management Services, Inc. (HCMS). Harold H. Gardner is the founder, owner, and president of Human Capital Management Services, Inc.; Chairman of the Health as Human Capital Foundation; and the organizing partner of Clinical Prevention Information Services, LLC.

Printed in the United States of America
Published by the Health as Human Capital Foundation

13 12 11 10 09   2 3 4 5

ISBN: 978-0-9800702-0-0

Lynch, Wendy D.
Aligning incentives, information and choice : how to
optimize health and human capital performance / Wendy D.
Lynch and Harold H. Gardner.
p. cm.
Includes bibliographical references and index.
ISBN-13: 978-0-9800702-0-0
ISBN-10: 0-9800702-0-1

1. Medical economics--United States. 2. Personnel
management--United States. 3. Human capital--United
States. 4. Medical care, Cost of--United States.
I. Gardner, Harold H. II. Title.

RA410.53.L96 2008   338.4'73621'0973
                           QBI07-600337

Library of Congress Control Number: 2008920910

Health as Human Capital Foundation
1800 Carey Avenue, Suite 300
Cheyenne, WY 82001
Phone: 307.433.9619
www.hhcfoundation.org

This book is printed on acid-free paper.

Contents

CONTENTS

Illustrations

ILLUSTRATIONS

TABLES

Foreword

Incentives and Behavior

Incentives, information, and choice. Combined alignment of these three concepts form the backbone of this book.

The concept of alignment, or "lining up," has multiple implications: aligning incentives toward a well-defined common goal (toward a specific destination); aligning incentives among stakeholders in a system (encouraging parallel movement); and aligning incentives with information and choice (so people are equipped to succeed). When incentives are aligned in this way and when people have both sufficient information on which to make informed choices and freedom to choose, social systems work better. Businesses are more successful, workers achieve more, and healthcare will be more affordable and more effective if incentives are aligned among the parties involved, and toward the desired health outcome.

Since these concepts are so critical, it would seem to be important to define them and how they affect human decisions. To do this we will refer to other sources that we have found helpful. The dictionary defines incentive as:

> *"1) inciting; stimulative. 2) That which incites, or tends to incite to determination or action; motive; spur."*[1] At the core of this definition is the transitive verb "incite" defined to *"arouse to action; spur or urge on."*[2]

In short, ***an incentive is what motivates, drives, and sometimes justifies human decisions.***

Incentives are not always defined and measured in the currency of money. Tyler Cowen, an economist, explains: "Quite simply, an incentive is anything that motivates human behavior, or encourages an individual to make one decision rather than another. An incentive can be money, but it can also be a tip, a smile, or an act of praise."[3]

Hence, the incentives relevant to a given choice are rarely simple or one-dimensional. Rather, most choices are likely to be affected by multiple incentives which themselves might be complex in character. Hence,

Cowen concludes, "the fundamental economic insight, oddly enough, is that not everything can be bought with money."[4]

Incentives affect the process of making choices—but they will affect some individuals differently than others, based on the unique set of perceptions held by each individual. "Incentives matter through the medium of how a person perceives what is at stake in the choice. It is not just getting the mix of incentives right, you also have to know something of the values or cultures of the people you are dealing with."[5] In short, people's ordering of preferences is always nested in and primarily determined by the mores and values of the culture of which they are a part.

In a market system, however, monetary incentives will almost always influence choice. When there is a direct transaction between a buyer and a seller in markets, monetary incentives are important and perhaps decisive motivators in choosing one thing over another.

Allowing choice is crucial to efficient markets. Individuals must be free to choose what they really prefer if their utility is to be maximized in the choices they make. Cowen also observes, "The real purpose of economics is to get more of the good stuff in life. . . . It is a profoundly important fact that you can't understand how incentives work if you don't understand the importance of a respect for human liberty."[6] If someone else does the choosing, there is no mechanism for individual preferences to be registered in the choice process and, therefore, there is no hope that people can get what they most want. Likewise, if someone else pays the bill, it is impossible for individual consumers to reckon the true costs to them of alternative choices and their decisions will not reflect their true preferences. Hence, if people are free to choose among alternatives available to them, and each alternative can be evaluated with respect to what it is worth and what it costs, then we can be confident that choices made will maximize the net benefits to the chooser.

This all implies that certain information is available for efficient decision making. Sufficient and reliable information about alternative choices allows decision makers to assess their relative costs and how different decisions can be translated into well-being. "Small improvements in understanding can bring a much better use of incentives, leading to much better decisions and much better lives."[7] Some of the information relevant to any choice, however, is objective and knowable to an outside observer, such as product or service quality and price (cost). But other relevant knowledge is purely subjective and unknowable to anyone but the decision makers themselves, such as what a given product or service is worth to them. Given the opportunity to make market choices, however, people will demonstrate the value of a product based on what they are willing to pay. Hence, in a competitive market where consumers are unhindered in their consumption and choices, the value of the product to consumers will be approximately revealed by the market price.

Employers and healthcare policy makers can make use of incentives in attempting to reach desirable goals. "If you (an employer, for example) want to control more of what happens around you, you need to know how to balance the kinds of incentives you offer. . . . It is obvious that economies without good monetary rewards perform poorly."[8]

So, if incentives are numerous and complex when do financial incentives work and when do they not? In essence, financial incentives influence the likelihood that an individual will engage in an activity that they might not otherwise feel inclined to do. The activity could be a job task, or an effort in choosing a healthcare provider. To have influence, the size of a financial incentive must be sufficient to have importance to the individual; the more money involved, the greater the impact of the incentive.

The philosophical approach used in this book emphasizes the power of individual choice in an environment of varying incentives and information. This approach assumes that individuals make their own choices, and that individuals are assumed to choose that option which they anticipate will enhance their own interests the most.

In more economic terms, this paradigm is known as methodological individualism. This paradigm establishes the formal problem "as the familiar one of maximizing the utility function (of an individual) subject to the constraints imposed by the opportunity set" of choices available.... *Each decision maker is assumed to be motivated by self-interest and to move efficiently toward the most preferred operating position open."*[9]

The proposition that people act in their own best interest may be impossible to prove one way or another. But what rational person could be expected to act otherwise? It goes without saying that the considerations a person uses to make choices will go beyond pure dollars and cents. And self-interest is not the same thing as selfishness. Any individual may have strong altruistic beliefs that imply that making others happy is a strong element in one's own happiness. And none of this qualifying discussion negates the point that, all other things being equal, an enhancement in the tangible economic wealth of an individual will always be preferred to an option that results in less wealth.

Incentives, information, and choice are three concepts that, when combined and well-aligned, help us find opportunity for solutions to some of our most perplexing and difficult challenges in human capital management and healthcare access, cost, and quality.

B. Delworth Gardner
Professor Emeritus
Department of Economics,
Brigham Young University

Harold H. Gardner, MD
Chairman
HCMS, Inc.

Fall 2007

References

1 *Webster's New Collegiate Dictionary.* Springfield, Mass.: G. & C. Merriam Co., 1961, 420.

2 *Webster's*, 420.

3 Cowen, T. *Discover Your Inner Economist.* New York: Dutton, 2007, 2.

4 Cowen, 3.

5 Cowen, 18.

6 Cowen, 4.

7 Cowen, 10.

8 Cowen, 11.

9 Furubotn, E.G. Pejovich, S. *The Economics of Property Rights.* Cambridge, Mass: Ballenger Pub. Co., 1974, 2-3.

Preface

This book is a selection of blog entries posted from 2005 to 2007 that were researched and written by the Health as Human Capital Foundation, a non-profit research and education organization affiliated with Human Capital Management Services, Inc. The intent of the blog is to establish health as a key component of human capital by providing objective, empirical information about the economics of inefficient use of health resources, and by proposing market solutions to healthcare access, cost, and quality problems.

Unless otherwise noted, the data analyzed for these blogs came from the foundation's access to a database of over 600,000 employees, based on records from numerous employers around the country. Using the database, we have been able to isolate employees' reactions to incentives created by their employer-provided health and paid-time-off benefits. By collecting the blogs into a physical book, we hope to reach a broader audience with the message about the link between healthcare and economics, and the importance of looking at healthcare reform through the lens of market economics.

Although always a team effort and reflective of both authors' opinions, most were actually written by me. Where the text speaks in the first-person, it refers to my personal experiences. But readers can "hear" the voices of both authors—and our many colleagues—throughout the themes of the book.

Why read this book?

If you are like us, you are busy. We understand that you don't have the time or energy to read every opinion about healthcare and business strategy—and you certainly don't have time to spend reading about the same solutions, packaged in a different way (neither do we).

This book is different.

This content comes in bite-sized pieces, each a story with a point to make. It comes from a three-year internet blog, covering current issues and management opportunity in human capital management and healthcare.

It challenges traditional thinking, and asks you to do the same. We tell you that some common strategies don't work, and why they don't.

If you let it, this book will change how you do your job. We tell you how incentives drive behavior, why current incentives might be working against you, and how to change them.

It shares discoveries we have made in our careers. Sometimes answers come where we don't expect them. In this case, they came from applying an economic lens to business and healthcare.

This book has no mystery or magic, just sound and often simple economic concepts. This is not a special formula. We simply invite you to consider a new paradigm with which to see (and solve) old problems.

You will see that our mini-chapters cover a wide variety of seemingly-unrelated topics: Why don't workers take better care of their health? Why are absence rates different in one country compared to another? What makes high performers quit their jobs? How is gasoline consumption in Iran like prescription drug consumption in the U.S.? Who chooses high deductible health plans?

Actually, these questions are all connected. It boils down to valuing people and aligning incentives to promote and reward positive behaviors. Whether we know it or not, we—in our businesses, our government, or communities—have created incentives that influence what employees and citizens value, consume, and protect. When we learn to see those incentives, we also see how to align them with our goals (health, success, growth).

Wendy D. Lynch
Research Director, the Health as Human Capital Foundation
Fall 2007

Acknowledgements

Our intent when we started our blog in the fall of 2005 was to provide bite-sized, regular, thought-provoking content worthy of a peer-reviewed journal. Posting an accurate, timely, sometimes analytical, and (hopefully) interesting blog entry every two weeks requires a team effort. We knew we needed input, critique, and quick turnaround from people with a variety of perspectives, skills, and talents.

First and foremost we thank our content reviewers, whose opinions and expertise have eliminated muddled thinking, and refined and improved every topic. Invaluable input about economics has been provided by our professor, B. Delworth Gardner, PhD, and his colleague Richard Butler, PhD, from Brigham Young University. Our primary internal analytical contributor has been Nathan Kleinman, PhD, with support from Arthur Melkonian, MD, Dustin Wingenbach, and Justin Schaneman. A clinical perspective about the interface between health and human capital has come from Shawn Petrini, as well as Marcie Lee Thomas. Real-world critiques, regarding what matters to professionals and how to best position our messages have been provided by Chuck Reynolds, Neil Sullivan, Julie Stone, and Tobi Wickham.

We have technical support from Matt Leininger, who helps make the site work and look nice. Plus, we have not regretted our original decision to use Google's Blogspot site, which has been reliable, useable, and easy to track.

For both the blog and this book, we have relied heavily on Anita Waller for her expertise and attention to detail. Without her "final review," editing, formatting, questioning, creating and checking citations, and oversight of the book development process, the quality of our content would have certainly suffered. And last but not least, we thank Kathryn Lasky for her ability to keep all projects moving and on schedule, doing her own job, and making our jobs easier.

A final thanks goes to everyone at HCMS Group, Inc., whose human capital integrated database has made much of the research presented possible, and our blog sponsoring organization the Health as Human

ACKNOWLEDGEMENTS

Capital Foundation for their continued support of this educational effort. And lastly, thanks go to the many blog readers from whom we have received encouragement, challenges and feedback, and to our current and past mentors who have challenged us to think differently.

Harold H. Gardner, MD
Chairman
HCMS, Inc.

Wendy D. Lynch, PhD
Research Director
Health as Human Capital Foundation
and
Vice President of Strategic
Development
HCMS, Inc.

Fall 2007

Introduction

   Are incentives aligned or misaligned? The answer to this question is a strong predictor of how well a social system is working. Essentially the question asks whether multiple parties within a system all have a shared reason to move toward a common end. If we are all in the same boat, will we all benefit from getting to shore?

   In this book, we consider incentives in their ever-present and aggregate sense: *the entire array of pros and cons* a person experiences making decisions in daily life. We focus less on isolated incentives, such as small cash rewards for specific behaviors, except to point out whether or not they align with the broader incentive environment. To understand alignment in business and in healthcare we may ask:

- Have we designed an employment contract so that employers and employees have aligned incentives to achieve the same goals (e.g. business success and growth)?
- Have we designed a healthcare system where doctors, patients, and insurance companies have aligned incentives to achieve the same goal (e.g., better health and efficient services)?

   More aligned incentives: better results. Misaligned incentives: worse results. Based on the direction of misalignment, we can also predict what the problems will be. In later chapters, we will describe seemingly inexplicable occurrences that result from misaligned incentives. For example:

   Why would an employee intentionally gain 40 pounds in four months?* Why are over 30% of all visits to primary care for a reason that is recommended *against* by the American Medical Association?† Why did workers in Sweden average three more sick days *per worker* one year compared to the year before (with no reason to believe there was more sickness)?‡ Why is there a huge increase in sick days in December in some companies and not

---

   * See Blog 4.7 Should you pay less for healthcare if you are sicker? Opening a can of incentive worms.
   † See Blog 5.5 Annual physicals and patient sensitivity to copayments.
   ‡ See Blog 3.5 Your time, someone else's money.

others?§ Why does your likelihood of a serious medical procedure change depending on what month it is?¶ Why would the size of a person's pay bonus affect his interest in health?**

Incentives, that's why. Every social system—businesses, communities, healthcare—has incentives imbedded in its rules and structure. Similar to the force of gravity, incentives pull behaviors in a particular direction. Whether designed on purpose, or simply an unintentional byproduct of other policies, incentives are pulling people to behave in certain ways. For example, an insurance policy that has a deductible that lasts for 12 months and resets to zero each year in January creates incentives regarding how to spend money leading up to January first (when the consumer will pay more). If a company pays workers by the hour rather than by the completed task, workers have a greater incentive to maximize time than to maximize output. The incentives exist. Sometimes incentives affecting behavior are obvious and sometimes they must be ferreted out. Almost always, we don't pay enough attention to them.

Becoming aware of incentives requires that some of us shift our frames of reference. As one would expect, proposed solutions vary widely between (and within) groups of politicians, employers, patients, clinicians, lawyers, and public health professionals. Given the inherently different motives and interests of each group (or individual) it is unlikely that any single group will design a universally satisfactory solution. Almost without fail, each group's interest will be myopic. Broader perspectives are required.

---

§ See Blog 6.1 Getting value from health benefits: Use them or lose them.

¶ See Blog 3.9 Moral Hazard and the New Year's Effect.

** See Blog 6.2 There are wellness incentives, and then there are incentives that increase the importance of being well.

Incentives matter: steps, clocks, and camp sites

Taking a page out of reality television, let's imagine a competition called Get There Together! The game involves three teams each trying to walk across a remote area and get the most members to a series of campsites first. Team leaders are rewarded handsomely for getting their entire team to each destination first, with greater rewards for quicker arrival. Team members are paid by the team leader using a specified strategy.

Let's imagine that our three team leaders choose rewards that are common in business and healthcare: rewarding employees who do more each day, rewarding employees for how many hours they spend, or rewarding employees for reaching goals. In addition, our team leaders set policies to try and keep their teams together in the event of an injury or illness: paid sick time, free health assistance, or other means. More specifically, let's meet our teams and their strategies:

Team A: Step-Takers

Leader A pays his members individually for the number of steps they take. If injured, they can get paid for 50% of the steps they usually take while they recover. A replacement team member will walk in the place of anyone injured.

Team B: Time-Keepers

Leader B pays his members a set amount per hour, up to a maximum number of hours, and for an hour of rest. Because there are no roads, an expensive helicopter is made available to transport sick members if there is an emergency. Team members are told that an unspecified bonus may be rewarded if they are the winners.

Team C: Camp-Reachers

Leader C pays his members a small base amount for each day, plus significant individual and team bonuses for reaching a destination as a group, by a specified time. Members are not paid on days they do not walk, but are given pre-paid helicopter vouchers to use if they are sick or injured. Unused vouchers can be turned in at the end for cash.

Incentives will affect behavior

Although members of each team have intrinsic motivation to win the contest (and look good for the television audience!), let's consider how each type of reward strategy creates behavioral incentives for contestants along their journey. If we look at rewards from the eyes of each team member—whose goal is mostly to earn the highest amount possible—then payment strategy matters a lot. Team A has a direct incentive to travel more steps per day, Team B has incentive to walk for a longer time, and Team C has incentive to maximize progress toward each new site with the least amount of time or wasted effort.

Pros and cons

To maximize their incomes, Step-Takers will likely walk quickly, generating as many steps as possible. The team will attract go-getters who think they can generate many steps per day. Steppers will learn that a few extra steps, even steps that do not get them closer to the destination, result in higher pay, leading to inefficiency and higher expenditures for the leader. Team Leader A may have to set up measurements and rules about allowable and unallowable steps to reduce this behavior. Strong Step-Takers may excel, especially early in the process. However, because there is a partial payment for "injury time," team members may be willing to take a risk of illness or injury in order to earn a higher reward in the short term. If team dynamics and terrain are difficult, tired or unhappy individuals may decide that half payment is more beneficial to them than continuing to endure the challenge. Interestingly, if the team members find a shorter route to the next destination, they will actually earn less than if they stay on a longer, less direct route.

Time-Keepers will show up on time and keep track of their hours. They are likely to be steady walkers, but not particularly fast. There is less incentive on this team to move quickly, although some members may be more motivated than others by the possibility of a bonus. Because helicopter assistance is paid for, individuals may find it tempting to make use of that service when terrain is difficult. Team Leader B may find that this team makes less progress than the other team, leading to a logical decision to offer bonus pay (say, time and a half) for longer hours (say, more than eight) on days when insufficient distance has been traveled. When overtime is available, the actual member incentive is to fall short of goals during the normal day in order to be eligible for more money in extra hours.

The Camp-Reachers have the most aligned incentives with their team leader. Their earnings will increase when the leader's earnings increase. There is a shared motive to make progress as individuals and as a collective group. This team will attract walkers who believe they can win through good strategy. There are no perverse incentives to add extra activity (like Team A), or artificially influence progress (like Team B), because efficient progress is rewarded most directly. If the team can get to the next camp site through a shorter alternate route, that will be rewarded. If the team travels in less time, that is also rewarded. Because team members will benefit in both daily pay and bonuses from not using helicopter assistance, there is a balanced incentive to both avoid injury (to save vouchers) and get help if they have to (get everyone there).

The Winner? Which team will win our reality series, arriving first with their members in good condition? On any one day, it is impossible to know for certain—unexpected events can occur even when incentives are aligned. But over time and many of these races, we are quite certain that Team C will make it there first, with fewer injuries, and spend the least in their efforts to *Get There Together!*

Work incentives affect work performance and worker health

Unlike reality show contestants, workers rarely have stardom or public visibility driving behavior. Instead, workers operate within an employment contract exchanging work for pay. The most common work arrangements are pay for time spent (hourly) or pay for a year's work (salary). Like our Time-Keeper team, these arrangements create interesting incentives to behave in ways that may not encourage efficient results. Working *longer* does not necessarily mean better output.

Another typical work arrangement is pay for volume of activity. A good example of this is our healthcare system. In many provider arrangements, a clinic earns more by conducting more procedures and tests. Like steps taken in any direction, backwards or forwards, providers learn that more activities result in better pay, even when the activity provides little value to the patient. If a system rewards *more* activity, members respond as such—a higher quantity at the expense of optimum quality.

Readers will notice that several examples in this book connect employee health and healthcare consumption to their employers' rewards strategy. As illustrated in our examples above, policies regarding pay and pay during injury or illness can create incentives to take better care of one's health. Reward policies and strategies combine to create environments encouraging specific types of behaviors. Some companies encourage clock-watching, others encourage lots of activities, and others—in our experience, surprisingly few—encourage a shared dedication to achieving goals such as high levels of worker productivity and good health.

Aligned Incentives Mean Common Goals and Shared Rewards

Our Step-Taker team demonstrated how rewards that *seem* aligned, e.g., taking more steps, may produce incentives that actually interfere with an efficient and successful result. Team C, the team rewarded for getting to their destination most efficiently, was the only team whose pay was determined by achieving the *exact* same goal for which their leader was paid. When we investigate the effectiveness of incentives, it becomes clear that when two parties both benefit by achieving the same outcome, the arrangement works better. While this may seem simple and obvious, one look at common practices in business and healthcare tells us that well-designed, "win-win" incentives are not the norm.

Let's consider some simple (seemingly obvious but not commonly demonstrated) messages that align incentives through common goals and shared rewards.

Message 1: *"My success is your success."*

Businesses that tie individual rewards to business outcomes tend to perform better and have fewer difficulties with inefficient behavior (such as high rates of unscheduled absences from work only one-third of which are due to health[††]). Yet our research suggests that a minority of businesses make such a link.

Three conditions help a team share success and rewards effectively. In keeping with the themes of this book, they involve incentives, information, and choice.

A) **Shared rewards tied directly to common goals.** Feedback from our survey of employees around the country indicated that only half were eligible for a bonus, and of those eligible, only one-third knew how their bonus amount would be determined.[‡‡] Optimal incentives have meaningful size (the amount matters to me), meaningful timing (it will happen soon enough to motivate me now), known rules (if X happens, I get Y), and shared influence (what I do can affect the result). Two of the more common examples of known, shared rewards are quarterly sales commissions and realtor fees. The person knows how much, when, and for what they will be rewarded.

   Clear rules about rewards lead to efficient work. If I am rewarded for answering phones, I will take calls and direct them where they ask to go. If I am also rewarded when the company has higher revenues, I will have a greater incentive to investigate what services the caller has interest in buying. Workers who have awareness of how their efforts affect business success and know how their contribution will be rewarded have aligned incentives.

B) **Transparency of information about success.** Do all team members understand what success looks like and how they are moving towards achieving it? Do employees know (even generally) about revenues and expenses for the business, or their unit? Without a clear definition and understanding of the goal, and timely updates about progress, team members will be less likely to

---

[††] CCH Unscheduled absence survey. 2006. http://www.cch.com/absenteeism2006/Images/Reasons2006.asp

[‡‡] See Blog 6.2 There are wellness incentives, and then there are incentives that increase the importance of being well.

stay on track—or even know exactly what track to stay on. Shared rewards also imply shared responsibilities and shared consequences. When all parties understand and contribute to success, they also share responsibility for failure. Employees should understand that inefficiency and waste affect profits, and share both some benefits of higher profitability, and some consequences of lower profitability.

C) **Some discretion in decision making.** When teams share rewards for success and efficiency, members have incentives to make decisions that benefit the organization (and themselves). Like Team C in our reality show, we want to encourage teams who figure out how to get to the destination more quickly, more efficiently or more safely. When workers share success in ways that align with the success of company owners, they are more likely to think and behave as owners would think and behave.

How does "my success is your success" relate to healthcare? In the current healthcare-business system, it rarely does. Other than some uninsured services like Lasik surgery, healthcare providers rarely get rewarded for achieving better outcomes.[§§] Incentives, in the form of pay, almost never align with a common goal for both patient and provider.

Message 2: "A day's work for a day's pay."

The practice of paying people for days they don't work became popular during and after WWII. Employers could not raise salaries (a wage-price control law was in place during wartime), and decided to offer other forms of compensation—like paid vacation and health insurance —to attract and retain workers. Because paid holidays, vacation and sick leave are now an accepted (and expected) part of benefits for employees working for U.S. businesses, the practice is rarely questioned.

However, from the standpoint of aligning incentives, paid sick-leave is as misaligned as a benefit can be. Setting aside tradition and paternalism, let's examine the incentives created by paid sick-leave. First, when a worker receives equal pay for a day not working versus a day working,

---

[§§] See Blog 5.2 Getting paid more for doing worse…only in healthcare.

the decision to not work has no immediate monetary consequence for the worker. The employer, by contrast, will be paying a wage despite receiving no effort from the worker. One party (worker) suffers no financial consequence, the other party (company) loses 100% of its investment. Rather than creating common goals and common consequences, paid sick-leave places workers and employers in opposing positions.

A second implication inherent in all sorts of paid time-off, is that workers provide as much value working as not working, which is clearly false. Employees of some large employers actually can receive full pay for six months if they experience an illness or injury. By some standards this is considered caring and kind. From an economic perspective, a policy that provides full pay for not working erodes other incentives to succeed, undervalues and penalizes those who are at work, and encourages use of a paid-time-off system for other reasons (job searching or avoidance of work conflict). Readers will see later[¶¶] that the more a person is paid while absent, the more likely he will be absent,[***] and the longer he will stay absent.[†††]

Lastly, and least talked about, is the message paid sick-leave sends about the value of one's health. If only someone else (my employer) suffers the economic consequences of my illness, I have less incentive to protect my health. We often hear objections to this argument along the lines of: "people don't ignore their own health simply because they have sick leave."[‡‡‡] Yet, one only has to be self-employed, without disability insurance, for a short while before realizing that we do avoid risky situations (choosing not to take snowboarding lessons or try bungee jumping) when we know there are significant potential consequences to our income. There is a rational reason why nearly all professional sports have owner-imposed rules that prohibit athletes from engaging in risky pastimes during the sports season. Their message is clear: the employee's health matters to company success.

[¶¶] See Chapter 3: Your time and money matter more to you than someone else's.
[***] See Blog 3.2 Money matters in decisions about disability.
[†††] See Blog 3.3 Hoping for absolutes in a subjective world.
[‡‡‡] See Blog 1.6 Please don't complicate things with new information. I like the old (wrong) answer better.

In the past decade, many companies have moved from offering paid sick-days and paid vacation to offering a combined "bank" of days that can be used for any reason. This better aligns incentives, since taking a sick day will reduce the number of available paid vacation days a worker will have. Further alignment can be created by paying workers for unused sick days, such that both the worker and the employer will benefit from an extra day working.

In our own small firm, we do not provide paid time-off, but instead pay workers more (in the amount that would cover a typical number of days off). For example, 15 days amounts to just under 6% of the work year. This means that employers who pay for 15 days of sick leave and vacation purchase 94% of the year. Instead, we purchase 100% of a year in a daily rate and allow the worker to take days off for no pay. It is the workers' choice to choose the ideal balance of time off and pay to suit their life needs; they choose to work without pay at their own discretion. This way, incentives are aligned. Workers are rewarded (only) for the days they work and individuals own the full benefits and consequences of their decisions not to work. We have very low absenteeism.

An additional implication of "a day's work for a day's pay" is a clearer separation of work from the rest of life. When an employer pays employees during a vacation day or a sick day—officially the worker is still on the payroll. The modern-day practice of work "bleeding" into time-off likely evolved in part from employers' awareness that workers are (although officially away) still "on the clock." If workers are paid during vacation and illness, why should employers feel reluctant to ask them to continue working a little during vacation? When a worker chooses to take time, without pay, no conflicting incentives exist.

Logically, the two messages "my success is your success," and "a day's work for a day's pay," work best in tandem with each other. Reliable, tangible rewards for good performance reinforce the value of being at work. Both principles bolster efficient efforts toward a common mission. In fact, we find that larger performance-based bonuses have a dramatic effect on absenteeism rates. This is because workers understand that "being there" leads to a tangible reward. Applied well, these principles lessen the need for oversight, management, and rules about work. The individual has significant incentive to do well, the employer will pay more to workers who are more successful, and—because there is more disclosure of information and less misalignment of incentives—workers and employers trust each other more.

Message 3: We support active decision making by workers/consumers through: "aligned incentives, better information, and freedom of choice."

Can individuals be trusted to make "good" decisions? Readers will see in several of the blog entries that this question is often posed with respect to healthcare and human resource management. Doctors question whether patients should enroll in consumer-directed healthcare plans. Human resources managers wonder if employees can make good decisions about health benefits. Inherent in this question are both a value judgment about what constitutes a "good" decision and a concern that individuals are not well-enough informed or qualified to make a good decision.

Our opinion: people make "good" decisions in the sense that they choose what benefits them. By itself, more information will not result in better decision making. Instead, better decision making results from having incentives aligned with common goals, having freedom to choose among options, and having good information about benefits and risks. The concept that human beings own themselves (their health, their career) in a free society is crucial. It means they will invest in themselves if they have opportunities and incentives to do so.

For healthcare decisions, we believe that no approach can solve our healthcare cost problems unless consumers' economic incentives are aligned with efficiency and quality. Until the consumer pays directly (at least in part) for services with his own money, he has little incentive to care about price or value. Further, if a consumer is given limited or no options about where he can receive services, he has no incentive to compare or shop around. In an environment where someone else (employers or government) pays and choice is limited, better information has limited impact on the quality of decision making.

Where policy makers insist that individuals require more or better information *before* they can be allowed to make choices, we argue the reverse. Until individuals have incentive to make decisions and choices to make, they will have little use or demand for information. Some decry that information is not adequate for consumers to make decisions. But why should information be expected to be available when the decisions lie outside the consumer? Give consumers freedom and incentives to choose and the information industry will respond as it does in every situation when consumers do choose.

In business, there has been significant investment in health education programs. The hope has been that with more information, employees and their families will take better care of themselves resulting in lower healthcare costs and absenteeism. However, results from such programs (both in terms of engagement and in terms of health improvement) have been disappointing.§§§ In our perspective, this is a predictable outcome given misaligned incentives between employee and employer about who will experience the financial consequences of poor health. For employees of large companies (who are most likely to provide health education), the employer pays most of the cost of healthcare and all of the pay during sick leave. Unless workers have a health savings account (fewer than 10% of employees), they experience little financial benefit from spending less on healthcare or avoiding illness.¶¶¶ Unless they have cash back from unused sick leave, employees experience no financial rewards from avoiding sick days. Further, employees do not choose whether part of their pay is spent on sick leave and health education—it happens without their input.

The recipe for better decision making requires an incentive to participate (because the cost and quality affects me), a set of options (where my choice will make a difference), and sufficient information to distinguish the cost and quality between options. But the true value of information is realized in an environment of aligned incentives and choice.

Creating work environments and social systems that encourage efficient performance and health protection requires aligned incentives.

---

§§§ See Blog 2.4 The episodic nature of illness. Part 1.
¶¶¶ See Blog 8.3 PTO Banks and Health Savings Accounts.

This book uses economic principles to provide an over-arching perspective about current inefficiencies in healthcare and business, as well as discusses natural tensions resulting from competing or misaligned motives.

Giving examples of incentives, information, and choice in real life

How do economic principles present themselves in one's daily existence? Do patients, employees, and providers actually respond to aligned and misaligned incentives in ways economists predict? Yes, they do.

The series of blogs posted online**** and published in this book give empirical evidence—everyday examples—of how incentives influence behavior. Rather than simply stating expected results from economic theories, these examples show how such theories manifest themselves in the real world. Using a very large, unique database and a team of research colleagues, this work provided an opportunity to find, test, and tease apart choices actually made. The blogs show real data from real people, and interpret them from a perspective of economics. Our examples show what people actually do in response to economic incentives, rather than general assumptions about what one might expect them to do. Certainly, many authors have discussed theories and principles of incentives with much more rigor; we hope this work helps readers translate why such principles matter to their lives.

Many of our examples describe unintended consequences from a rule or policy that may have been designed for an entirely different purpose. These examples illustrate how many of the problems we face today in healthcare and business are problems we have created (mostly by accident) ourselves. Like trying to ignore gravity, until we begin to see these underlying forces, we will remain at their mercy and wonder why we can't change the outcome.

**** See www.hhcf.blogspot.com.

SECTION 1

Health as Human Capital

Chapter 1
Health as Human Capital:
A Different Paradigm

Like your skills and your motivation, you own your own health. In combination, these personal assets—health, skills, and motivation—comprise the package of resources that a person can offer in a job market: a person's human capital. How workers apply their human capital goes a long way towards determining what the employment market will pay in return.

As a part of one's human capital, health is an asset worth augmenting and protecting. It is a personal resource that has great influence not only on one's lifetime earnings, but also one's general quality of life. Because health matters most to the individual "owner," we believe its protection is primarily the responsibility of the individual.

While health ownership is simple in concept, the implications of "health as human capital" are far-reaching. Owning health means making decisions about lifestyle and medical treatments. It means earning rewards for good health and taking responsibility for negative consequences of illness. The health as human capital paradigm rejects the premise that someone else (one's employer, or one's government) should be primarily held responsible for health and healthcare. In fact, this paradigm shows us how our employment and government programs have evolved over the past 50 years to actually discourage individual health protection by misaligning incentives. The following set of blogs will help illustrate this point.

When a worker receives as much money when he is sick as when he is well, there is less incentive to be well. When a worker has a greater potential for earnings when she remains injury free, she will pay more attention to safety. How we design our work contracts affects not only how we work, but how we protect all of our human capital assets, including health.

To begin our discussion about *aligning incentives, information, and choice*, we start this book with our perspective about health as a human capital asset.

Blog 1.1   Health as human capital. How is this perspective different than the medical paradigm?

The health as human capital paradigm[1] is not just another label on the same-old solutions. Some people assume that it is a re-packaging of "total cost management" or "health and productivity management." Not so.

It begins with this simple concept: health is one of three important assets that a person brings to his or her job (as well as to family and community). Health, like skills and motivation, belongs to the individual and is influenced by individual choices. Better health allows us to earn a better living. Having the capacity to function well, mentally and physically, with high energy and few limitations, improves the quality of life, the productivity of work, and the pleasure of leisure. Health is one of our most precious personal resources.

Because it is inherently ours, no one can influence and care for our well-being better than ourselves. For the majority of us, our personal actions (how we eat, exercise, sleep, avoid harmful substances, choose safe practices) and our choices (follow known guidelines for screening and take needed medications) have far more influence on our functioning and well-being over a lifetime than any miraculous medical procedure. Yet, too often we take this personal resource for granted or place responsibility for its protection on others.

Somewhere along the way, our culture accepted a medical premise that the normal human experience is interrupted by a series of flaws and afflictions that others (in the healthcare system) can fix for us.[2] Rather than treating health as a personal resource to develop, nurture and protect, we hear that our well-being is best trusted to highly-trained professionals who will intervene to eradicate the offending germ or molecule, or alter the course of a misbehaving bodily process.

FIGURE 1.1   HUMAN CAPITAL, DEFINED

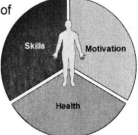

The potential value an individual or group of individuals brings to an organization.

That Human Capital is a function of:

- Skills: education and experience
- Motivation: attitude and incentives
- Health: physical and mental capacity

When responsibility for illness is placed mostly on outside causes, and responsibility for wellness is assigned to external technicians, we naturally place great value on access to medical treatment. My economist friends point out that our preference for medical solutions is reinforced by economic subsidies. Whenever the price to the consumer is subsidized (the price borne by the consumer is only a fraction of the total production costs) by insurance plans or government programs, consumers will demand more than is economically efficient.

Combine a culture that believes that medicine is the answer with a system that subsidizes its cost and we get an appetite for healthcare consumption. As a result, when there are societal health problems, they are often expressed as something like the following common assumption:

People are not getting sufficient, high-quality care from the system.

Defining the problem as one of insufficiency (quality and/or amount), leads to solutions that naturally focus on delivering *more* services. More subtly, we imply that the system is not "making us healthy enough," encouraging us to demand more of this externally-provided "health." It also implies that there are solutions out there to which we are entitled. We seldom hear about risks inherent in medical treatments, even though medical errors and side-effects are common, and their consequences sometimes dire.

In recent years, "total cost management" and "health and productivity" initiatives have contributed more momentum to the medical paradigm by quantifying even *more* consequences (absences and lost time) that occur because we don't get enough care (drugs, treatments, procedures). Almost every solution proposed in these initiatives involves more interventions or medical care. Virtually none suggest greater responsibility by the individual to avoid or manage illness.

The health as human capital paradigm states "the problem" differently:

> **Due to perverse economic incentives, poor information, and the lack of true market forces, people undervalue their own ability to manage and improve their health, leading them to consume health services inefficiently.**

In this paradigm, the problem is an economic one. People don't pay directly for healthcare and are over-protected from the consequences of illness. When individuals pay only a small portion of the true cost of care, it is more attractive. When it is inexpensive *and* perceived as an "easy" option, consumption is high *and* effectiveness is compromised. We have created a system that not only allows, but encourages, healthcare consumption in lieu of personal health protection.

Entries in this blog have illustrated several examples where economic incentives in healthcare influence consumption of services. We have seen:

- How rates of disability[*] increase when more salary is covered during an absence.
- How duration of disability[†] increases when salary is fully covered during an absence.
- How insurance moral hazard[‡] leads to higher consumption when services are less expensive (unrelated to health status).
- How consumers respond logically to anticipated greater medical needs[§] (they change insurance to reduce out-of-pocket costs), or

---

[*] See Blog 3.2 Money Matters in Decisions about Disability.
[†] See Blog 3.3 Hoping for Absolutes in a Subjective World.
[‡] See Blog 3.1 Remembering the RAND Health Insurance Experiment.
[§] See Blog 6.4 Do Anticipated Health Events Affect the Choice of Health Plan?

higher cost sharing (they accellerate consumption to avoid new costs).

- How consumption is higher when individuals reach their deductible** earlier in the year.

These are examples of inefficiency *and* of perverse incentives—where one gets more value from using the healthcare system than not using it. Essentially, current benefit designs ensure that sicker individuals receive more value from their benefits than well individuals. Employee compensation shifts from wages to health-related benefits.[3] This trend cannot continue if we wish corporate and governmental budgets to remain solvent, and businesses to compete well in the global market.

Unfortunately, the medical paradigm of insufficiency takes a "more is better" approach. In this paradigm, society rejects suggestions that perhaps we have more than we need in many cases. It asks: if people are suffering and so many have limited access, how can you say we have enough? Well, economic theory suggests we have too much.[††] Medicine has made incredible contributions to the quality of modern life, but we would contend that this contribution should be in addition to the many ways we can keep ourselves well, rather than as a substitute for caring for ourselves. Excusing individual responsibility from the equation, while well-intended in some cases, is a little like driving with our eyes closed, blaming traffic for what happens and letting insurance pay for the damage.

What can be done? Look honestly at how policies in your organization contribute to the de-valuation of personal health. Are employees being rewarded for being healthy? Are employees protected from feeling *any*

¶ See Blog 3.6 The Challenge of Insuring Discretionary Events.

**See Blog 3.9 Moral Hazard and the New Year's Effect.

††Subsidized prices mean that over-consumption will inevitably occur if consumers are free to take all of the care they desire at discounted prices. A rational consumer will maximize total utility from the expenditure of a specified budget when the marginal utility per dollar spent is equal among all consumption alternatives. If these marginal utilities are not equal, then a consumer can shift expenditures from a lower to a higher marginal utility and thus gain total utility. If the price (dollars spent per unit) of, say, good "A" is held artificially low, then the marginal utility per dollar spent for A will rise, leading to a higher consumption of A than is efficient. In terms of healthcare, this means that we will over-consume medical treatment, which is subsidized, and under-consume preventive health measures, which are not.

consequences for illness? What messages are being sent?

October 29, 2006

References

1 Gardner, H., Butler, R. Beyond Biomechanics: Psychological Aspects of Musculoskeletal Disorders in Office Work: In *Human Capital Perspective for Cumulative Trauma Disorders: Moral Hazard Effects in Disability Compensation Programs.* Eds. S.L. Sauter, S.D. Moon. 1996, Taylor and Francis, London, http://www.hcmsgroup.com/hcms/reserach/papers/BeyondBioCH14.pdf (accessed October 27, 2006).

2 For more on the development of the authoritative medical profession see: Starr, P. *The Social Transformation of American Medicine.* New York: Basic Books, 1982.

3 Fuhrmans, V. Health-care premiums rise 7.7% outpacing wages and inflation. *The Wall Street Journal.* September 27, 2006 http://online.wsj.com/article/SB115927289880274192.html (accessed October 27, 2006).

Blog 1.2   Can't buy me health

"The reality is: you can't buy your health. You already own it. It's yours, not someone else's to sell to you."

My colleague, Hank Gardner, M.D., made this statement a few weeks ago. The conversation stuck with me because it expressed some complex issues quite succinctly. Health is one form of human capital, and like all forms of human capital, it is not traded in the marketplace. Just as you cannot increase your knowledge without a commitment of your own time and effort, you cannot increase your health without being personally involved in that effort. While simple, the concept that good health cannot be purchased has profound and important implications.* I will list a few that have occurred to me.

1) We have the greatest influence on our own health.

Over a lifetime, our own behaviors and actions have the greatest

---

* We certainly acknowledge that healthcare services can be purchased for the purpose of treating illness. Our point is that society under-values an individual's role investing in and protecting his own health assets; we often assume that "someone else" will be able to fix any physical problem. Buying healthcare is not the same as purchasing health—a characteristic a person already has.

impact on our level of wellness or illness. We make choices every day that alter our likelihood of illness or subsequent recovery. For the most part, we know what the choices are.

FIGURE 1.2   LIFESTYLE NOW…AND CUMULATIVE LIMITATIONS 25 TO 30 YEARS LATER

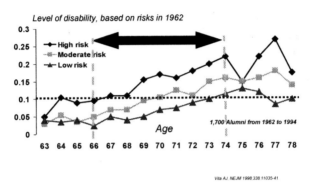

Level of disability, based on risks in 1962

1,700 Alumni from 1962 to 1994

Age

Vita AJ. NEJM 1998.338.11035-41

As one profound example of how our lifestyle choices affect our health, figure 1.2 shows the rate at which people in their 60s and 70s reached a level of physical limitation that necessitated living assistance.[1]

The three lines show three groups, defined by their health behaviors 25 to 30 years earlier. The y-axis indicates the average level of physical limitation experienced for people in the group. The 0.1 level was identified as the point at which individuals first reported not being able to perform at least one of their normal living activities without assistance. What we see is that individuals who had positive health behaviors in 1962 (non-smoking, moderate exercise, and healthy body weight) experienced fewer physical limitations eight years later than those who had the least healthy behaviors.[†]

How many external influences can you think of—or purchase—that could affect wellbeing this dramatically?

---

† There are many interesting findings of this study not discussed in this space. Among them:
A) Limitations were higher for those with unhealthy habits at all age levels.
B) Among individuals who died during the study, low-risk individuals experienced less limitation prior to death than high-risk individuals.

2) We place too much responsibility on others for our own health (and we place too little responsibility on ourselves).

Too often, we assign responsibility to the medical system without acknowledging that it is only one influence input, and not the most important influence, in the production and protection of our health capital. When Dean Ornish demonstrated that many aspects of coronary artery disease and diabetes could be reversed with a program of strict diet, exercise, and meditation, the program was criticized by medical professionals (not on the basis of results) because it required too much of the patients themselves.[2] Their position: one could not ask patients to behave responsibly when other alternatives were easier. Similarly, studies have shown that relatively small amounts of weight loss can reduce onset of diabetes by 60% in pre-diabetic patients.[3]

Is there enough incentive for each of us to do what we can to manage our own health, or has the public been convinced (by media and the medical establishment) that "someone else" can fix us?

3) We often portray more intervention as "better" care.

As we saw in the last blog entry,[‡] medical professionals and the public are often convinced that more extraordinary interventions will produce better outcomes than less-invasive approaches. We are a society of action; we like to "doing something." More often than not, this implies having someone *else* do something to us. It follows a basic perception that, with enough intervention, we should be able to fix what is wrong.

4) We assume that spending more on healthcare gets us more health.

Except for those who do not have access to basic preventive services or adequate primary care, there is limited evidence that additional spending produces better health. Plus, there is clearly a point of diminishing returns after which no amount of spending will cure an illness or ensure recovery.

It is difficult to accept that the richness of a health insurance plan (for example, a $3,000 out-of-pocket maximum versus a $4,000 out-

---

‡ See Blog 5.7 When the most expensive option isn't the best option.

of-pocket maximum, or capping the maximum at \$5 million versus \$4 million) translates directly to differences in the overall health status of a population. Instead, it is a statement about access to the most expensive technology for very few—much of which has questionable known impact on health or longevity. While this issue poses difficult ethical questions about what types of care should be universally available, the underlying assumption (which is not necessarily true) is that spending equates to better health.

Likewise, buying health insurance does not equate to buying good health. Insurance lowers the financial risk associated with illness and treatment, but it does not inherently make us healthier. Too often, we confuse coverage with access, and access with health. But coverage is a financial issue, and "access" does not necessarily produce good health. Access may provide a ticket to receive beneficial care, but it does not absolve an individual from investing in his or her own wellbeing. Having insurance does nothing to prevent becoming ill, it just changes the mechanisms through which services will be paid, or changes one's likelihood of seeking care.

5) If more money doesn't necessarily result in better health outcomes, how does it change healthcare policy or human resource practices?

If reducing medical expenditures does not *always* mean restricting necessary care or sacrificing health, perhaps the debate changes. Too often, stakeholders argue as if all dollars have equal value to the health of a population. They don't; in some cases, dollars spent in proactive care go farther than those spent in reactive care. In fact, some spending is actually dangerous or harmful to the individual.

These are just a few of many implications of the concept: "you can't buy your own health." Certainly there are many, many more. If we acknowledge that health is not for sale, but instead something we own and must protect, does it change how we behave?

February 11, 2007

References

1 Vita, A.J., Terry, R.B., Hubert, H.B., Fries, J.F. Aging, health risks, and cumulative disability. *N Engl J Med* 1998; 338:1035-1041.

2 Cardiologists aware of life-saving diet, yet failing to recommend it, new survey shows. *Medical News Today*, February 24, 2006, http://www.medicalnewstoday.com/medicalnews.php?newsid=38192 (accessed February 9, 2007).

3 Diet and exercise dramatically delay type 2 diabetes. United States Department of Health and Human Services, August 8, 2001, http://www.hhs.gov/news/press/2001pres/20010808a.html (accessed February 9, 2007).

Blog 1.3   "It's more important to understand the person with the illness, than the illness the person has"*

We saw in a previous blog† that, among a group of people, having a specific health condition is not a strong predictor of who will be expensive in the future. Instead, having many different health issues predicts future high medical expense costs better than any specific health condition. Hence, our position is that outside the treatment a patient receives directly from his or her provider, add-on disease-focused programs are an inefficient, and perhaps counterproductive, method of managing healthcare expenditures.

In this entry we extend this topic to include broader human capital concepts. We don't question whether medical care for specific diseases

---

* Hank Gardner, M.D. has articulated this position as long as we have known him. We don't know who first said it, but Hank has pointed out examples of this for decades, as a clinician, a researcher, and a thought leader.

† See Blog 2.6 Should we focus on specific diseases?

can and should improve.‡ However, the broader view—beyond the narrow, clinical realm of medicine—recognizes that illness always occurs within the context of a human life. Everything people experience, including their past episodes of illness and future fears or expectations, will affect their perceptions of and responses to illness.

The health as human capital paradigm emphasizes that health interventions will not fix problems that are the result of poor benefits design, poor management, or low pay.[1] Additionally, since investments in health programs may detract from a company's ability to invest in better pay or training for employees and managers, disease-focused programs may actually contribute to human capital risk. Consider the following possibilities:

- Imagine yourself having an illness and working in a workplace where
  —workers feel undervalued by low wages
  —conflicts are frequent and poorly handled
  —disability insurance provides 100% pay during absence
  —medical insurance has a $0 deductible and low coinsurance
- Then imagine yourself having the same illness and working in a workplace where
  —workers are paid well, and receive bonuses for high performance
  —managers receive extensive training in personnel issues
  —disability insurance provides less than 100% pay during absence
  —medical insurance has a high deductible and employees have a health savings account (HSA).

If your doctor asks whether you are ready to return to work, will these circumstances matter? Of course they will, consciously or unconsciously.

---

‡ We absolutely accept that patients who have specific illnesses often fail to receive optimal care and that compliance by providers and patients with established recommendations (both treatments and behavior change) would improve quality and cost outcomes in the long run. Similarly, if everyone practiced optimal prevention and maintained known healthy habits, far fewer of us would develop chronic illnesses in the first place. These are realities. The question is not whether things could be better, the question is which, if any, investments made by employers are most effective in improving these outcomes. And are they effective enough to warrant spending money on them instead of something else, i.e., considering the opportunity cost of doing one thing rather than another.

A person reacts to the experience caused by the disease. This experience includes their physical sensations (pain, fatigue, itching), emotional discomfort (fear, anxiety), functional limitations (I can't lift my arm, I can't concentrate), and expectations (I need to perform well today). The same person, experiencing similar or identical discomfort, functional limitations, and expectations, may react differently to them on different days. This is because, from an economic perspective, costs and benefits that result from an illness are time-dependent and vary from day to day.

Many[§] who have studied the phenomenon of the illness experience point out that illness is far more than a mechanical, biological mishap. Illness has meaning and "being sick" (also referred to as the "sick role" phenomenon) has strong social implications. In relation to others, one's roles, responsibilities, expectations, and entire patterns of living will alter with illness. This applies to families, co-workers, neighbors, and communities. Serious illness provokes a variety of behavioral reactions from the sick persons and those around them.

Being sick can alter priorities, excuse responsibilities, forgive arguments, attract assistance, and quiet adversaries. The experience of sickness can alter how we see life, or life can alter how we experience illness. A small child may say his tummy hurts when he doesn't want to go to school, a grandmother who wants visitors may explain that her back is hurt, a stressed mom may ask the kids to be quiet so she doesn't get a migraine. We may behave differently than someone else with the exact same illness; the "tough guy" who ignores chest pain until he collapses, versus the worrier who has every lump or pain checked by the doctor. While we like to think of medicine as a science, the illness experience and our reactions to it are more individual.

---

§ We acknowledge and encourage you to explore some wonderful works by the following authors:
- Kleinman, A. *The Illness Narratives: Suffering, Healing and the Human Condition.* New York: Basic Books, 1988.
- Kerr White Health Care Collection, University of Virginia Health System, http://www.med.virginia.edu/hs-library/historical/kerr-white/home.html (accessed October 14, 2006).
- Angel, R., Thoits, P. The impact of culture on the cognitive structure of illness. *Culture, Medicine and Psychiatry* 1987;11 (4):465-94.

And, there are certainly many others.

A medical label also has power in the work setting. It can be a threat to being taken seriously (mental health), a potential detriment to advancement (pregnancy), permission for light duty (back pain), or a career ender (serious injury). A doctor's note can legitimize escape from pressure at work in a way that is unavailable through any other avenue. No other option can provide (sometimes) full pay while not working.

Does this imply that all illnesses are a way to manipulate other people or situations? Of course not. But it does remind us that *all* illnesses occur within the context of a person's life, circumstances, and incentives. Estimate the amount of performance loss or healthcare expenditure that will occur in the following pairs of situations:

- A person with moderate back pain who has just had a significant disagreement with her boss, or the person who is newly diagnosed with Stage 2 breast cancer who loves her job and has strong family support?
- A person with carpal tunnel syndrome, three previous instances of workers' compensation and two years until retirement, or a person with high performance ratings and a strong career orientation who has a heart attack?
- A person dealing with depression, caring for a dying elderly relative, or an insulin-dependent diabetic with a foot problem who considers her co-workers her best friends in the world?

It is hard to ignore the power of context in these (or any) situations. The person with a more serious clinical issue is not necessarily the person one might choose as having greatest risk—or who might need the most support. Nor would one assume that advice regarding medication compliance, lifestyle, or tests is what would reduce risk most effectively. So, for these employees, what disease management program will be helpful? Mental health? Cardiovascular? Diabetes? Or does it depend on the person and the situation? You get the point.

This perspective may help you understand why we encourage employers to think about their compensation structure, their policies, and their benefit design *first* before they consider investing in a program for a specific disease.

October 16, 2006

References

1 Lynch, W.D., Gardner, H.H., Health as Human Capital Research Group. "A Hierarchy of Aligned Incentives: Health in the Context of Broader Human Capital Enhancement." Health as Human Capital Foundation, September 2006, http://www.hhcfoundation.org/hhcf/pdf/hierarchy_paper.pdf (accessed October 14, 2006).

Blog 1.4   While everyone argues whether corporations or government should "pay for" healthcare—it's your money they're spending

Our rational alternative to current healthcare proposals

We would propose that if the focus of healthcare reform first acknowledged some basic truths currently not heard in the healthcare debate, it may be possible for true reform:

- It's your money.
- Having health insurance is not the same as having healthcare.
- Our healthcare options are not limited to "red" or "blue."
- You can do more to protect your health than anyone else can.

First, we will explain why these matter, and then we will propose a rational alternative.

1) It's your money

Whether Uncle Sam or corporate execs pay the bill, it's still your money.

Corporations pay with workers' wages, and government pays with citizens' taxes. In either case, we pay. Think of it this way: from each pay check, we take some hard-earned money out of our own pockets and hand it to our employer or our congressman and say, "Please decide how to best spend this on health services for me and my family."

Even if you trust your employer or congressman to do their jobs well, are they really more qualified than you to make personal decisions about what to buy for your family?

Our opinion: individuals spend their money on what matters most to them, and will do so more efficiently than companies or government.

Note: we understand that it is more complicated than this. Some among us pay more (in wages or taxes) than others, making the distribution of this burden unequal across citizens. So, one does not usually get services equivalent to what one pays; it may be more or less. That said, in aggregate we supply the money, others spend it.

2) Having health insurance is not the same as having healthcare

Much of the national healthcare debate centers on who is insured and who is not. However, insurance is an administrative payment system, not to be confused with actual medical care. Further, insurance is not the same as access. Some uninsured people get access to care through public systems. And some insured people may have limited access to good care. Depending on the plan, being insured does not guarantee a person will get proper prevention and primary care.

Plus, people do not always have the option of buying a product that suits them. Each state creates laws that mandate what *must* be covered in health plans, such as infertility treatments, acupuncture or chiropractic care.[1] Each mandated item (often the result of lobbying by specific interest groups) increases the price of coverage, whether you value that service or not. Federal law prohibits insurance carriers from selling their products in other states, so consumers are stuck with the package their state legislature defines.

When politicians suggest that insurance should be required, it implies that everyone will be "cared for." Not so, because required insurance really just means everyone will be asked to pay for a full 'bells and whistles' insurance package designed through legislation, and not shaped by the specific and unique needs of each individual. True "insurance" is a way to spread risk of an unlikely event across a population of people, such as car insurance for accidents. When routine and extra items get added to insurance, it no longer functions the same way—which leads to a higher priced (and sometimes unaffordable) product. Mandating the current—overloaded—product is wasteful and inefficient.

3) Don't assume there are only two options: red or blue

Our political system is driven to a great extent by agreements between candidates and their major financial backers. Each party has interests to protect. For example, Democrats avoid placing limits on malpractice law suits because they are supported disproportionately by trial lawyers. Republicans will not threaten the control (and incomes) of medical professionals, because they are supported disproportionately by the medical industry (over two-thirds of the AMA donations go to Republican candidates).[2]

Over 35,000 lobbyists worked in the nation's capital in 2005 (over double the number as recently as 2000). Thousands represent the interests of the pharmaceutical, medical, legal, and insurance industries. In fact, three of the top five highest-spending lobbying organizations in the past ten years were in the medical industry.[3]

By accepting political solutions designed by elected candidates, we necessarily accept solutions that are well-financed by that candidate's funders. This system discourages every politician from suggesting true reform. Regardless of one's political leanings, everyone would benefit from acknowledging that neither party has suggested a solution that truly solves the healthcare problem at an individual level.

4) You can do more to protect your health than anyone else

The national discussion today continues to perpetuate a notion that the secret to a healthy America is "out there" in a well-designed insurance system to pay for medical care. Rarely do citizens look in the mirror and remind themselves that over half of chronic illness is preventable, and that lifestyle is often as effective as medication in treating expensive illnesses. We often insist that we have a "right" to all medications, services, and procedures, but ignore the responsibilities that balance such rights.

Yes, bad things do happen, like cancer and car accidents. In those times, we are grateful for care and coverage. We expect insurance to cover such things, but in return are we each making a reasonable effort to do what we can to avoid them?

When someone else pays for the consequences, we worry less about risk (the 'moral hazard' phenomenon). So, have we further created a system that encourages riskier behavior? If we set fire to our own house, the insurance company won't pay for the loss. Car insurance costs more after multiple speeding tickets. Life insurance costs more for smokers and pilots. If lung cancer treatments were more costly for smokers than non-smokers, would we be more likely to quit smoking? If auto insurance paid more for medical care after a car accident if we had been wearing a seatbelt, would we always wear our seatbelts? While not everyone would protect themselves, perhaps more of us would. How much do we encourage risk-taking because the consequences are "covered?"

The common thread in these observations? Self-responsibility. Too often we abdicate responsibility for our health, our money, and our choices to someone else (pick one: government or private industry). We need an approach that acknowledges and eliminates the irrational aspects of our current system. Such an approach does *not* just lump a multitude of services into one product that gets paid by government or industry using our money. Instead, in our opinion, a rational solution features:

A) **True insurance**: financial protection from very serious, high cost, rare events (above $10,000 or $20,000).

B) **A lower premium** on insurance made possible by a national standard that reduces the number of required "extra" covered services.

C) **Insurance** products that can be **sold across state** (perhaps national) borders, providing greater choice.

D) **Uniform access to primary care and preventive services**—which everyone needs—using vouchers or income-rated discounts for low-income individuals (not insurance).

E) **Funding for an individual health savings account** for every citizen that gives consumers control and choice on moderate-cost services.

F) **Shared responsibility** for premiums and accounts among individuals, employers, and government.

It's time to re-shape the healthcare debate away from mandatory, pre-defined insurance products for all, and instead toward a design that allows affordable coverage and encourages personal ownership for health. We need an approach that allows individuals to purchase basic products and services at a reasonable price, supports them in times of misfortune, and rewards those who protect their health and wellbeing. None of the current proposals do this.

October 7, 2007

References

1 Health Insurance Laws and Benefits Tool, Insure.com, http://www.insure.com/articles/interactivetools/lawtool/lawtool.jsp (accessed October 4, 2007).

2 Sharfstein, J. The AMA's cigarette PAC - American Medical Association supports politicians who are not against tobacco industry. Washington Monthly, March 1999, http://findarticles.com/p/articles/mi_m1316/is_3_31/ai_54098103 (accessed October 5, 2007).

3 Lobbying Overview: Top Spenders, 1998–2007, Lobbying Database, http://www.opensecrets.org/lobbyists/overview.asp?txtindextype=s (accessed October 4, 2007).

Blog 1.5   An option rarely mentioned in the current healthcare debate

Recent pre-election political discussions have featured significant debate about who should pay for healthcare. Imbedded in these debates are strong beliefs about who should bear responsibility for the cost of health services. First, it is important to differentiate healthcare from health insurance. While the terms are used interchangeably, one refers to services, and the other refers to a system that defines and pays for a set of specified services. The usual debate focuses on insurance (who will pay for what we deliver now), rather than how to alter care delivery to improve its value. As such, this blog discusses arguments about who pays.

Recently, proposals in politics and the media focus on one of two options: universal health insurance provided by government, or private insurance coverage provided (for the most part) by employers. These often appear to be the only alternatives. Employers call for government to free them from responsibility for an ever-increasing cost burden. Advocates for low-income families call for government to cover the un- and under-insured. Health technology and pharmaceutical companies insist that a government solution will kill all scientific innovation. Others argue that a government system will eliminate waste.

Experts from other government-run systems in Europe, Canada and Asia provide a mixture of promising reports and scary outcomes—depending on the author's vantage point. In universal-coverage systems, one can find wonderful examples of effective, high-quality care, as well as frightening tales of long waiting lists and rationed access. Quality may be inferior or superior, depending on the metric and one's definition of "better."

There are three problems we hear about in healthcare: we spend too much **(cost)**, too many people get left out **(access)**, and what we do get could be significantly better **(quality)**. Yet, solutions get oversimplified to a single issue: who pays.

While loud voices debate the merits of one payer versus another, seldom do we stop to wonder if we are asking the right question. Will a choice between employer and government fix the problem? Are these our only alternatives? Putting aside rigid red or blue positions about private industry and government, consider the following misconceptions and realities about who pays.

Misconception 1: Employers pay for health insurance for workers. Reality: Workers pay the majority of the cost of health insurance in lieu of better wages or other benefits. Depending on industry and salary level, between 56% and 85% of costs are likely shifted back to employees as lower wages.[1, 2]

Misconception 2: Universal health insurance means the government will pay for healthcare. Reality: Any additional health insurance provided by government will be paid for by taxpayers through higher taxes, inflation, or the substitution of health benefits for other governmental services.

Misconception 3: Finding the "right" party to pay will fix the problem. Reality: Changing who pays will have minimal effect—because inefficiencies in healthcare delivery will not change. Unless payments are structured to align incentives relative to peoples' values, we will be wasting money in healthcare.

In the world of the economist, if the price, quantity, and quality of service remain the same, changing who pays is an issue of income redistribution only and will not affect the true allocation and delivery of resources. **Changing who pays does not change the price or efficiency of healthcare.** However, if price changes, the demand by consumers will change, both in respect to quantity and quality of service. This makes it a resource allocation (efficiency) issue rather than an income distribution issue.

While the primary debate centers on who should write the check for health insurance coverage on behalf of workers/citizens, rarely do we acknowledge that in reality workers and citizens provide the real resources. In either case, citizens and/or workers place trust (and money) in the hands of another party (government agencies or employers) to purchase healthcare for them. Further, in most cases it is these purchasers who choose criteria for eligibility, define what services will or will not be covered and how much will be paid for them.

Certainly, this "we-pay, others-purchase" system evolved over time, guided by many more forces than we can cover in this blog entry. Some include the following:

- Employers received tax breaks for providing healthcare instead of wages, a policy started during WWII for reasons related to wage and price controls, not better healthcare.
- Employment in the 1950s and 1960s consisted of a more paternalistic and long-term arrangement than it does now. Pensions and medical coverage for life were part of this arrangement.
- Government began covering healthcare for older and poorer citizens in the mid-1960s, as an amendment to the Social Security Act in an attempt to cover some of the gaps not included in an employer-provided system.
- A powerful medical industry developed, aware that its paying customer was not the patient, but a private or public agency (or the insurance companies payers asked to make arrangements on *their* behalf).

By fighting over which one of *them* (government or employers) will provide health insurance for U.S. citizens, we ignore a significant question. Do we need someone else to set rules, define prices, and purchase services on our behalf? Isn't there an alternative to choose no one? We already pay for health insurance through taxes or reduced wages—do we need to pay someone else to manage this for us, or could we create a more efficient system without the middle-man?

There is another choice

The same moneys collected from wages and taxes can be distributed to individuals in the form of savings accounts or vouchers or other venues in the consumer's control. This can include money for premiums to cover catastrophic illness, and funds for routine care according to individual choice. Distribution can occur over a lifetime, in amounts weighted by need, or circumstance, or other factors. Money governed by individuals is more portable (eliminating loss of coverage during job transitions), less prone to moral hazard (where people spend more because someone else pays), and applies market forces to encourage cost transparency and competition based on access and quality.

Because individuals, through their decentralized decisions, can alter the dynamic of healthcare delivery in ways that a third-party cannot, this is really the only choice that has potential to address all three problems: cost, access, and quality. It requires a true consumer-based system rather than the pseudo-system* which exists now; a new system based on the belief that all individuals deserve to choose their own care path.

This leads us to addressing misconception #3: changing what (and how much) we pay for. The most efficient transactions will occur when patients pay providers directly for services. Individuals paying directly for services they value, rather than groups lobbying third-parties for what they think society should have, give us the best chance of creating a rational system, inspiring innovation and competition.

---

* For example, current consumer-directed programs often require forfeiture of funds when leaving a job, required use of a defined network in order to qualify for the deductible, and place many restrictions on health plan parameters. These issues limit true consumer behavior.

Current debates do not often include this alternative; we are used to assigning this responsibility (and to some extent blame) to someone else. Most likely, politicians will decide that assigning responsibility for payment to government or employers is a better option than allocating it to individuals.[†]

But hopefully, in the next debate about either-or, you will remember a third option.

March 25, 2007

References

1 Blumberg, L.J. Who pays for employer sponsored health insurance? Health Affairs (Millwood) 1999; 18(6):58-61.

2 Pauly, M., Percy, A., Herring, B. Individual versus job-based health insurance: weighing the pros and cons. Health Affairs (Millwood) 1999; 18(6):28-44.

[†] This occurs, in part, because our political system tends to protect the interests of large organizations (all doctors, all unionized workers, all health plans) over individual people. Politically powerful interest groups can offer significant support in exchange for political favors whereas individuals are so unorganized that they cannot offer politicians such inducements.

Blog 1.6   Please don't complicate things with new information. I like the old (wrong) answer better

Sometimes we would rather not hear that our usual way of thinking is insufficient or incorrect. It is easier and more comfortable to stay put than to change.

A medical example

It is now known that most ulcers are caused by a type of bacteria called Heliobacter Pylori, the discovery of which won the 2005 Nobel Prize.[1] Before the 1980s, it was well-accepted that a) ulcers were the result of lifestyle factors—such as stress, alcohol, and spicy food, and b) bacteria could not live in the acidic environment of the stomach. With that understanding of cause, the standard way to treat an ulcer was to control the level of acid produced by the body. When word came of a bacterial cause, it forced a difficult change in thinking for doctors and patients alike.

Believe it or not, patients and doctors were so entrenched in the old and wrong understanding of ulcers, standard medical practice did not adopt antibiotic treatment for more than a decade, leaving patients largely unaware. The delay in new treatment occurred despite its clear advantages—it was one tenth the cost, one tenth the duration, and much more effective than ongoing acid-reducing therapy.[2]

In science, as in all aspects of life, old belief systems die hard. The new paradigm regarding ulcers challenged long-held belief systems and coping behaviors of both doctors and patients. It was quite disruptive. Executives who popped acid-reducing pills and believed they worked themselves sick, wives who cooked bland meals and advised children not to stress dad out, doctors who had learned the "proper" practice of acid-reduction, suddenly faced a very different world view. Even when it represents a clear opportunity for improvement, humans are not anxious to change their minds. (For a wonderful explanation of how changes in thinking occur (or don't) in science, see Thomas Kuhn's work.[3])

A health as human capital example

We find that paradigms are also tightly held in human resources and business. For example, we were asked recently to take part in a project to help businesses estimate the potential to reduce absences and lost productivity in their workforces. It was part of an initiative focusing on health in the workplace and finding ways to improve well-being while achieving positive business results. We were asked to partner with a team of decision makers, supporting the effort with our database and analytic expertise.

Excitedly, we volunteered what we know:

1) Health status influences business costs; however, it is quite difficult to significantly change a population's health status using outside interventions and programs.

2) In contrast, economic incentives in corporate policies, which can

be changed, seem to produce a cascade of measurable effects. First, these policies influence costs, and second, perhaps more importantly, they seem to affect how employees view and manage their own health.

When asked what (*in the world*) we were talking about, we listed evidence from well-designed compensation policies, paid-time-off policies, health-plan benefits, retirement benefits, and training policies. In other words, the structure of how companies pay people, reward people, and help them become more productive by enhancing their human capital. Our data show that when companies share rewards and responsibilities with their employees and invest in their growth, not only does performance improve, but so does attention to health. Bonuses affect employees' ratings of health importance; salary reimbursement levels during paid time-off influences medical disability rates; health plan design contributes to workers' compensation costs; and compensation practices affect healthcare costs. Our point: it's all connected.

The response? Reluctance and frustration. Clearly, we were making something more difficult than it needed to be. Everyone knows that to reduce healthcare costs, we just need to make people healthier. Like fighting the acid to get rid of the ulcer instead of treating the bacteria really causing the problem, this project team was not interested in broad systems issues that increase medical utilization and discourage health protection. Instead, they just wanted to focus on what they believe to be the "real" causes of health costs, specifically related to the health status of workers.

So, unless we could help make a business case for continuing the old way of thinking by improving health status, as in medical interventions, our input was considered disruptive, not constructive.

Those pesky economic incentives

Any new perspective creates opportunities and threats, winners and losers. The discovery of a bacterial cause for ulcers presented a significant opportunity to alleviate, and oftentimes cure a very painful condition. It also provided opportunity for antibiotic manufacturers to build significant revenue. Conversely, the new "bug" discovery threatened the livelihood of anyone who sold stress-reduction services for ulcer sufferers as well as the market for antacid medications.

Our own underlying incentives will influence whether we embrace or refute a new discovery, whether historical or modern, whether in business, medicine or any field.

Case in point, we find that describing health in a broader human capital context also poses perceived threats. Current providers of health programs and medical interventions, insurance carriers, and those wedded to separate management and budgeting across corporate departments often find the all-inclusive human capital discussion worrisome. The project organizers asked us instead if we could present our ideas but "leave out the part about economics and compensation, and focus on wellness." The meeting organizers felt their audience, who had no influence on compensation practices in their organizations, would rather not hear about such matters. (We declined the invitation.)

If a company can fix many of its health and human capital problems by changing broad employment policies, some corporate department managers will have less control over turf and budget. Similarly, vendors selling the "problem" solely as a health problem, and the "solution" solely as a health solution will lose business. Accepting that many traditional employment arrangements between companies and employees actually discourage high performance and undermine health is frightening to those invested in the status quo. New answers, even right answers, are often the most disruptive.

You can pretend economic incentives are not driving health and business outcomes...but they are. Like pretending that the cause of ulcers is stress, ignoring reality only prolongs the problem.

Wanted: those not threatened by reality

We will continue to seek out organizations whose incentives are aligned with, rather than threatened by, this new paradigm. And in those cases, we find like-minded decision makers who actually spend less, but achieve better work performance, greater human capital growth, and lower costs.

We will also seek ways to share our ideas...including the parts about economics and compensation.

October 21, 2007

References

1 Graedon, J., Graedon, T. Infectious ulcers win Nobel Prize. HealthCentral.com, September 17, 2005, http://www.healthcentral.com/peoplespharmacy/408/61189.html (accessed October 18, 2007).

2 Lynch, N.A. Heliobacter pylori and ulcers: a paradigm revised. Breakthroughs in Bioscience, Federation of American Societies for Experimental Biology, http://opa.faseb.org/pdf/pylori.pdf (accessed October 18, 2007).

3 Forster, M.R. Guide to Thomas Khun's The Structure of Scientific Revolutions. March 19, 1998, http://philosophy.wisc.edu/forster/220/kuhn.htm (accessed October 18, 2007).

SECTION 2

Some Things Worth Knowing about Healthcare

Chapter 2
Some Things Worth Knowing about Healthcare

Before we discuss optimal healthcare and human capital strategies, it is important that readers understand some key issues about the nature of healthcare spending. Unless you have seen detailed healthcare data, there are things you might not know. The media doesn't spend much time explaining specifics, so most of us only get some general facts. There are some widely-held assumptions about how much healthcare services cost, and where the dollars are spent that simply aren't true. Even more often, there are known general truths that oversimplify and misrepresent the big picture.

We all know healthcare is expensive, and we know that some diseases cost more than others. What we don't know is that these general truths can lead us to propose the wrong solutions. For example, you may have heard that on average, individuals spend over $5,000 per year in healthcare services. Yet, over 80% of people cost less than that, some far, far less. You may have heard that people with diabetes require very expensive care. However, in a given year, most diabetics do not have high costs. You may think that people who receive really expensive care are the ones with a really serious disease. But more often, costs are in proportion to the number of different illnesses an individual has, not the severity of any one condition. You may think that you will be able to find good information about healthcare options when you need it, but some important facts about your local hospitals are kept hidden.

As we work as a nation to find solutions to the cost and quality problems in healthcare, it is important that we understand the true nature of the problem, not just its magnitude. The next group of blogs help clarify the nature of some of our challenges.

Blog 2.1 What would "Goldilocks" say about healthcare utilization?

Rarely are we "just right."

Many discussions about our nation's healthcare crisis focus on substantial numbers of uninsured people and their lack of access to health services. We worry about those who do not receive sufficient care. Rarely do we hear about services that happen too much.

Some might claim that there is no such thing as "too much" care. Or that a bit too much would be hard to find objectionable—like being too clean, or too careful. Isn't more care always better? Or, like Goldilocks, should we all be seeking an amount of healthcare that is just right for us?

According to many statistics, Goldilocks was on to something. There are convincing indications that Americans often get too many healthcare services. Perhaps the most convincing data come from the Dartmouth Atlas of Healthcare.[1] The *New York Times* posted an interactive graphic from the Atlas showing huge variations in costs and procedures across regions of the country.[2] Amazingly, costs and rates of procedures, such as hysterectomies and heart bypass vary as much as four-fold—for people with similar health status. Yet, evidence suggests that additional services do not produce better health outcomes overall.[3, 4]

What causes the staggering variation (and likely excess) in care? Two simple economic principles:

1) The law of supply, and
2) Moral hazard.

The Law of Supply

The law of supply (separate from the law of demand) says that the higher the price of something, the greater the quantity that will be supplied. It is not surprising then, that higher rates of service strongly correspond with the degree of availability of specialists, hospital beds, and testing devices in a geographic region. Health organizations make money by keeping their highly-priced personnel and resources in use, and increasingly, suppliers are headed down a path that makes illness easier to find and diagnoses easier to declare. We keep lowering the standard of what constitutes illness, advancing the sophistication of interventions, and increasing our ability to detect diseases before they become symptomatic. As much as we tend to appreciate access to medical technology, there is great potential for harm as well.* Further, we rarely acknowledge that spending more on healthcare means we have less money to spend on other things (like education or higher wages).

Someone living in a region with a significant supply of advanced, specialty hospitals will be more likely to receive surgery than someone with equal levels of disease in a region without these resources. Yet, in many cases, the people receiving additional care are not healthier.

In an efficient market, the law of demand will balance the tendency of suppliers to provide expensive services. The law of demand states that the more something costs, the less of it consumers will buy. The equilibrium between supply and demand is the point at which the price is acceptable to the consumer (to buy) and the supplier (to sell).

Without the consumer in the equation paying his or her own money, we experience the second economic phenomenon: moral hazard.

Moral Hazard

Stated simply, people naturally consume more of a product or service when someone else pays for it. In the case of healthcare, individuals rarely pay the full cost of a medical treatment because it is covered by insurance or through a government program. As one might expect, people demand a higher quantity of healthcare than they would if they had to pay the full price themselves.

The combined effects of higher supply and consumer moral hazard.

When a high quantity supplied of expensive services goes unbalanced by cost-conscious consumers, the result is higher-than-efficient quantity demanded. This helps to explain why a metropolitan area with a high

---

* For a wonderful description of this phenomenon, see E.S. Fisher and H.G. Welch. Avoiding the unintended consequences of growth in medical care: how might more be worse? *JAMA.* 1999 Feb 3;281(5):446-53 and N.M. Hadler. *The Last Well Person: How to Stay Well Despite the Health-Care System.* Montreal: McGill-Queens University Press, 2004.

concentration of specialists will have costs three or four times as much per person than an area with fewer hospitals and specialists, but there will be no significant difference in the health of the residents.

How will Goldilocks find an amount of healthcare that is "just right" when society insists that more is better, and that she has little responsibility to pay for it?

The next time you hear someone imply that "more is better" consider this Swiss study published in 1993, called "Revisiting the most informed consumer of surgical services: the physician-patient." The national dataset focused on how frequently doctors themselves undergo surgery. Remember, for Swiss citizens, there were no financial barriers to services. The authors found that controlling for other factors, physicians were significantly less likely to undergo almost all types of surgery compared to non-physicians of similar demographics (an exception was appendectomy).[5]

There could be many reasons for the difference (e.g., physicians were healthier), but it does make one wonder, if *more* care is a sign of better care. Why would doctors, who know the most about it, seek less? Perhaps they know what Goldilocks did: sometimes less is "just right."

July 1, 2007

References

1 Mahar, M. The state of the nation's health. *Dartmouth Medicine*. 2007 Spring;31(3):26-35, http://dartmed.dartmouth.edu/spring07/pdf/atlas.pdf (accessed June 26, 2007).

2 Aigner, E., Bloch, M., Nguyen, V. Regional differences in costs and care. *The New York Times*, June 11, 2007, http://www.nytimes.com/ref/business/20070611_GAP_GRAPHIC.html (accessed June 26, 2007).

3 Fisher, E.S., Wennberg, D.E., Stukel, T.A., Gottlieb, D.J., Lucas, F.L., and Pinder, E.L. The implications of regional variations in medicare spending. Part 2: health outcomes and satisfaction with care. *Ann Intern Med*. 2003;138(4): 288-98.

4 Fisher, E.S., Wennberg, D.E., Stukel, T.A., Gottlieb, D.J., Lucas, F.L., and Pinder, E.L. The implications of regional variations in medicare spending. Part 1: the content quality, and accessibility of care. *Ann Intern Med*. 2003;138(4): 273-87.

5 Domenighetti, G., Casabianca, A., Gutzwiller, F., and Martinoli, S. Revisiting the most informed consumer of surgical services: the physician-patient. *Int J Technol Assess Healthcare*. 1993;9(4): 505-13.

Blog 2.2   What the mean does and doesn't mean: when average isn't normal

According to the Kaiser Family Foundation Annual Survey, the average cost of employer-sponsored healthcare in 2005 was $4,024 per individual employee. The average for family coverage was $10,880, leading to an overall average of about $7,000 for each employed person.[1] These are daunting numbers, but what do they really represent? For things like healthcare costs, the average is not really a helpful description of the true pattern of spending across a population.

From an accounting perspective, an employer uses the average to understand total spending on benefits, by converting total spending to one per-employee amount. For some things, the average is a reasonable indication of what is typical in most cases. For example, things like weather (daily temperature) or human characteristics (height, weight, and IQ) are normally distributed—more data cluster neatly around a middle point and only a few are at high or low extremes. The mean is a good indication of a true typical middle point for such things. But other things, like medical costs or disability costs, don't cluster as neatly around a middle point but have outliers on one side that pull (skew) the average upward. For skewed data, such as medical costs, it is important to look at the whole range.

Healthcare spending is relatively low for most people and is high for relatively few. Figure 2.1 shows the typical skewness in medical costs, using 2002 data we analyzed from a company of about 15,000 people. Dividing costs into five equal buckets of money, we see that 30% of these employees spent 80% of all the healthcare dollars (the four bars on the right side of the graph). In the lowest quintile, 70% of all employees spent 20% of the total healthcare dollars; an average of $901. The average overall cost is $3,150. Clearly, while accurate, $3,150 does not represent a typical amount or an extreme amount. The costs of the high outliers pull the overall average up.

We often hear that people who have chronic illnesses are expensive, on average. In one analysis, we studied costs for diabetics and found that diabetic employees spent almost three times as much on healthcare

FIGURE 2.1   QUINTILES OF ANNUAL HEALTH COSTS

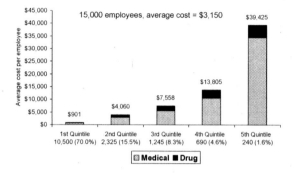

on average as individuals having no chronic illnesses, and twice the average for non-diabetics. Two percent of diabetics fell in the costliest group, compared to fewer than one percent for the entire population. However, almost three-quarters of diabetics still spent less than $2,500 on healthcare. Even for people who have serious conditions, the average is not representative of a typical person with that condition. The average, once again, is higher than what is spent by 70% to 80% of all diabetics.

Why is this important to understand? Because when we try and "manage" costs through policies, programs, and plan design, we have to know what sort of costs we are managing. If we manage people assuming that they are all "average," we may assume that there are considerable savings to be had for each person. However, knowing that 70% of people spend less than $1,000, it becomes apparent that large savings are unlikely for most people. The next time someone says that the average person with Condition X costs $8,000 and that an intervention will save you $1,500 per person...consider how much most of them actually spend and for whom such savings can be achieved.

November 21, 2005

References

1 The Henry J. Kaiser Family Foundation. Employer Health Benefits 2005 Annual Survey, http://www.kff.org/insurance/7315.cfm (accessed November 20, 2005).

Blog 2.3   Illness is about likelihood, not certainty

Recently, some accomplished health researchers challenged our findings regarding how much individuals' healthcare costs change from year to year. We were showing that the vast majority of expensive people become less expensive the following year.* The researchers insisted that our findings must be incorrect—everyone knows that chronically ill people get progressively sicker and more expensive over time. Many studies comparing average costs for groups of people prove their case.

Although paradoxical, both perspectives are correct.

Most health issues make a person *more likely, but not certain*, to have a serious (i.e. expensive) event. I learned this lesson early in my career from a set of studies published in 1991[1] and 1992.[2] My colleagues and I looked at the excess cost of smokers compared to non-smokers. While there was a difference in cost, on average, it was due to smokers disproportionately being among the most expensive in every disease group.

Specifically, comparing smokers to ex-smokers, in the oldest age group, there was a $265 average difference in medical costs (see figure 2.2). This did not occur because all smokers are $265 more expensive each year, but instead because older smokers had 5.5 more people (22.5) per 100 in the high cost group than ex-smokers (17 per 100). But this is still a minority of people. At the medians (the midpoint of costs for all smokers and all ex-smokers), smokers were actually less costly. The differences in likelihood are even smaller in younger age groups, where only 4%- 7% were expected to have high costs.

When studies use averages to describe differences like this (such as $265), we naturally translate that into a general difference. But actually, most smokers are not more expensive; a few are a lot more expensive. The same phenomenon applies for other risk factors and chronic illnesses. Not every person with hypertension and high cholesterol will have a stroke or heart attack, but the likelihood of such events is higher. So, as a group,

---

* For a similar graph, see Blog 2.5 The episodic nature of illness and its implications, part 2.

FIGURE 2.2 HOW LIKELIHOOD OF HIGHER COSTS INFLUENCES AVERAGE COSTS

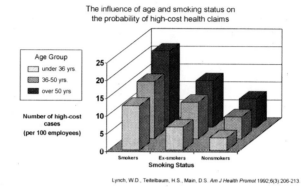

The influence of age and smoking status on the probability of high-cost health claims

Lynch, W.D., Teitelbaum, H.S., Main, D.S. *Am J Health Promot* 1992;6(3):206-213.

average costs will be greater for people with illnesses—but those averages often reflect big cost differences in a small subset of people.

In a similar way, the health researchers we spoke with recently were correct in saying that sick people get progressively more expensive over time—on average. The longer a person has an illness, and the more co-morbidities the person accumulates, the higher his likelihood of requiring more healthcare and experiencing a severe event. Despite this progressive increase in likelihood, however, most people will not be expensive in a given year and very few will repeat in multiple years.

In figure 2.3, we see the reality of small likelihoods over time. In this analysis we combined all costs for medical care, absence, disability, and workers' compensation. In the circles are the percent of people who accounted for the top 40% of costs in a specific year.[†] The complex web of arrows shows how employees in the circles migrate into and out of the expensive group over time. To understand what happens to an expensive group the following year, add the percents in all the outgoing arrows. For example, of the expensive people in 2003, 75.3% became less costly, 12.1% repeated as high cost in 2004, and 12.6% left the company.

In this population of approximately 10,000 people, between 2%-6% (260 to 610 people) accounted for 40% of all health-related costs in a

---

† Although the exact amount needed to qualify in the high cost category varied by year, those in this group exceeded $20,000 in total costs.

given year. In each year, between 73%- 83% were in this high-cost group for the first time. As seen on the horizontal line between the circles, only 12%-18% of these expensive people, which is between 0.4% and 1% of the total population (18% of 6.1% =1.09%), were expensive in two consecutive years. If we combine those who never repeat as high cost and those who leave the company, seven in ten expensive people are only expensive once in the four-year period.

FIGURE 2.3   FOUR-YEAR TRANSITION ANALYSIS

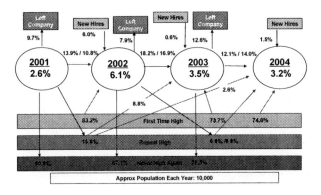

Why did we choose to show this complicated diagram, instead of using a simpler representation we have shown before?‡ Because sometimes it is important that we recognize how complex these issues are. We could simply say that averages are misleading and fewer than 1% of people are high cost repeatedly over time. But sometimes our efforts to simplify lead us to incorrect assumptions—like our researcher friends who challenged migration based on previous summary data.

This figure demonstrates the instability of health costs and infrequency with which individuals in an employed population have high use of health benefits. Despite our awareness that the workforce is becoming more expensive in general, it is not as common or repetitive an occurrence as we often imagine.

---

‡ See Blog 2.5 The episodic nature of illness and its implications, part 2.

It's how you ask the question

Are people with illness more costly than those without illness, on average? Absolutely. Do most people with chronic illness receive expensive healthcare in a given year? Not necessarily.

Do people with chronic illness get more costly over time, on average? Yes. Are most people who are expensive in one year also expensive in subsequent years? No, the majority are not.

It's about likelihood

When a person has a health risk (smoking, obesity) or an illness (hypertension, high cholesterol), he increases his likelihood of being expensive sometime in the future. If this were a game of dice, his chances of landing on an unfortunate number are higher. But, nothing is certain.

January 1, 2007

References

1 Lynch ,W.D., Teitelbaum, H.S., Main, D.S. The inadequacy of using means to compare medical costs of smokers and nonsmokers. *Am J Health Promotion* 1991; 6(2):123-129.

2 Lynch, W.D., Teitelbaum, H.S., Main, D.S. Comparing medical costs by analyzing high-cost cases. *Am J Health Promotion* 1992; 6(3):206-213.

Blog 2.4   The episodic nature of illness and its implications. Part 1

Why don't more people participate in disease management programs? In a previous blog entry,* we suggested a few reasons based on market economics. In this entry (and the next) we will look at another possible reason—the episodic nature of illness and medical treatment.

One misconception about chronic disease is that "chronic" implies a steady, ongoing experience of illness. We know that people with chronic illnesses have higher medical costs, on average, so we assume that every person with chronic illness is more expensive all the time. Not so. Contrary to what one might think, very few illnesses produce high costs

---

* See Blog 5.6 Interpreting attrition rates in disease management through a lens of market efficiency—who is paid, by whom, to do what?

in a given year. Most people—even people with chronic illnesses—do not incur high medical costs. Our research team analyzed data from 200,000 employees in 2001. Only 14% of diabetic employees, 11% of hypertensive employees and 9% of employees with high cholesterol (hyperlipidemia) had costs over $7,500. The "average" cost for people with these conditions reflects, in part, the number of people in the expensive "tail" of the curve. A person with chronic illness is more likely to be expensive, but not certain of being expensive in any given year.

Even when an individual does have high costs, his or her costs usually do not stay high over time. A good example is acute myocardial infarction (heart attack). This is one example where the event is expensive (over $7,500) for almost everyone (70%) who has the diagnosis. However, the following year, only 25% of the same people will have high costs. Not many illnesses result in a greater chance of being expensive in year-two as well as year-one. Diabetes, hypertension and hyperlipidemia are exceptions. They do result in a slightly higher likelihood of being expensive in the second year—rising by 2.1%, 1.2% and 1.1%, respectively. Still, even after the increase, 80 to 90% of employees with these illnesses will have medical claims under $7,500.

What these patterns mean is that serious problems occur in episodes. Only a small portion of people will have a serious episode in any given year. If few people have high costs (translation: utilization), it is difficult to intervene with the whole group and save money. It is also difficult to find the right ones at the right time who need help.

An example: Musculoskeletal Issues

Let's use musculoskeletal issues to illustrate the possible implications of episodic illness. Our analysis found that 14% of patients with back problems (intervertebral disc disorders), had high costs in a given year, and the exact same percent had high costs the subsequent year. Patients with back sprains and strains had a 10% rate in both years. So, again, for these issues, few will be expensive in any given year. In other words, the problems are episodic.

Using an example from a large employee population from 2002 through 2004, the following analysis examined 1,200 employees who were

FIGURE 2.4   PERCENT HAVING ZERO, ONE, OR MORE PHONE CONTACTS IN A DISEASE
MANAGEMENT PROGRAM

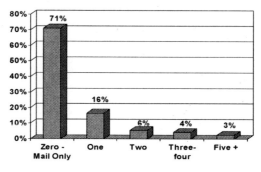

Percent having this many phone contacts

identified for a musculoskeletal DM intervention.† As seen in figure 2.4, few of those identified were contacted. Of those identified, 71% received mailed information. Of those who were called, over half (16% out of 29%) only had one phone contact. (This is not unlike the patterns in the last blog, where participation is below what one might consider desirable.)

Since musculoskeletal conditions are episodic, with only a portion of people experiencing high utilization in a given year, what does the pattern of costs look like? People expensive in one year are not likely to be expensive the next. Figure 2.5 shows the pattern of musculoskeletal costs before and after the start of enrollment into the DM program.‡ Overall (solid line), everyone who had musculoskeletal issues in the year before

---

† The premise of DM programs is to support individuals with chronic illness, hoping to slow progression of the disease and avoid serious and costly problems. To succeed financially, interventions need to help sufficient numbers of people who have large enough savings to cover thier cost. Some programs have been marketed using the logic that on average, "people with chronic illness are expensive," without clear explanation that the yearly average is not representative of most cases.

‡ For those who want more detail, the cost trend analysis included all people with musculoskeletal issues, including those *not* identified by the DM vendor. To be included, the person had to have two consecutive years of medical claims and employment prior to enrolling in the program. Individuals *not* enrolled were given a "hypothetical" start date at the median time in the program. We removed all cases in the top quintile of cost (to remove the effect of outliers in the graph), but their peak costs did occur before the start of the program as well.

FIGURE 2.5   MUSCULOSKELETAL COST TRENDS BY LEVEL OF INVOLVEMENT IN
DISEASE MANAGEMENT

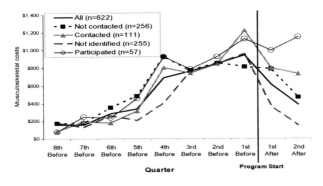

the program—whether chosen for the intervention or not—had an episode whose costs peaked before the program started. People who were not identified (dashed), identified but not contacted by phone (squares), and identified and successfully contacted (triangles), all had similar decreases in cost after the program began.

Those who were contacted and agreed to participate in more than one call (n=57, circles) were in the only group that continued upward. One is left to wonder why. Were they contacted when the episode was still active? Were they in the midst of treatment decisions that others were not?

With the exception of the small group of active participants, it does appear that enrollment lagged behind the episode. Knowing that few people will be expensive, and that those who **are** will not remain expensive, it is not surprising that many of those identified will not be costly after the program begins, and the rest might be well on their way to being less costly. Perhaps many people don't sign up for a program because they already feel better.

It is important for decision makers to understand this episodic pattern, as well as the difficulty one has in predicting expensive episodes before they happen. We should not be surprised when programs misidentify many potentially-expensive cases for every one correctly identified. Nor should we be surprised that most interventions chase after events which have already occurred. These are natural consequences of the episodic aspects of illness.

41

In the second part of this topic, we will look at the dynamics of change in medical cost.

June 11, 2006

Blog 2.5　The episodic nature of illness and its implications. Part 2

When people get sick, will they be consistently expensive from year to year? In the last blog entry, we described how only a portion of people with a condition will have expensive treatments in a given year. And their costs will inevitably change the following year. Figure 2.6 illustrates the distribution of costs for over 13,000 male employees in 2003.

FIGURE 2.6　PERCENT OF PEOPLE IN QUINTILES OF COST

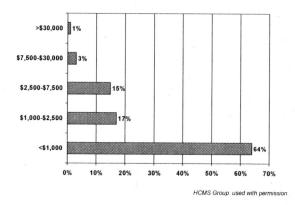

HCMS Group used with permission

The cost categories were as follows: Very Low cost = under $1,000; Low cost = $1,000 to $2,500; Moderate cost = $2,500 to $7,500; High cost = $7,500 to $30,000; Very High cost = over $30,000. We see a familiar distribution of costs, where about 65% of the population had costs under $1,000, 81% (64% plus 17%) had costs under $2,500, and only about 4% had costs above $7,500.

So, how much do costs change? Figure 2.7 shows the direction of change in costs from 2003 to 2004. For each bar we see where people in each category in 2003 ended up in 2004. As we see, most of those in the <$1,000 cost category in 2003 stayed (light gray) in the same category

42

FIGURE 2.7   PERCENT OF PEOPLE AND DIRECTION OF CHANGE IN COSTS FROM
2003 TO 2004

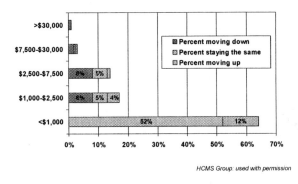

HCMS Group: used with permission

in 2004. But the other categories show a significant portion of people
changing to higher (dots) or lower (dark gray) categories.

To see it better, we changed the graph (fig. 2.8) to show the percent of
people from the category in 2003 who changed to different categories in
2004.* For example, in the center row of the people with moderate costs in
2003, 55% had lower costs, 36% stayed the same, and 9% became more
expensive.

FIGURE 2.8   PERCENT AND DIRECTION OF PEOPLE CHANGING COSTS FROM
2003 TO 2004 (AS A PERCENT OF 2003)

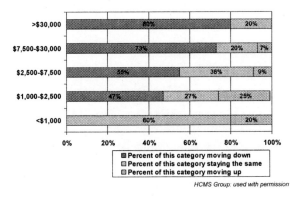

HCMS Group: used with permission

---

* The two graphs are the same, except they have been converted so each bar totals
100%. For instance, in the bottom bar 52% is 80% of 64%. And 12% is 20% of 64%. So,
52 and 12 become 80 and 20.

In terms of overall change in the whole group (figure 2.7), 63% stayed in the same cost category (light gray), 18% moved higher (dots), and 19% moved lower (dark gray). The people in the very low cost category were the most stable, with four of five remaining in the lowest category. But that is the only group where the majority stayed put. Of everyone who had costs over $1,000 (above the lowest level) in 2003, only 30% stayed in their category in the subsequent year. The small group in the highest two categories were the least stable, with only one out of five remaining in the same category.

We wondered whether employees with a chronic illness were more or less likely to change categories. We created the same matrix for members of the population with diagnosed diabetes (*n*=898). As shown in figure 2.9, far fewer of the diabetic employees fall into the lowest category.

FIGURE 2.9   PERCENT OF DIABETIC PEOPLE IN QUINTILES OF COST

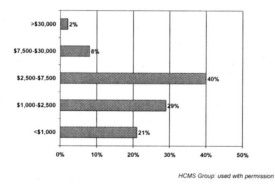

HCMS Group: used with permission

However, only 10% fall in the top two categories (>$7,500). More diabetic employees fall into the moderate category than any other.

As we see in figure 2.10, there is even more movement (dark gray bars and dotted bars) in this graph than in the overall migration chart above (fig. 2.8). The answer to our question: those with illnesses change categories more often. Across all cost levels (not shown) only about 50% of the people with diabetes stayed at the same cost level, while about 25% went up, and 25% went down.

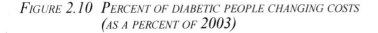

FIGURE 2.10 PERCENT OF DIABETIC PEOPLE CHANGING COSTS (AS A PERCENT OF 2003)

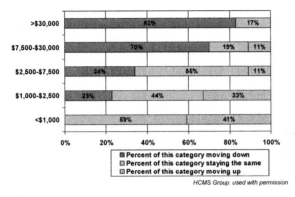

HCMS Group: used with permission

Why should decision makers be aware of the dynamic nature of costs? Several reasons. First to keep in mind is that people move. When we refer to "regression to the mean," we are referring to the top levels in the matrix—where the majority move downward no matter what we do. Having episodic costs means that high-cost people do not stay high cost. What we see here is that 80% of the highest-cost people (whether they have chronic illness or not) will be less expensive next year.

We often classify people in general terms; healthy people are low cost and chronically ill people are expensive. Actually, people in every level can move to every other level of cost in the next year. The concept of "targeting" should be evaluated with movement in mind. "Targeting" diabetic employees, even those who were expensive last year, may result in chasing people who are already on their way to lower costs. Unless an intervention can identify those at risk prospectively, there will be far more "misses" than "hits."

Second is a reminder for why we must interpret single-group evaluations with caution. If this degree of movement happens naturally in the absence of an intervention, it is difficult to know whether movement after a program is meaningfully different—unless you have a true control group.

Most people need care in episodes, meaning that a minority will be costly, and those who are costly will likely cost less next year. Remember

45

these facts the next time someone tells you about an intervention where people became less expensive after participating…would the participants have become less expensive anyway?

June 26, 2006

Blog 2.6 Should we really be focusing on specific diseases? An argument in favor of focusing on people instead

Recently I was asked, "If you were to advise a group of employers about what disease to pick next as a focus for disease management, what disease would you tell us to pick?" My answer: I would tell you not to pick one, because *single diseases are not the most useful way for employers to address the cost problem.*

In a future entry* we'll address other factors surrounding a person with an illness. This entry will focus on the mathematics of cost for single and multiple diseases. We will explain healthcare utilization using the Agency for Healthcare Research and Quality (AHRQ) disease classification system, which categorizes medical claims data into 261 different disease categories. While there are thousands of diseases, this standardized classification system makes them more manageable.

Our research team has spent considerable time looking at what factors contribute to individuals being expensive and what makes them continue to be expensive over time. One might hypothesize that many aspects of healthcare utilization could be indicative of who will become expensive in the future. A disease-focused approach assumes that specific diseases result in high costs and that better interventions for those illnesses will reduce those costs. But what if specific diseases are not what makes people costly over time?

We will test three possible hypotheses here to predict whether someone will be expensive in the next year:

_____

* See Blog 1.3 It's more important to understand the person with the illness, than the illness the person has.

46

A) How much someone spends overall in year 1—regardless of reason— predicts their likelihood of being expensive in year 2. We will test this hypothesis using the following metric.

Metric 1: A person's total costs for medical care in year 1.

B) A person who has a single expensive condition in year 1 will be more likely to be expensive in year 2. We will test this hypothesis using the following metrics:

Metric 2: Maximum <u>amount</u> spent on a single condition.
Metric 3: Maximum <u>percent</u> of costs spent on a single condition.

C) A person who has more conditions in year 1 will be more likely to be expensive in year 2. We will test this hypothesis using the following metrics:

Metric 4: Total number of different conditions in year 1.
Metric 5: Total number of unique prescriptions in year 1.

We looked at how each of these factors—measured in year 1— predicted the likelihood of being high-cost in year 2 (defined here as higher than $7,500). The analysis was done on about 250,000 employees and their dependents. As we see in figure 2.11, across this large population all patterns of use in year 1 were predictive of higher expenses in the following year.

FIGURE 2.11   LIKELIHOOD OF HIGH COSTS ACROSS A POPULATION

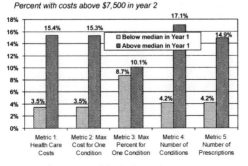

Health as Human Capital Research Group, 2006

For example, people who spent above the median in total costs in year 1 were five times as likely to be high cost (15.4% compared to 3.5%) than those whose spending was below the median in year 1. Our hypothesis that a person spending a lot on a single condition in year 1 will be expensive in year 2 also holds true for metric 2. Of the people who spent below the median of dollars on their most expensive, single condition in year 1 (metric 2), 3.6% were high cost in year 2, compared to 15.3% for people above the median in spending on a single condition. Lastly, having a higher number of diseases also results in a higher likelihood of being expensive in year 2; 17.1% of those who had above the median number of conditions in year 1, while only 4.2% of those below the median number had high costs in year 2.

An interesting pattern is evident with metric 3—having a high portion of costs in one condition. What we see is that individuals who have a high portion of costs spent on a single condition in year 1—in other words, the majority of spending was on one problem—were only slightly more likely to be expensive in year 2 than those spending a smaller portion on any one problem. Having most costs for a single condition means the person is less likely to have many diseases, suggesting that a single, expensive episode is not a strong predictor of subsequent expenses.

To look at the likelihood of repeating as a high-cost patient, we limited the population to 20,000 people who were expensive in year 1 (over $7,500 in healthcare costs). In figure 2.12, we see how these cost patterns contribute to a person repeating high-cost utilization in a subsequent year.

FIGURE 2.12 LIKELIHOOD OF REPEAT HIGH COSTS

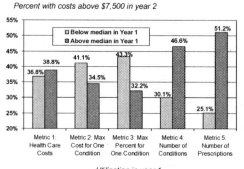

Percent with costs above $7,500 in year 2

	Below median in Year 1	Above median in Year 1
Metric 1: Health Care Costs	36.8%	38.8%
Metric 2: Max Cost for One Condition	41.1%	34.5%
Metric 3: Max Percent for One Condition	43.3%	32.2%
Metric 4: Number of Conditions	30.1%	46.6%
Metric 5: Number of Prescriptions	25.1%	51.2%

Utilization in year 1

Health as Human Capital Research Group, 2006

Testing overall costs, it appears that the magnitude of costs in year 1 (metric one) is not very predictive of being expensive in year 2. Just being costly was not very predictive of repeating in the high-cost group. Testing the effect of a single, expensive condition revealed that a person who had a high portion of costs in a single category was actually *less* likely to be expensive in year 2. Only 32% of people who had a high portion of costs in one single disease repeated as high cost, compared to 41% of those who had more dispersion in costs across multiple illnesses.

The alternative hypothesis, testing the effect of the number of conditions, shows more predictive power. A person with a higher number of conditions or prescriptions was much more likely to repeat with high costs the following year.

What does this analysis tell us? As we mentioned in a previous entry[†], very few single illnesses are predictive of increasing costs in multiple years. Because illnesses tend to be episodic, for the vast majority of AHRQ-defined conditions we find that an expensive year is most often followed by lower expenses the following year. This explains why individuals in this study who had a large majority of costs in one condition were actually *less* likely to repeat their high costs. Those experiencing multiple issues and receiving multiple treatments today are the ones who most drive costs tomorrow. It is not *what* you have, but *how many* things you have that seems to drive costs. Really expensive medical cases are almost always complex ones involving multiple conditions and coordination of multiple treatments.

What this implies is that when we try to manage a cost problem in an incremental illness-by-illness fashion, we may not be aiming at the right target. Finding an expensive person with a serious illness may not be as important as finding people who have many things wrong but may not be expensive yet. Further, a program focusing on a single problem might complicate things *even more* by adding yet another independent provider who may not see the whole picture. So, by picking out the next most expensive condition, we may actually miss opportunities to support the employees who most need attention.

---

† See Blog 2.4 The episodic nature of illness, part 1.

So when someone asks you to pick the next illness target, just say no. Focus on people instead.

October 2, 2006

Blog 2.7　Which conditions do we spend the most money on? It's not what you might guess

In a recent meeting among human resources professionals from large companies, the discussion turned to the types of health conditions that contribute to total spending. Several in the group assumed that severe conditions account for the majority of costs in a population of employees and their families. Actually, no. While it is a common assumption that serious illnesses (the "outliers") contribute the most to costs, in fact spending has more to do with the prevalence of an illness than its severity.

This surprising fact has implications when policy makers think about solutions to our healthcare problems. If common issues contribute most to costs, perhaps there are signifcant opportunities in the ways we prevent and manage those issues.

So which conditions really drive cost by virtue of being prevalent? Let's look at some actual data from our Research Reference Database to find out.

First it is important to distinguish between three different topics:

a) There are *people* who have high healthcare costs.
b) There are *expensive treatments* per person for certain conditions.
c) And there are *conditions* that accumulate a lot of spending in a population of people.

First topic: People who accumulate a lot of healthcare costs. We have talked in other blogs about *people* whose combined treatments cost a lot. What our data show us is that individuals with high, prolonged costs tend to have many conditions, not limited to one serious diagnosis. In fact, a person with one primary, serious condition may drive a single high-cost episode, but is *not* as likely to be expensive for very long.

Second topic: Conditions that are very expensive to treat per person. Specific conditions that have the highest cost per person tend to be severe and require highly technical treatments. Using a year of data* for about 250,000 employees, we sorted conditions by the cost of treatment in that year per person with the condition. As shown in table 2.1 below, conditions are listed by their Agency for Healthcare Research and Quality (AHRQ) category name, which is a labeling system that condenses tens of thousands of diagnosis codes into 261 conditions.[1]

TABLE 2.1   TOP TWENTY MOST COSTLY CONDITIONS (PER PERSON)

AHRQ Category	Cost per Person	Total Cost	Percent of People in Population	Average Cost per Service	Average Services per Claimant	Percent of Total Cost	Cummulative Percent of Total Cost
CANCER OF ESOPHAGUS	$ 15,150	$363,596	0.01%	$459	33	0.07%	0.07%
OTHER CNS INFECTION	$ 11,986	$551,369	0.02%	$768	16	0.10%	0.17%
ACUTE MYOCARDIAL INFARCTION	$ 10,213	$4,759,166	0.19%	$608	17	0.88%	1.05%
CANCER OF STOMACH	$ 10,044	$341,505	0.01%	$429	23	0.06%	1.12%
CHRONIC RENAL FAILURE	$ 9,962	$3,705,710	0.15%	$221	45	0.69%	1.81%
MULTIPLE MYELOMA	$ 8,384	$226,375	0.01%	$122	69	0.04%	1.85%
CANCER OF OVARY	$ 8,358	$1,111,549	0.05%	$209	40	0.21%	2.06%
NON-HODGKIN'S LYMPHOMA	$ 7,826	$2,363,387	0.12%	$215	36	0.44%	2.50%
CANCER OF BRONCHUS LUNG	$ 7,368	$1,068,420	0.06%	$229	32	0.20%	2.69%
MAINT CHEMO/RADIOTHERAPY	$ 7,252	$2,668,593	0.15%	$343	21	0.50%	3.19%
CANCER OF PANCREAS	$ 7,134	$242,566	0.01%	$181	39	0.05%	3.24%
LEUKEMIAS	$ 6,754	$823,934	0.05%	$237	28	0.15%	3.39%
CANCER OF RECTUM AND ANUS	$ 6,688	$1,049,994	0.06%	$197	34	0.20%	3.58%
ASPIRATION PNEUMONITIS	$ 6,669	$213,404	0.01%	$827	8	0.04%	3.62%
CANCER OF BREAST	$ 6,019	$8,336,335	0.56%	$166	36	1.55%	5.17%
HODGKIN'S DISEASE	$ 5,713	$656,945	0.05%	$163	35	0.12%	5.30%
SECONDARY MALIGNANCIES	$ 5,502	$1,562,495	0.12%	$377	15	0.29%	5.59%
CANCER OF BRAIN AND NS	$ 5,500	$555,515	0.04%	$310	18	0.10%	5.69%
CANCER OF COLON	$ 5,138	$1,505,459	0.12%	$148	35	0.28%	5.97%
APPENDICITIS/APPENDICEAL	$ 5,021	$2,234,497	0.18%	$441	11	0.42%	6.38%
		$34,340,814					

HHCF 2007

Rare illnesses are in the top twenty conditions with the highest cost per person. The most common condition in the list is breast cancer, a diagnosis given to only about half of one percent of this population. By contrast, cancers of the esophagus and stomach were diagnosed in only

---

*   The analysis used in this example came from 2002 data.

one one-hundredth of a percent, or one in 10,000. The cost per person in one year, for treatment of these specific diagnoses, ranged from about $5,000 to $15,000. An important characteristic of spending for these costly conditions is that they usually involve numerous services, some more technical than others. As we see, cancer diagnoses often reflect 30, 40 or even 60 services per year. Plus, the average cost per service is also high (Note: this includes many services with a variety of fees). So, a condition with a high per-person cost likely includes multiple technical services and a prolonged series of treatments.

The last column of the table makes our point: the top 20 most expensive conditions to treat only account for a total of about 7% of all spending for the population (about $34 million out of $504 million). So, despite having expensive treatments per-person, these conditions do not drive total population spending.

Third topic: Total healthcare spending in a population. What surprised some in our meeting was seeing that the primary factor determining total spending on a condition is how commonly the condition occurs. In addition, a condition that is both common and requires repeated treatments (chronic) will accumulate the most costs.

Which condition almost always has the highest spending in an employed population? Back problems. In the AHRQ labeling system, back problems fall in a category labeled Intervertebral Disc Disorders. As we see in table 2.2, twelve percent of the population, receiving an average of 17 services (even though the average service cost was only $66) generated more overall fees than any other condition. Back problems generate almost twice as much spending as the second condition on the list, coronary artery blockages. In fact, for this population, the cost of treating back pain was about the same as the combined costs for all 20 of the most costly rare conditions in our other table. Notably, the 29 conditions listed in this table account for one half of all spending for the population.

Anyone who gets familiar with datasets like these begins to notice that some general assumptions about healthcare spending do not hold true. It's not always the serious things that generate costs. We spend a lot on things that are less life-threatening and more problematic for everyday living. A great many of the conditions with greatest accumulated spending are

TABLE 2.2   MOST COSTLY CONDITIONS OVERALL

AHRQ Category	Total Cost	Percent of People in Population	Average Cost per Service	Average Services per Claimant	Percent of Total Cost	Cummulative Percent of Total Cost
INTERVERTEBRAL DISC DISORDERS	$33,655,753	12.08%	$66	17	6.7%	6.7%
CORONARY ATHEROSCLEROSIS	$14,646,585	2.06%	$272	11	2.9%	9.6%
NONSPECIFIC CHEST PAIN	$12,897,611	6.80%	$126	6	2.6%	12.2%
OTHER CONNECTIVE TISSUE DIS	$12,885,943	11.79%	$61	7	2.6%	14.7%
OTHER NERV SYS DISORDERS	$12,012,048	5.39%	$134	7	2.4%	17.1%
ABDOMINAL PAIN	$10,040,222	7.76%	$105	5	2.0%	19.1%
OTHER BENIGN NEOPLASM	$9,955,112	6.29%	$193	3	2.0%	21.1%
OTHER FEMALE GENITAL DIS	$9,933,718	21.31%	$55	3	2.0%	23.0%
TRAUMA-RELATED JOINT DIS	$9,093,512	2.86%	$97	13	1.8%	24.8%
SPRAINS AND STRAINS	$8,679,622	8.24%	$47	9	1.7%	26.6%
CANCER OF BREAST	$8,336,335	0.56%	$166	36	1.7%	28.2%
OTHER NON-TRAUMATIC JOINT DIS	$7,916,250	9.40%	$62	6	1.6%	29.8%
NUTRIT/ENDOCRINE/METABOLIC	$7,830,366	2.78%	$194	6	1.6%	31.4%
BILIARY TRACT DISEASE	$7,661,250	0.90%	$410	8	1.5%	32.9%
OTHER UPPER RESP INFECTIONS	$6,745,317	18.07%	$54	3	1.3%	34.2%
OTHER UPPER RESPIRATORY DIS	$6,715,373	7.92%	$61	6	1.3%	35.5%
NORMAL PREGNANCY/DELIVERY	$6,474,086	2.51%	$103	10	1.3%	36.8%
AFFECTIVE DISORDERS	$6,453,862	3.25%	$68	12	1.3%	38.1%
BENIGN NEOPLASM OF UTERUS	$6,279,882	1.61%	$299	5	1.2%	39.4%
OSTEOARTHRITIS	$6,113,040	2.37%	$159	7	1.2%	40.6%
CALCULUS OF URINARY TRACT	$5,974,553	1.13%	$218	10	1.2%	41.8%
NON-MALIG BREAST CONDITIONS	$5,628,141	4.64%	$127	4	1.1%	42.9%
MENSTRUAL DISORDERS	$5,475,073	4.71%	$101	5	1.1%	44.0%
OTHER GI DISORDERS	$5,447,813	4.40%	$142	4	1.1%	45.0%
CARDIAC DYSRHYTHMIAS	$5,372,073	2.79%	$128	6	1.1%	46.1%
HEADACHE INCLUDING MIGRAINE	$5,105,182	4.81%	$92	5	1.0%	47.1%
OTHER LOWER RESPIRATORY DIS	$5,095,454	6.61%	$87	4	1.0%	48.1%
COMP OF BIRTH/PUERPERIUM	$5,091,660	1.45%	$209	7	1.0%	49.2%
ACUTE MYOCARDIAL INFARCTION	$4,759,166	0.19%	$608	17	0.9%	50.1%
	$252,275,002					

HHCF 2007

day-to-day problems like colds, menstrual cramps, headaches, joint pain, muscle pulls, and digestive problems.

Only two conditions from our first table (expensive per person) are in the second list (high spending overall): breast cancer and heart attack (AMI). Both are in the second list because of the high average number of services a person receives.

Another interesting observation is that the two conditions responsible for 10% of all spending have been the focus of recent scrutiny about ineffective treatments. New findings suggest that a significant number of back surgeries[2] and as many as half of heart angioplasties[3] have little therapeutic value,[†] and may in fact do more harm than good. It certainly makes one wonder how much of the $50 million this population spent treating backs and coronary artery disease was well-spent.

Why should we know this?

Decision makers faced with the challenge of improving the quality of healthcare and managing ever-increasing costs should be aware of where the money goes. So often, we focus on the *really expensive* and *really serious* conditions and forget that not all decisions are life-or-death. Further, we spend huge amounts of money on treatments that have questionable value.

These data also illustrate that a large portion of our nation's spending goes to managing common issues that are to a great extent preventable and also can have a significant self-care component. Self-management and self-assessment resources can be effective tools for improving the appropriateness of care (for example, recognizing when headaches, stomach aches, and muscle pain are serious warning signs of a need for medical attention.) Even in the case of coronary artery disease, we now know that lifestyle and compliance with medications (behaviors controlled by the patient, not the healthcare system) are just as effective as angioplasty in at least half of cases.

For those who share our optimism about consumer-directed approaches, this reinforces the importance of giving consumers an incentive to participate actively in decisions about their own care. The vast majority of people spend healthcare dollars, thankfully, on services and treatments that do not involve rare forms of cancer or neurological disease. And, as we've seen here, the vast majority of spending does not stem from these conditions either. Instead, most of us will be faced with decisions about how to best manage the functionally-impairing symptoms of everyday life. Perhaps this type of information can also reassure those

---

† See Blog 5.7 When the most expensive option isn't the best option.

who fear that consumers should not be involved in medical decisions, since most medical decision making is around conditions that consumers already deal with everyday.

November 18, 2007

References

1 Healthcare Cost and Utilization Project (HCUP), Clinical Classification Software (CCS). Agency for Healthcare Research and Quality, November 6, 2007, http://www.hcup-us.ahrq.gov/toolssoftware/ccs/ccs.jsp#overview (accessed November 20, 2007).

2 Consumer Reports: Ten Overused Medical Tests and Treatments. FindLaw.com, October 1, 2007, http://news.corporate.findlaw.com/prnewswire/20071001/01oct20071927.html (accessed November 15, 2007).

3 Hochman, J.S., Lamas, G.A., Buller, C.E., et al: Coronary intervention for persistent occlusion after myocardial infarction. *N Engl J Med* 2006;355(23):2395-407.

***

Blog 2.8   Why don't high deductible health plans have low(er) premiums?

We saw in a previous entry* that high-deductible health plans (HDHPs) are priced at a level that is neither attractive to the consumer, nor encourages significant deposits by employers into health savings accounts. This may seem illogical. Why can't we just shift the money from the premium to the deductible and call it even? Well, that's not how insurance works.

The *real* risk in healthcare is the possibility of something very expensive happening. If we rank order a group of employees from lowest to highest healthcare spending and divide them into ten equal groups of people, we see how uneven the spending really is. As shown in the graph, the bottom 80% of people spend about 20% of the dollars. The top 10% of a sample group of employees account for about 70% of costs. The top

---

* See Blog 3.10 Proof that consumers can and do make logical, economic choices in healthcare—they bypass poorly priced 'consumer' plans.

5% spend almost half of all the healthcare dollars.[†] Thus, for about 90% of the consumers in the plan, more will be paid in premiums each year (some *a lot* more) than the value of services they get. That extra payment is to cover the *possibility* that they *might* be expensive.

FIGURE 2.13 WHERE ARE HEALTHCARE DOLLARS SPENT?

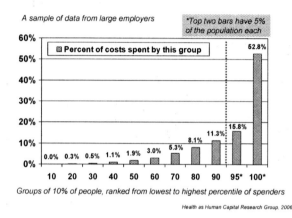

So, of the total spent on healthcare, how much is coming out of consumers' pockets? We will show two hypothetical scenarios—assuming that consumption stays the same. In one scenario, there is a $300 deductible and a $4,000 out-of-pocket maximum. In the other there is a $2,500 deductible and a $4,000 out-of-pocket maximum. In both, we make the assumption that after the deductible (and before the OOP maximum) the consumer pays a 20% co-insurance.

Figure 2.14 shows the percent of total healthcare spending that each group of people will pay out-of-pocket. Under the $300 deductible scenario, consumers will pay 15% of the total cost out-of-pocket (see the bar at the far right). The group that spends the most will be those in the top 10%, where people at this level of spending will pay 3% of all costs.

---

† Note that we broke the top 10% into two bars of 5% each.

FIGURE 2.14 WHERE ARE HEALTHCARE DOLLARS SPENT, AND BY WHOM?

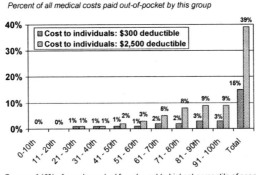

Percent of all medical costs paid out-of-pocket by this group

Groups of 10% of people, ranked from lowest to highest percentile of spenders

Health as Human Capital Research Group, 2006

In the $2,500 deductible, a total of 39% of the total costs are paid out-of-pocket by the consumers. Those spending above the 70th percentile (meaning the top 30% most expensive people) will spend the most—26% of all costs (eight plus nine plus nine). The overall difference in out-of-pocket spending between the two scenarios described here is 24% (39% versus 15%). If the average cost (out-of-pocket plus coinsurance plus amount paid by insurance) among the people in the plan is $3,000, that means the average difference in spending by individuals is about $750.‡ So, despite the $2,200 difference in deductible, the predicted difference in spending by the insurer is only $750.

The maximum any *one* person can pay is always the same in either scenario: $4,000. The only thing changing is the likelihood of paying amounts above $300 and below $4,000.

In both scenarios, the insurer pays the vast majority of overall costs—including 91% or more of the cost for the most expensive people. Here is where insurance companies must cover their risk. Any spending above the out-of-pocket maximum is the sole responsibility of the health plan. Because the highest-cost cases often exceed $1 million, the insurer sets its premium to cover potential losses that result from the possibility

---

‡ We tried changing plan design assumptions to include different plan features (co-insurance and out-of-pocket maximum), and our hypothetical scenarios still resulted in cost differences ranging from 15% to 25%.

of a bad year of having more-than-usual expensive cases. The risk is almost exclusively at the high end of the spending distribution. The job of actuaries at insurance companies is to estimate the extent of risk and price products at a rate that covers the risk, based on past experience.

While it is important to understand these aspects of insurance, there are still some questions we have about the price of premiums for HDHP. While a HDHP may not justify a huge discount, our experiences leave us to wonder about three issues:

1) Whether current pricing takes into account behavior change. The usual method used by actuaries is to model the difference in overall spending *if utilization stays the same* when the responsibility for payment changes—as we illustrated here. However, the RAND experiment and several of the previous blog entries[§] suggest that when people spend their own money, they spend less. Thus, we would expect that the same group of people facing two different deductible levels would spend less in the higher-deductible plan.

    Because we expect lower utilization, premiums can be lower. While some would argue that deductibles only influence utilization of low-cost items, RAND showed a 30% difference in rates of hospitalization between the highest and lowest cost-sharing levels.[1] We have also shown that the rates of surgical procedures[¶] are sensitive to economic incentives (moral hazard) as well.

    In another blog entry,[**] we showed that employees who chose a high-deductible plan had half the average cost of those who chose alternatives. We estimated that about 80% was due to the effect of the deductible, while 20% of the difference was due to the characteristics of people who chose the plan.

2) Whether pricing reflects self-selection (or the opposite of adverse selection).

    Human nature dictates that those least likely to need expensive care (young, single, healthy) and most able to handle unexpected

---

[§] See Blog 3.1 Remembering the RAND Health Insurance Experiment and Chapter 3: Your Time and Money Matter More to You Than Someone Else's.

[¶] See Blog 3.6 The challenge of insuring discretionary events.

[**]See Blog 3.8 Is it the plan or the people select the plan what influences consumption the most?.

expenses (higher income, professionals) are most likely to sign up for a high deductible. As such, when offered as one option, an employer can expect that sicker people will sign up for the lower deductible—and the premium on the high-deductible plan can be lower.

Further, humans are naturally risk averse, so we know they will select a smaller deductible unless the price is attractive. Thus, those anticipating higher risk of expensive care will be less likely to choose HDHPs.

Are HDHP products priced to reflect selection bias?

3) Whether current pricing has strategic motives.

Is there concern that the few who sign up for HDHP will cause adverse selection in the more popular plans, such that decision makers are afraid to make HDHP too attractive? Are there other reasons to price these plans higher than they have to be?

Our sense is that the HDHP market continues to evolve. Some reasons that HDHP prices are not lower reflect the realities of insurance and catastrophic costs. However, we suspect some of these other factors are also influencing the difference in price. Stay tuned as we analyze the actual effects of HDHP with our research partners.

November 19, 2006

References

1 Newhouse, J.P. *Free for all? Lessons from the RAND Health Insurance Experiment*. Cambridge, Mass.: Harvard University Press, 1993.

Blog 2.9   How does compliance affect costs? Well, it depends

Regular readers of this blog know that we have discussed how:
· Most people have low medical costs in a given year;[*]
· Averages can be misleading;[†]
· Illnesses are episodic;[‡] and
· People with high costs this year are likely *not* to be as expensive next year.[§]

All these findings have implications about medical treatments or interventions. One often hears a general statement that high rates of medical compliance with recommended medications result in lower future health costs.[¶] As a generalization, this is probably correct to state that, on average, people of similar characteristics and severity of illness will have lower costs when their illness is better controlled than when it is not. Many chronic diseases can be managed well with adherence to medication and a healthy lifestyle. Thus, we hear that taking medicine regularly reduces overall costs.

Indeed, take a look at the study published in 2005.[1] The authors tested the effects of medication adherence on four different chronic illnesses. They showed that individuals who were more adherent had lower costs and lower rates of hospitalization than individuals who were less adherent to their medications. The population was large, over 130,000 people, followed over a two-year period from 1997 to 1999. These patterns illustrate pronounced effects, shown in figure 2.15.

---

[*] See Blog 2.3 Illness is about likelihood, not certainty.
[†] See Blog 2.2 What the mean does and doesn't mean—when average isn't normal.
[‡] See Blog 2.4 The episodic nature of illness and its implications, part 1.
[§] See Blog 2.5 The episodic nature of illness and its implications, part 2.
[¶] We emphasize that this discussion refers to short-term costs, not long-term clinical value of adherence, which is an entirely different discussion.

FIGURE 2.15 MEDICATION ADHERENCE AND COST OUTCOMES

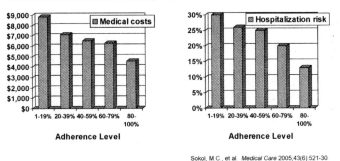

As medication adherence increases, cost outcomes decrease

Sokol, M.C., et al. *Medical Care* 2005;43(6):521-30

We tried to replicate these findings on our dataset of over 245,000 enrolled employees and found that these conclusions should be interpreted within the context of several important observations. First of all, in 1999 dollars, our cases of chronic illness (such as diabetes) were much less expensive than in their study. Because the study reported some detail about selection criteria, people we selected using their method were much less expensive than they report. For some reason, the cases in their study were particularly expensive. Indeed, to create a study group with similar costs to their study, we had to restrict our selection to males over 50 years old with complications, and remove anyone with medical costs under $3,000. Once we selected this group, namely those with high severity, we could replicate the general findings—on average, higher compliance resulted in lower hospitalization rates and costs (although not as big a difference as theirs).

However, even in this higher-severity group, not everyone gets less expensive with constant adherence to their medications. The most expensive people with high adherence may experience great reductions in cost. However, the least expensive people, with high adherence may actually become *more* expensive because of the cost of the medication.

To illustrate, we analyzed data for just under 1,000 insulin-dependent diabetics over the age of 50. We divided them into five cost groups, ranging from "below $1,000" to "above $35,000." We calculated how many months of insulin they refilled in the first year and then looked at their healthcare costs in the second year. Then using regression analysis, we estimated the effects of adherence (controlling for gender, marital status, and job classification). What we see is that projected costs depend directly on the individual's room for improvement. Figure 2.16 shows projections of cost reduction in year 2, based on cost and adherence in year 1.

FIGURE 2.16 HOW ADHERENCE CONNECTS TO FUTURE COSTS

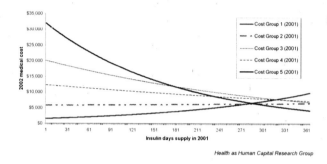

Health as Human Capital Research Group

The least costly groups (lower lines) become more costly on average (likely due to higher medication costs, more appropriate visits, and the tendency for people who have worsening illness to be more adherent). The highest-cost group (top line) shows the most dramatic drop in projected year-two costs when adherence is higher.

As we see, the more expensive the group one selects, the more pronounced the effect of high adherence is expected to be. The key learning here is that—in the short term—*overall* cost improvements will be determined by the portion of *high cost* people who improve adherence. The difficulty is that only a small portion (19% in this example of people over the age of 50) are in the top two groups and the majority (56%) are in the bottom two groups).

The older and sicker the group, the more people will have high costs, and the easier it is to demonstrate an overall cost improvement due to adherence. For example, say an intervention causes five people who would have only taken their insulin successfully for six months, to actually take their insulin for 11 months. If one of the five people comes from each of the cost groups, our model predicts that spending (for all five people combined) will be less than it would have been without the intervention. However, to achieve equal numbers of successful adherers in each group, the intervention must have a much higher *success rate* in the high-cost groups, where there are fewer people. Having greater numbers of costly people to begin with makes this task more likely. This explains why it is easier to see an association between adherence and short-term cost reduction in older, sicker groups.

In general, it pays to adhere to recommended lifestyle and medication regimen. And the most important, positive effects will likely be evident over longer periods of time. But one-year *cost* effects (which are frequently the focus in business) depend on the starting point, the level of illness, and the expense in the population we select.

February 25, 2007

References

1 Sokol, M.C., McGuigan, K.A., Verbrugge, R.R., Epstein, R.S. Impact of medication adherence on hospitalization risk and healthcare cost. *Medical Care* 2005;43(6):521-30.

Blog 2.10 Hospital infection rates: a secret that needs to be told

The CDC estimates that in 2002, 1.7 million patients acquired an infection in U.S. hospitals and about 100,000 died as a result.[1] On *average*, one in every 22 hospital admissions will result in an infection, which means in facilities with the highest rates the incidence is even higher.[2] More worrisome, the rate of a "superbug" called methicillin-resistant Staphylococcus aureus (MRSA), is increasing in hospitals,[3] where over 75% of equipment (such as blood pressure cuffs) in patient rooms tested have the resistant bacteria.[4] In all, the Committee to Reduce Infection Deaths (RID) estimates that infections add an additional $30.5 billion to the cost of healthcare in our country.[5]

Almost all healthcare-associated infections are avoidable with appropriate levels of cleaning and hygiene by healthcare providers and facility managers.[6] One hospital reported a 62% reduction in infections using methods described as "easily and cost effectively reproducible in any organization."[7] Further, patients who are aware of the risk can also take personal steps to help avoid infection.[8] So, the rates can be lowered with care and effort—using existing methods of cleaning, ventilation, and personal hygiene, such as better hand-washing practices and disinfecting door knobs and bed rails.[9]

If you knew the hospital infection rates for the hospitals in your area, would it affect your decision to go there? It just might—*if* you could access that kind of information. Unfortunately there is one small problem with that strategy:

> *In most states, hospitals are not required to report infection rates, so they don't.*

Not surprisingly, the hospital lobby opposes reporting requirements[10] and has been influential in discouraging congress from mandating standard reports. Unlike industries like transportation,[11] which is mandated to provide safety information, healthcare facilities have only voluntary reporting guidelines, and few participate.

Since most states do not report rates, with a few exceptions like Pennsylvania and Florida,[12] the public has little information on which to base decisions or compare risks.

Let's examine the economic incentives and disincentives in this hidden problem. Hospitals do not have to report negative events that are, in part, avoidable. Because fee-for-service medicine charges by the service, more services result in more revenue. By avoiding errors, hospitals help their patients, but decrease fees. Thus, a hospital with a higher infection rate actually receives additional revenue, due to longer stays and more treatments, than hospitals with better safety ratings (at least until late 2008 when Medicare will stop paying for treatment for some avoidable errors).[13] Since patients have no information about poor infection records to dissuade them from choosing the most dangerous facilities, those facilities do not lose business.

While no one wants to suggest that facilities would allow infections intentionally, the economics are actually aligned to reward facilities whose patients do worse. The consumer site Stopinfectionsnow.org, part of Consumer Reports, has begun collecting anonymous information from patients in an attempt to make safety issues more transparent.[14] Perhaps increasing media attention will place pressure on providers to report accurate safety records, or self-police through voluntary systems of confidential reporting by healthcare employees (similar to the transportation industry).[15]

At a minimum, all patients would benefit from increased transparency by having more accurate information on which to base decisions. In any industry, when consumers base their purchasing choices on accurate information about quality, overall levels of quality improve. Thus, if this information were public, hospitals would have a strong incentive to reduce infection rates in order to maintain market share.

While our culture tends to hold medicine in high esteem, it seems unacceptable to us that consumers tolerate the added risk, discomfort, and cost associated with undisclosed infection rates. Cars have safety ratings, individuals have credit ratings, airlines have ratings on rates of lost baggage…all to allow consumers and businesses to assess their risk and make informed choices. One has to wonder how health facilities have avoided requirements to report such an important safety issue.

In this era, where anyone selling products regularly on E-bay receives a rating from his buyers, and almost any product on Amazon.com gets a rating of one to five stars from purchasers, the absence of patient-reported outcomes represents a missed opportunity. It could be that patients presume that insurance companies and Medicare—the purchasers—would protect them from facilities that have poor infection control. Or consumers may assume that if patients are getting infections more often at specific hospitals, the media would know about it and publicize it.

Unfortunately, neither of these assumptions is true.

Hopefully, new efforts by Google[16] and Microsoft[17] to create a home for consumer-held health records will include mechanisms for more transparency regarding safety and quality among healthcare users. If so, market forces from consumers demanding clear, accurate information about the healthcare they purchase may reform the system after all.

December 17, 2007

References

1 Klevens, R.M.; Edwards, J.R.; Richards, C.L. Jr.; Horan, T.C.; Gaynes, R.P.; Pollock, D.A., and Cardo, D.M. Estimating healthcare-associated infections and deaths in U.S. hospitals, 2002. *Public Health Rep.* 2007; 122(2):160-6, (page 160) http://www.cdc. gov/ncidod/dhqp/pdf/hicpac/infections_deaths.pdf (accessed December 4, 2007).

2 Klevens.

3 Zeller, J.L.; Burke, A.E., and Glass, R.M. JAMA patient page. MRSA infections. *JAMA.* 2007; 298(15):1826, http://jama.ama-assn.org/cgi/content/full/298/15/1826 (accessed December 4, 2007).

4 McCaughey, B. *Unnecessary deaths: the human and financial costs of hospital infections.* 2nd ed. New York: Committee to Reduce Infection Deaths; 2006, http://www. hospitalinfection.org/ridbooklet.pdf (accessed December 4, 2007).

5 McCaughey.

6 McCaughey.

7 Joint Commission. The 2007 John M. Eisenberg Patient Safety and Quality Awards: Innovation in patient safety and quality at the local level, Evanston Northwestern Healthcare, http://www.jointcommission.org/PatientSafety/EisenbergAward/07_ eisenberg_award.htm (accessed December 4, 2007).

8 Committee to Reduce Infection Deaths. 15 steps you can take to reduce your risk of a hospital infection, http://www.hospitalinfection.org/protectyourself.shtml (accessed December 4, 2007).

9 Centers for Disease Control, Healthcare Infection Control Practices Advisory Committee. Guidelines for environmental infection control in health-care facilities, 2003, (page 74) http://www.cdc.gov/ncidod/dhqp/gl_environinfection.html (accessed December 4, 2007).

10 McGiffert, L. Washington lawmaker takes aim at hospital infections. ConsumersUnion.org, February 17, 2006, http://www.consumersunion.org/pub/core_ health_care/003178.html (accessed December 4, 2007).

11 National Transportation Safety Board. Reporting an accident to the NTSB, aviation, http://www.ntsb.gov/aviation/report.htm (accessed December 4, 2007).

12 McGiffert.

13 Medicare will not pay for preventable conditions acquired at hospitals. Senior Journal.com, August 20, 2007, http://64.23.76.120/NEWS/Medicare/2007/7-08-20-MedicareWillNot.htm (accessed December 5, 2007).

14 Consumers Union. Share your hospital infection story, Stop Hospital Infections. org, http://cu.convio.net/site/PageServer?pagename=SHI_shareyourstorypage (accessed December 4, 2007).

15 Office of Transport Safety Investigators. Confidential safety information reporting scheme (CSIRS), February 23, 2007, http://www.otsi.nsw.gov.au/CSIRS/ (accessed December 4, 2007).

16 Allen, J. Health grades, inc.: a google a day. SmallCap Investor.com, November 9, 2007, http://www.smallcapinvestor.com/articles/11092007-health_grades_inc_a_ google_a_day (accessed December 4, 2007).

17   Microsoft electronic health records solutions. Microsoft.com, http://www. microsoft.com/industry/government/solutions/electronichealthrecords.mspx (accessed December 4, 2007).

SECTION 3

What Economists Already Know

Why Economics?

Although many people think of economics as primarily a financial or mathematical field, economists will tell you it is primarily a behavioral science that uses rigorous concepts and tools to better understand human decisions. In short, the field provides a logical framework for understanding decision making. Underlying economics is the basic premise that *individuals, in general, will behave in ways that maximize personal benefit and minimize potential loss. Individual choices are influenced by personal incentives and preferences.*

This is an appropriate scientific framework to use in understanding work performance and health benefits utilization because incentives and preferences apply not only to patients and doctors, but also to all levels of decision makers and stakeholders throughout the system. People will consider, naturally, their own potential for gain and loss in every choice they make.

Another underlying premise in economics is that while *the wants (wishes) of humans (consumers) are virtually unlimited, the supply of goods and services is finite.* This is true because natural, human, and capital resources are limited and must be allocated (rationed) among competing goods and services desired by consumers. This principle is useful in debates about services, because it necessitates an acknowledged upper limit to the amount of resources available to supply wants. It also encourages consideration of choices about what can and cannot be included within the constraints of that limit.

How Markets are Important

Economists recognize and explain how markets (transactions between buyers and sellers) evolve in a free-enterprise economy to guide how resources are being allocated and priced. In a market economy, buyers and sellers come to the market with their own interests to make mutually beneficial exchanges: to buy and sell. Prices reach equilibrium as a result of the bargaining that occurs so that buyers and sellers can be simultaneously satisfied. When a price equilibrium is reached in the natural bargaining exchange (the price at which the demander is willing to pay and the supplier is willing to sell), economists refer to the market as efficient because no better mutually-beneficial trades can be made.

Markets demonstrate what consumers value.

In an efficient market, consumers are very aware of price and expect to get more when they pay more. For example, a consumer may be willing to pay hundreds of dollars for a fancy haircut at her favorite salon because she values the service. Yet the same consumer would expect to pay much less at a drop-in barber shop. Another consumer may not value hair styling enough to pay more than $20. Because the consumer knows what product and price to expect—and because consumers pay directly for their haircuts—the market is quite efficient in allocating resources to haircuts. (A shop giving terrible haircuts at a high price is not likely to be in business very long.) If you want fancy hair styles, you pay more.

Open markets encourage innovation and competition.

When direct transactions occur between buyers and sellers, buyers naturally shop for the best value they can find—the item with the features they want at the best price. Sellers compete amongst themselves to produce, price, and position their services in ways that attract customers. A supplier who can reduce production costs with a new method (innovation) has an advantage to attract customers with lower prices. We have seen dramatic demonstrations of this phenomenon in the electronics industry as internal components have become progressively smaller, faster, and less expensive.

When outside forces interfere with free and direct interactions between buyers and sellers, price is unlikely to achieve a natural equilibrium. The more outside interference a market experiences, the more *inefficient* it will likely be. Interference can come in many forms: manipulating supply, fixing prices, or inserting a third-party to negotiate prices or handle payment. In healthcare we see inefficiency from several outside influences: patients do not pay directly for the services they receive and doctors are paid a pre-negotiated amount for services regardless of how well the service is delivered. As a result, innovation may, in many circumstances, be resisted. There are numerous examples where a new, less invasive and less expensive procedure is invented, but not quickly adopted by providers—because they will make less money using the less expensive procedure.* Patients, who are not paying directly for care, are often unaware of price differences and do not demand the less expensive option. Just the opposite effect compared to electronics.

In employment markets we see inefficiency because salaries are often determined independently from specific performance criteria or are negotiated as a group (where high performers and low performers get the same rewards). Like any other market, to be efficient, the price paid by the buyer (salary paid by the employer) will reflect the value of the service purchased (work done by the worker). Like haircuts, if we pay the same amount to two hair stylists, we expect the same quality of haircut. A good stylist who is underpaid will look for better opportunities; a poor stylist who is overpaid will have little incentive to improve. Any system that allows a price (even salary) to be set, rather than respond flexibly to market forces will be inefficient. As we will see in the blogs discussed later, market inefficiency results often from among the parties involved.

> *The result of market inefficiency? Higher-than-necessary costs for less-than-optimal results.*

The following chapters present some economic principles related to inefficiencies in healthcare and employment markets. Each principle is followed by short examples, selected from a series of blogs we have presented that illustrate and validate the principle. The basic economic principles discussed here are well documented and widely accepted by economists, but are often overlooked in general discussions about health benefits. More careful attention to and application of these economic principles would lead towards significant improvements in the efficiency of the healthcare and business system.

---

* See Blog 1.6 Please don't complicate things with new information. I like the old (wrong) answer better; Blog 2.10 Keeping hospital infections a secret; and Blog 5.7 When the most expensive option isn't the best option.

Chapter 3
Your Own Time and Money Matter More to You than Someone Else's

When a person is spending someone else's money, he or she will spend more. This tendency applies to both small spending (a dinner allowance for business travel) and larger spending (insurance coverage for emergency room visits). The economic term for this tendency is *moral hazard* and it refers to the excess amount a person would spend (e.g., steak instead of a burger) when someone else pays the bill, compared to what they would spend if paying their own money. The "law of demand" says that as the price to me goes down (because someone else pays for part or all of it) the quantity I will demand goes up. However, since there is no way of knowing if I would have had the steak if I were paying the full price, it is impossible to estimate just how much excess is being consumed. This is why moral hazard is difficult to estimate.

Most excess consumption resulting from moral hazard falls into a category of discretionary spending, the extra bit one might add when it is perceived as "free." At an all-you-can-eat buffet, people are much more likely to choose items that they won't actually eat than if there is a personal cost for every item. In fact, there may be an incentive to choose even more items to make the meal seem even more valuable "for the money." Similarly, if there is no (or little) extra cost to a patient, he or she may not question adding more tests or services, "just to be safe." This source of market inefficiency—extra consumption that occurs because the consumer doesn't pay—contributes to higher overall costs in the system. As you will see in the next section, the RAND Health Insurance Experiment in the 1980s showed that individuals who had free care consumed about 30%-45% more healthcare services than those who paid 95% of the cost. Yet, there was little indication that those consuming less experienced negative health effects.

The same phenomenon applies to paid-time-off benefits. When there is no obvious cost to an employee, he or she will have fewer barriers to being absent. Economists have estimated a 13% increase in the number of employees who use sick days when those days are paid days.[1] Again, compared to paying full costs, when the individual can acquire services at low or no cost, some level of excess consumption—of time off or services—will occur.

As one might imagine, the more indirect the transaction between the consumer and the service provider, the more opportunity there is for inefficiency on both sides. In the case of healthcare services, a consumer may have insurance subsidized by his employer, who pays the insurance company, who contracts with a doctor's office, who pays a nurse's salary. When a nurse chooses between two services, her decision is five steps removed from the contractual agreement the employee has with his employer regarding healthcare. Neither the nurse nor the patient (supplier or consumer) has a strong incentive to make cost-effective choices about care.

Read on for more examples of how all of us protect our own time and money more than someone else's.

References

1 Gilleskie, D.B. A dynamic stochastic model of medical care use and work absence. *Econometrica* 1998;66(1):1-45.

Blog 3.1   Remembering the RAND Health Insurance Experiment

One of the best studies ever conducted on the effects of economic factors on healthcare consumption—the RAND Health Insurance Experiment (HIE)—occurred in the 1970s.[1] Its findings are still very relevant today, especially in light of current trends in consumer-driven care.

A main question of the study was whether consumers change their utilization of healthcare in response to cost sharing. Families were randomly assigned to plans providing free care (zero copayment), or to plans requiring copayments of 25%, 50%, or 95% of the cost of the

FIGURE 3.1   HEALTHCARE UTILIZATION BY LEVEL OF CO-INSURANCE

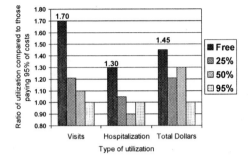

Newhouse, J.P. *Free for all? Lessons from the RAND Health Insurance Experiment.* Cambridge, Mass.: Harvard University Press, 1993

service. Figure 3.1 indicates that cost sharing matters. Compared to families who had to pay 95% of costs, those receiving free care were 70% more likely to visit a doctor and 30% more likely to be hospitalized. Overall, the cost of their total healthcare consumption was 45% higher.

Because participant families (about 2,000 of them around the country) were randomly assigned to health plans with specific economic features, the effects of these features could be determined independently from other factors. Random assignment insures that the differences measured between plans were not due to differences in the characteristics of people, such as their health status, their attitudes, or their income. The study confirmed virtually no significant differences in dozens of these variables. Hence, differences in consumption can be attributed *specifically* to the differences in plans.

Families in this experiment who used less care ended up being as healthy as families using more care because it was free. The study found very few instances where health status was better for those receiving free care.* In fact, free-care families were more likely to use all types of care—including care that was defined as inappropriate and possibly dangerous. Those receiving free care also missed more work than those who paid 95% of fees.

---

* Low-income individuals who were ill did better in the free group, mostly due to earlier detection of problems. But surprisingly, very few advantages were detected from having free care.

77

This study illustrates that utilization of healthcare is driven by economic incentives—and the effect is quite large.

I will cover a few more issues from the HIE in the next few weeks,[†] but if you are interested in more detail about the HIE, the entire study is presented and discussed in Newhouse's book.

October 10, 2005

References

1 Newhouse, J.P. *Free for all? Lessons from the RAND Health Insurance Experiment*. Cambridge, Mass.: Harvard University Press, 1993.

---

† See Blog 5.1 Health insurance experiment: provider incentives.

Blog 3.2   Money matters in decisions about disability

Would it surprise you to learn that the closer my disability benefits will be to full salary during a short-term disability (STD), the more likely I am to file a STD claim? Using data from tens of thousands of disability claims across hundreds of paid-time-off policies, the HHC Research Group looked at how the level of salary reimbursement (for the first 180 days as calculated by the sick-leave, STD, and other paid-time-off policies)

FIGURE 3.2   *DISABILITY EVENTS IN NON-EXEMPT EMPLOYEES BY INCOME REPLACEMENT IN DIFFERENT AGE AND GENDER GROUPS*

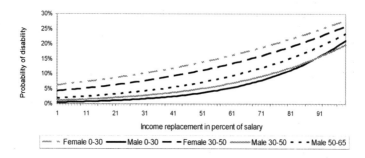

affected the rate of filing a disability claim.

Correcting for type of job and salary, results showed that for all groups except females age 50-65, rates of STD were related to the percent of pay the employees could anticipate receiving during their absence. These graphs represent the patterns for all types of disability cases combined. Interestingly, there was no such relationship for fractures or pregnancy and delivery. Disability claims for those events happened at the same rate regardless of salary reimbursement levels.*

Question: Do people who are eligible for a higher percent of their pay during an absence from work have more severe injuries and illnesses? Probably not. But, those eligible to be paid more—other things being equal—will be more willing to apply for time off. Salary reimbursement during disability was intended as a protection against unanticipated loss of income. At what point does it create an incentive that encourages paid time-off rather than providing the intended protection? What level of shared consequence (any amount below 100% reimbursement) is appropriate? What we see here is that higher reimbursement will result in more cases of STD. That is natural human behavior.

From the standpoint of the employer, it appears that—in addition to the actual cost of higher pay during disability—higher payments for disability also increase overall costs due to:

1) the increased likelihood of absence, and
2) the resulting decrease in efficiency and productivity.

September 27, 2005

---

* Our research team often uses fractures to compare a very concrete physical problem with ones that include some discretion about when to treat and when improvement happens. Rates of fractures do not respond to financial incentives— meaning that individuals seem to seek care at the same rate regardless of cost. Pregnancies and deliveries are also quite 'inelastic' to salary reimbursement. Because illnesses that have more ambiguity in their identification and treatments (like sprains and stress-related syndromes) are more responsive to salary reimbursement, we infer that economic factors are playing a role in employee choices regarding STD. For more detail about the multivariate analysis, see Health as Human Capital Research Group. Generous salary replacement policies produce higher rates of short-term disability claims. January 2005, Health as Human Capital Foundation Research e-News http://www.hhcfoundation. org/hhcf/pdf/e-news_one-full_detail_sal_replacement.pdf (accessed September 25, 2007).

Blog 3.3 Hoping for absolutes in a subjective world

In a perfectly objective world, one would be able to define diagnoses, health status and functionality in absolute terms: afflicted or not, ill or well, able or unable. But in many instances, neither medical science nor human experience allows such straightforward classifications. We may not know what is wrong or what our prognosis might be. Plus, recovery from illness or injury usually includes diversions and setbacks rather than smooth, linear improvement. Thus, there is often no single, clear, identifiable point along the line between ill and well, or able and unable, that we can point to with certainty and say "now, I am better enough to return to my usual activities."

It is within this realm of uncertainty that companies apply health benefits policies. Disability insurance covers salary during the time that a person is ill and unable to work. This policy sounds simple enough, yet, the degree of subjectivity in both illness and ability allow different interpretations of what constitutes well enough or able enough. The degree of subjectivity also allows more opportunity for factors other than health and work to influence return-to-work decisions. As an example, a worker who loves her job may feel ready sooner than a worker who hates her job. A worker whose family responsibilities are overwhelming may take more time than a worker with strong family support.

In this entry, we will look at whether financial incentives affect the speed at which workers return from episodes of illness. We analyzed data from over 25,000 claims for short term disability (STD) insurance coverage. These claims came from multiple companies with a variety of jobs and STD policy rules. This same population was used in another entry[*] to demonstrate that policies that covered a greater portion of salary during a disability absence resulted in a higher rate of claims.

In this analysis, we tested whether, after filing a disability claim, the duration of the claim was affected by the percent of salary paid to the employee during the claim. A type of inquiry called "survival analysis" was performed, controlling for differences in age, gender, and other

---

[*] See Blog 3.2 Money matters in decisions about disability.

demographic factors. This analysis essentially measures how long it takes for a population of people to reach a specific outcome—in this case, how long before they have returned to work.

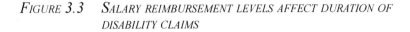

FIGURE 3.3   SALARY REIMBURSEMENT LEVELS AFFECT DURATION OF DISABILITY CLAIMS

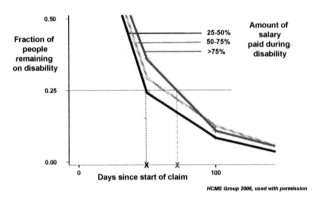

HCMS Group 2006, used with permission

What we see in the graph is that salary coverage influenced the speed of return-to-work. Generally, workers receiving a higher portion of pay (farthest right in medium gray) remained out of work longer than workers receiving a lower portion of pay (farthest left in black). In the group receiving between 25% and 50% of regular salary, we see that 50 days after the claim began one-quarter of workers had not yet returned to work. For those receiving more than 75% of pay during their illness, the same portion of workers remained on disability after 75 days.

Subjective readiness is sensitive to financial incentives

It should not surprise us that workers who share a greater portion of the cost of lost time assessed themselves as ready, or able enough, sooner than those who sacrificed a smaller portion of their salaries. It is human nature to make decisions within the full context of benefits and costs. Given that absolutes are rare in illness and functionality, each person responds subjectively to the set of circumstances he or she faces, including financial incentives.

We may wish every illness could be identified as clearly as a clean break on an x-ray, followed by an equally obvious picture confirming complete recuperation. But such is not the case for most issues. Knowing that workers will adjust their return in response to financial incentives, policies should reflect a conscious choice to balance support with shared responsibility for recovery. Paying 100% of salary reduces the incentive to become "ready." The smaller the portion of regular salary paid during a medical absence, the more incentive a worker will have to become ready sooner.

September 17, 2006

Blog 3.4 Good intentions: the curse of $3 prescriptions and $0.40 per gallon gasoline

Joke:

Q: How many (Chicago School) economists does it take to change a light bulb?

A: None. If the light bulb needed changing the market would have already done it.

Here at the Health as Human Capital Foundation, we believe that market forces are powerful and useful. Perhaps market forces can't actually replace a light bulb, but they do provide an essential rationality to consumption of goods and services. Consumers vote with their pocketbooks. If price increases, consumers purchase less. If a lower-cost alternative appears, some consumers switch brands. Markets, without external constraints, find a dynamic equilibrium that responds to changes in supply and demand.

In "efficient" markets (ones where prices and supply are not artificially too high or too low), consumer and suppliers engage freely in bargaining such that prices and quantities respond naturally to fluctuations in supply and demand. Technically, there are several criteria required to achieve market efficiency,* but—put simply—such a market is one without

---

* Efficient markets require many direct transactions between suppliers and

external interference in normal market forces. The competing pressures of buyers deciding how much to buy and suppliers adjusting quantity and price create a useful balance. When a third-party gets involved (paying on another's behalf, limiting supply, or subsidizing price), then inefficient outcomes are guaranteed.

> **If market forces are *not* present—even for well-intentioned reasons—it does not take long before things get messy.**

Take the recent energy difficulties in Iran, where the government has subsidized the price of gasoline for many years, making it cheaper (below 40 cents per gallon) than any other country in the world. Not surprisingly, Iranians have grown to consume more gasoline than people in most other nations.[1] In fact, consumption has increased so far beyond Iran's refining capacity that the government now imports billions of dollars of gasoline each year. This, on top of an estimated billion dollars of cheap gas smuggled out of the country, reveals the true expense of an artificial and imbalanced market.

In late June, the Iranian government announced a need to decrease the demand for gasoline. However, leaders felt that price increases would be politically unpopular and instead instituted a ration of 100 liters per month per citizen. Limited now to a small amount of inexpensive gasoline, some citizens responded with riots and protests. Regardless of the original intention behind gas subsidies, its unintended consequences have been costly and it will take painful measures to bring back the savings and efficiency only a balanced market can produce. From the other side of the world, one wonders why leaders won't simply let the price increase incrementally toward a more "real" level. Or, if government support for the poor is required, a better market solution would be an allowance placed in consumers' hands (perhaps a petrol savings account?) instead of price controls, because it allows consumer choice and direct purchases.

---

demanders, many purchasers and many suppliers (so that one party cannot monopolize the price or supply), and no interference that biases price or supply consistently in one direction or another. In an efficient market, price reflects the current value of the product and is neither artificially high nor artificially low.

Let's look at a health example.

In many health plans, consumers pay a small copayment when filling a prescription. For example, the actual cost of the medication may be around $50 or $100, but the perceived "cost" to the consumer is artificially low, at $3 or $5. The remainder is paid through insurance, which is often sponsored by employers.

At the copayment price, like drivers getting cheap gasoline, consumers have little incentive to conserve or look for a treatment alternative. In the case of moderate high-blood pressure or early-stage diabetes, we know a majority of people can avoid progression of illness with minor weight loss and moderate exercise—instead of medication. But consumers have less incentive to implement alternatives when prescriptions are $5, ignoring the potential savings of lower-cost alternatives. Increasing the amount a consumer must pay (for example a coinsurance of 10% to 20% of the full medication cost) may attenuate demand somewhat, but consumption will remain far from efficient. Paying $20 for a $100 product does not produce rational levels of consumption.

As spending on medications has increased, employers—not unlike the Iranian leaders—have looked for ways to "manage cost" without putting too much (unpopular) pressure on consumers who have grown accustomed to their highly-subsidized price. When consumers are protected from true price pressure, third parties subsidizing the cost must find other punitive ways of managing demand. Either they can negotiate lower prices from suppliers, steer consumers toward "preferred sources," or apply some rationing to the type or amount consumers are allowed. In the case of prescription medications, third parties have tried all three—to little or no effect.

In today's health plans, rarely can a consumer take any prescription to any pharmacy and know what price to expect. Some drugs are allowed, others are not. Some have a low copayment, others a high copayment. Some arrangements provide a price incentive when consumers purchase medication via mail-order vendor. Many of the same arrangements limit which local pharmacies a consumer can use.

The reason for all these cumbersome rules? Too many third parties getting between customers and the medications they want to purchase.

Whether gas or prescription drugs, these complications arise when someone interferes with market forces. In contrast, where individuals spend their own money, they make decisions based on a price that reflects real supply costs. This is the necessary force that brings markets into equilibrium, and a reason to support health accounts that consumers own and manage.

The next time you find yourself wondering why it is such a hassle to fill a prescription, realize it's the same third-party hassle Iranians face filling their gas tanks and ask yourself, "Who is paying whom to protect me from the real price?"

Perhaps if they just gave you the money and let you choose what to buy, the market would take care of itself in producing an efficient outcome.

July 30, 2007

References

1 Samii, A.W. Iran Considers Gasoline Rationing. *Daily Standard*, February 7, 2007, http://www.weeklystandard.com/Content/Public/Articles/000/000/013/255wbnfa.asp (accessed July 27, 2007).

Blog 3.5   Your time, someone else's money

What happened in Sweden when the government-paid sick leave program was changed in 1987 so that there was no longer a one-day waiting period and it now covered 100% of pay on any sick day? Well, sick leave went up.[1] And kept going up the next year to the point that people were averaging 25 absent days per year—four more days *per person* than in 1986! To try and manage the resulting productivity loss and expense, new policies were introduced that reduced payments in 1991 to 75% of pay, combined with waiting periods in 1992 of as long as 14 days before sickness insurance was provided.[2,3] Rates of sick leave came down by three days on average.

*FIGURE 3.4   AVERAGE ANNUAL NUMBER OF SICK DAYS USING SICKNESS
INSURANCE PER WORKER IN SWEDEN*

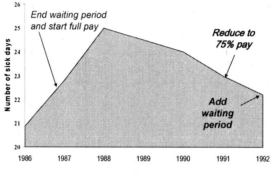

Henrekson, M., 2004; Johansson, P., 1996; Johansson, P., 2002; Voss, M., 2001.

Although this is just a short period of time during a series of many, many policy changes, it provided an excellent natural study of policy and utilization in the Swedish system. Scientists could not find any plausible explanation (such as unemployment rates) for the change in rate of absence other than the changes in reimbursement.[4]

Question: Were more people getting sick when pay was higher? Not likely. They did not get healthier when sick pay was reduced to 75% of salary, either. Instead, the lack of a small penalty (reduced salary) for taking time off made employees more likely to take a day off. They were simply responding to the incentives that the government's policy provided them.

November 6, 2005

References

1 Henrekson, M., Persson, M. The effects on sick leave of changes in the sickness insurance system. *Journal of Labor Economics* 2004;22(1):87-114.

2 Johansson, P., Palme, M. Do economic incentives affect work absence? Empirical evidence using Swedish micro data. *Journal of Public Economics* 1996;59(2):195-218.

3 Johansson, P., Palme, M. Assessing the effect of public policy on worker absenteeism. *J Hum Resources* 2002; 37:381-409.

4 Voss, M., Floderus, B., Diderichsen, F. Changes in sickness absenteeism following the introduction of a qualifying day for sickness benefit—findings from Sweden post. *Scand J Public Health* 2001; 29(3):166-74.

Blog 3.6   The challenge of insuring discretionary events

For many types of insurance—e.g., auto, homeowners'—policies serve to protect holders from some degree of financial loss that can result from unforeseen events generally beyond the control of the policy holder. In these cases, the covered losses include sudden accidents, natural phenomena or freak events. As homeowners in Florida have discovered in recent years, when certain covered events become more likely (such as hurricanes), insurance becomes more expensive or harder to obtain. This is because insurance is based on actuarial estimates that distribute the combined risk across a large pool of people. Since a minority of policy holders actually experience the loss, the pool invests their premium to cover the expected risk.

For another type of insurance, life insurance, policy holders are not insuring themselves against an unlikely event; obviously, death is inevitable, but the length of life is uncertain. Instead, insurers base premiums on the anticipated duration a person will hold the policy before they die. While the event is certain, insurance is often selected to compensate surviving family members in the case of premature death, which would be a heavy burden. On average, a person will pay life insurance premiums long enough to cover the value of the policy. This is because the insurer assesses the person's health and knows that the likelihood of death for young people is quite small. Usually, funds will accumulate over decades before a payout is required.

These insurance policies have a ceiling on the amount awarded for a loss. Policy holders receive up to the full market value of the car or house, or a pre-determined amount for a life policy. Known upper limits frame the scope and risk of payment so that the expected losses can be readily calculated by the insurer.

Health insurance is different. As we saw in an earlier entry,* health insurance policies have a short duration (usually annual) with an artificial calendar "reset" on January first. Because the likelihood of illness increases with age, premiums (for individual policies) also increase with

---

* See Blog 3.9 Moral hazard and the New Year's effect.

age. Rather than a long-term accumulating pool of funds similar to life insurance, the policy resets each year.

Health insurance is also different because it covers an array of problems and causes that other types of insurance do not. We expect our house and our car to experience wear and tear over time (the window sticks, the parts rust), and we also expect to do maintenance and upkeep. We do not ask insurance to cover new paint or new tires when they wear out, only when there is damage due to hail or vandalism. There is a much more liberal definition (and expectation) in healthcare that insurance should cover any and all efforts to make us better. A large portion of health issues develop gradually, take time to be recognized and diagnosed, and are a natural part of aging. Further, people have choices about when and how to respond ("it doesn't hurt *that* bad"). As such, health insurance must handle far more ambiguity in its domain than other types of insurance.

Traumatic health events such as broken bones are like an automobile accident: defining the extent of the damage is fairly objective. Most of healthcare is more subjective, depending on the individual's perceptions of the extent of a bruise, soft tissue damage, or fatigue, etc., self assessments often formed with the aid of healthcare providers whose judgments on these matters is no less subjective. Hence, for any given set of symptoms involving these more ambiguous health events, there will be a wide range of opinions about what (and when) constitutes necessary or optimal care; much more so than the assessment of damage to a car fender.

To illustrate the degree to which timing is discretionary in some aspects of health expenditures, we looked at how consumers responded to an announced change in the amount of money they would have to pay for procedures. Specifically, a large company announced (in mid-2004) that beginning in 2005 all employees would have a high-deductible health plan, along with a health reimbursement arrangement (HRA).† For the remainder of 2004, employees remained in their lower-deductible plan.

Figure 3.5 shows procedure rates before and after a health reimbursement arrangement begins. As we see, for these three procedures

---

† An HRA is an account for the employee to accumulate money to spend to cover the deductible and other out-of-pocket costs. Money in an HRA accumulates and is controlled by the employee until the person leaves his or her job.

(gallbladder removal, hysterectomies, and knee surgeries) there is definitely a response in the timing of procedures to the incentive changes brought about by the new policy. Facing a higher personal cost after the first of the year, some employees elected to schedule their surgeries before the insurance change (as seen in the highest rates compared to the previous seven quarters). This "bump" in procedures in late 2004 is a natural response to economic incentives…if I plan to have the procedure anyway, why not do it while I pay less and the insurance pays more?

FIGURE 3.5   CLAIMANT RATES FOR SPECIFIC PROCEDURES BEFORE AND AFTER THE IMPLEMENTATION OF A HEALTH REIMBURSEMENT ACCOUNT

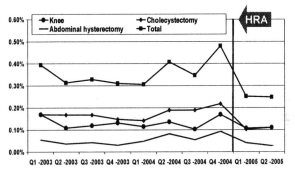

HCMS Group 2006, used with permission

But this response also reminds us that health "insurance" is somewhat of a misnomer. Some health expenditures are predictable. For example, some personal habits make higher costs more likely (smokers, or overweight policy holders, for example‡). Unlike methods of fixing cars or homes, there may also be many options to "fix" the medical problem, with a high degree of uncertainty about how successful the approach may be. As seen here, the timing of treatment can also be altered (predicted) in response to incentive changes in insurance coverage.

Health insurance may be perceived as a mechanism for protecting against unforeseen problems, but we must not forget that many aspects of healthcare border on the uninsurable. Healthcare involves much more complex decisions, a much broader set of services, and greater potential

---

‡ See Blog 4.5 Obesity: two perspectives.

for misdiagnosis of the problem than many other types of insurance. Appropriate "ceilings" are harder to quantify, and users often face overwhelming options about how and when to act on a perceived problem. Additionally, consumers lack awareness of the actual cost of care. This combination contributes to what is largely a dysfunctional and expensive system. It is important to realize that the degree of discretion makes a large portion of insured expenses non-random and subject to moral hazard.

Often we hear stories in the media about insurers not providing sufficient coverage of various treatments or procedures. Such stories typically characterize care as necessary and immediate, implying that delays or substitutions are virtually always harmful. This perpetuates public and legislative efforts to force insurance to "cover more!" Rarely, however, do we hear similar stories about how consumers use discretion to maximize their own use of limited health resources. Think of this the next time you hear someone say that he plans to have knee surgery before his next deductible kicks in, or to switch to an HMO before her baby arrives. Remember that all parties operate within this system of incentives, and in a majority of situations, we have choices.

September 4, 2006

Blog 3.7   Aging, medical costs, and absences: patterns you might not expect

We all know that as we get older, we tend to develop more medical problems. Insurance premiums increase with age because insurers expect costs to rise on average. Figure 3.6 shows this pattern. In a population of about 50 thousand employees we found that older groups of employees were progressively less likely to be in the lowest cost group (people costing less than $1,000) than younger employees. Expressed differently, 30% of 50 to 59 year-old workers had medical costs over $1,000, while only 12% of 20 to 29 year olds had costs that high. This pattern holds for any cutoff point: as we get older, the more likely we are to have high medical expenses.

FIGURE 3.6   PERCENT OF AGE GROUPS HAVING MEDICAL COSTS
BELOW AND ABOVE $1,000

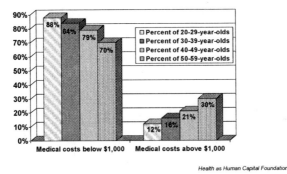

Health as Human Capital Foundation

One might expect that absences due to illness would follow the same pattern as medical expenditures. However, we happened to look at this a few weeks ago (using the same population as the medical costs) and were surprised. We looked at the combination of sick leave, short-term and long-term disability days. Instead of having a similar pattern, we actually found the opposite. Instead of the youngest employees (who are assumed to be the healthiest and *are* the least costly) dominating the low absence category (fewer than two days), they actually were the least likely to have fewer than two absences.

Further, younger employees were most likely to have five to ten absences. In case it was an artifact of gender, we checked and found that this pattern existed for both men and women.

There are many possible explanations for this opposite pattern of benefits use across age groups, none of which we will prove or disprove today. But it is almost certain that different phenomena are responsible for each pattern. At the very least, it demonstrates that illnesses resulting in high costs are not necessarily the same illnesses that produce frequent absences. More likely, factors other than poor health contribute to the absence of younger employees.

In another blog entry* we will talk more about known factors that increase absenteeism (such as lower wages, physically demanding jobs, or

---

* See Blog 6.3 Pay and use of paid time off: they are related.

FIGURE 3.7   PERCENT OF AGE GROUPS HAVING FEWER OR
MORE THAN FIVE DAYS OF ILLNESS ABSENCE

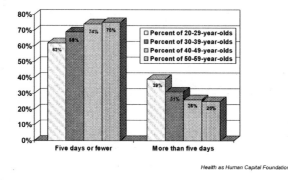

Health as Human Capital Foundation

the value of leisure time), several of which are more evident for younger workers. This entry is just another demonstration of how use of health-related benefits may reflect something other than health.

December 5, 2005

Blog 3.8   Is it the plan or the people who select the plan that influences healthcare consumption the most?

We know that employees who select a high-deductible health plan (HDHP) differ from those who do not select a HDHP* (see our white paper[1] for detail). HDHP enrollees are healthier, higher paid, and have fewer children. We also know that people in HDHPs have lower health costs overall. But how much of the difference in costs between the plans is due to the plan itself, and how much is due to the type of people who select HDHPs?

In figure 3.8, you see the answer. Despite known, significant differences in the type of people selecting high-deductible plans, we estimate that 82% of the difference in cost is due to the effect of the plan rather than the type of people selecting the plan. In other words, these

---

* See Blog 6.5 Kids, paychecks and healthcare deductibles.

types of plans have a significant impact on costs, and only 18% of the difference happens because low-cost users are more likely to sign up for HDHPs. The economic response to the incentives of a high-deductible plan seems to be far more influential than the type of person who signs up for the high deductible. In other words, you can expect an impact on costs regardless of who signs up for the plan.

Group characteristics (accounted for in the 18%) included age, gender, marital status, exempt/non-exempt status, full-time/part-time status, salary, number of children, eligibility for disability benefits, and the Charlson Comorbidity Index. Costs include insurance paid amounts, copayments, coinsurance, and deductibles.

FIGURE 3.8   COST DECOMPOSITION: EFFECTS OF PLAN VS. EFFECTS OF TYPE OF PEOPLE

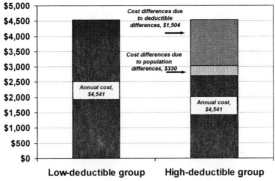

Costs include paid insurance, copayments, deductibles and coinsurance.

This does not contradict research that documents the phenomenon called "adverse selection." Employees who are healthier, expect lower health costs, and have higher incomes will be more likely to sign up for a HDHP option. This leaves higher-cost employees in traditional plan options. What our finding indicates is that the experience, once employees are in the plan, is *not* simply the result of having healthy people. Regardless of who enrolls, a significant change in cost is expected.

The rest of this entry covers the challenge of doing research in situations involving self-selection, and how we came to the conclusion above. There is also a short comment on the blog development process.

Self-selection

Researchers who study what happens in the real world often face the impossible task of trying to verify cause-and-effect in situations where the "cause" is a voluntary choice. For example, let's say a group of employees can choose to enroll in one of two health programs. After a year, employees who participated in Program A have lower costs than employees who participated in Program B. Because employees selected their own programs, we don't know if the difference in costs reflects the type of people who selected the program, the effectiveness of the program, or some combination of both.

This problem—not knowing what caused a difference—occurs in any circumstance where people are allowed to select among options that one wants to compare. Referred to as self-selection or selection bias, it is a limitation that researchers try to account for by "controlling for" other things. Essentially, this means they gather information about eligible employees to try and rule out the possibility that participants in Program A were healthier or less costly to begin with. Unfortunately, it is impossible to account for all possible differences between employees in each program (e.g., perhaps participants in Program A dislike going to the doctor more). So there is always lingering doubt that Program A produced lower costs. The only scientific way to prove a difference is if employees are randomly assigned to each program, eliminating all but random differences in the employees. Rarely can we apply that criterion in the real world.

As a side story…for anyone who wonders how tobacco companies could continue to deny that their products caused cancer for decades after scientific studies suggested otherwise—it was the selection bias issue. Because people could not (ethically) be randomly assigned to smoke or not, tobacco companies insisted that it was possible that individuals who were genetically predisposed to use tobacco were also genetically predisposed to getting cancer. Tobacco use was coincidental. Their claim could not be disproved completely, allowing officials to maintain their technically-correct, but shamefully-misleading position denying cause-and-effect.

The method: Decomposition

To separate plan effects from self-selection effects, my colleagues in the Health as Human Capital Research Group have been using an interesting statistical technique called decomposition. It allows the analyst to tease apart the portion of an observed difference that can be attributed to a specific factor and the portion of a difference that can be attributed to the people who self-selected that factor.

To get a more detailed explanation of the method, you can read our brief technical write-up.[2] As a general description, first the technique was used to estimate the overall difference in costs between high-deductible health plans and low-deductible health plans using separate multivariate regression models for people in the two types of health plans. The total difference is due to both the plan and the people selecting the plan. Second, these models are then used to estimate what would have happened if both groups of people had been in the same health plan. Using this result, we can estimate how much of the cost difference is due to the plans and how much of the difference is due to differences in the people who chose the plans.

It is important to note that although we included many important cost-related variables, one can never control for all possible contributing factors. If those who select the HDHP have a specific personality trait (risk taking, money saving) this is not accounted for. However, we are confident that most traditional predictors have been included.

In situations where we know that both an external plan and characteristics of self-selection contribute to a result, this method is useful in discerning the relative magnitude of each. Here, it helped us find that the plan had more of an effect than those who selected the plan.

Author's Note:

Although blog entries are written by one person, there is a wonderful team of individuals who contribute their thinking and effort to each one. This process makes every entry better. The analysis for this entry (and many others) was conducted by Nathan Kleinman, Ph.D. Our talented team of reviewers includes accomplished economists, healthcare providers, a professional writer, and multiple industry experts. Review of this entry, in particular, led to a flurry of emails among the group, re-analysis, complex methods of validation, and additional text because practitioners think differently than researchers and economists interpret things differently than health and benefits professionals. In the end, we come to a collective conclusion about what we find, and what it means. This author would like to acknowledge the team's contributions.

April 14, 2006

References

1 Lynch, W.D., Gardner, H.H., Kleinman, N.L., Health as Human Capital Research Group. "Selection of high-deductible health plans: attributes influencing likelihood and implications for consumer-driven approaches," Health as Human Capital Foundation, February 2006, http://www.hhcfoundation.org/hhcf/pdf/adverseselection_2_13_06.pdf (accessed April 10, 2006).

2 Lynch, W.D., Kleinman, N.L. "High deductible vs. low deductible decomposition analysis methodology," Health as Human Capital Foundation, April, 2006, http://www.hhcfoundation.org/hhcf/_pdf/entry_8.pdf (accessed April 16, 2006).

Blog 3.9   Moral hazard and the New Year's effect

By tradition, health insurance policies last one year.* For employees of large companies the new policy usually starts on January first. For small companies and individuals, the policy may start on other dates, but lasts until the same date the folowing year. Businesses and health plans are familiar with, and use, annual costs (pmpy: per-member-per-year) as a standard metric of expense. For the most part, an annual insurance timeframe is accepted as "the way things are." But we wonder, does a yearly policy really make sense?

While this topic is worthy of significant discussion, in this blog entry, we will focus on one implication of annual policies: moral hazard.

---

* Although some policy makers have suggested the creation of long-term health insurance resembling life insurance policies, we are not aware of such offerings in the market. See "Update on the individual health insurance market," CMS Report 6-A-05, June 2005 from the AMA. http://www.ama-assn.org/ama1/pub/upload/mm/372/a05cms6.pdf (accessed July 8, 2006).

Recent blog entries[†] have demonstrated the episodic nature of health issues and healthcare costs. Only a minority of individuals (even those who have serious illnesses) have high costs in a given year, and even fewer will have high costs in two subsequent years.

What are some of the implications of these episodes? If people do not repeat high cost in subsequent years, it follows that episodes usually happen within a 12-month period. Also, except for certain seasonal trends, we would expect that episodes will occur throughout the year. Some begin in March, others in August, others in December, and so forth. One might wonder whether timing matters. Let's consider the structure of traditional annual policies. From the perspective of the policy holder, there are three spending components:[‡]

My money: the amount the policy holder pays toward their yearly deductible. Below that deductible amount, the policy holder pays 100% of costs.

Shared money: the amount between the deductible and the out-of-pocket-maximum (OOPmax) of which the policy holder usually pays a percentage, and

Someone else's money: expenses paid in full by the insurer after the policy holder reaches the OOPmax.

There is good evidence that when we spend someone else's money, we behave differently than when we spend our own money.[§] This well-known phenomenon is referred to as moral hazard: the tendency to use more services when someone else pays, or when the items are pre-paid. Thus, in our calendar-year-defined system, it follows that the longer time a policy holder stays in the second or third level of spending, the more services they will tend to use.

To demonstrate this, we will use some findings that our research team produced a few years ago. They designed an analysis that included over 58,000 people who had consistent, single-person coverage over a two-year

---

[†] See Blog 2.4 The episodic nature of illness part 1; and Blog 2.5 The episodic nature of illness part 2.

[‡] We credit this description of three "types of money" to Dr. Hank Gardner, who has been using it to facilitate better policy design.

[§] See Blog 3.1 Remembering the RAND Health Insurance Experiment.

period (2001-2002), and a policy that renewed on January 1st. Annual deductibles ranged from $100 to $1,500 dollars, with most below $500. Of the group, more than 5,900 reached their deductible.

We wondered if the time between reaching one's deductible and when a new deductible started (so, in other words, the time between their deductible-reaching episode and the start of the New Year) would effect how much money they would spend in the next twelve months. Specifically, the twelve-month healthcare costs for people who reached their deductible in February were totaled from February until the following February (11 months before a new deductible started and one month after). For people who reached their deductible in March, we totaled their costs from March until the following March (meaning that three of those months were after their new deductible started). Clearly, those who reached their deductible in November and December of year 1 had very little time to consume services at the post-deductible price before a new period of full costs began again. Ten or eleven of their months occurred *after* a new deductible was applied.

As shown in figure 3.9, timing matters. Those reaching their deductible early in the year spent more in the next 12 months than those reaching their deductible later in the year. The effect is most visible in the first six months. After the policy holder reaches the point of subsidized spending, they tend to consume more services—until the deductible starts over. Those who reached their deductible in February used more services in the next twelve months than those who reached it in March. Those who reached their deductible in March used more services in the next twelve months than those who reached their deductible in April and so on. In other words, the longer an individual had subsidized spending, the more care they consumed. Because the analysis controlled for costs the month before the deductible was reached, only individuals reaching their deductible in February or later were included.

The team checked for other explanations for this pattern. The analysis controlled for demographics, income, health status, and other factors that might influence why early spenders might be sicker (there is more detail at the end of this entry). This appears to be a reflection of the timing of their spending, not their level of illness.

98

FIGURE 3.9   *HEALTHCARE COST DURING THE 12 MONTHS AFTER REACHING DEDUCTIBLE*

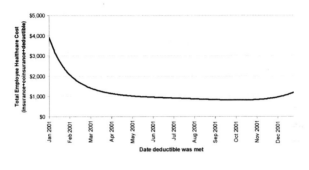

Health as Human Capital Research Group, 2006

Insurance moral hazard occurs when people are not spending their own money (or in this case, not as much of their own money). Under the annual policy design this is more likely to occur when a person has an episode early in the calendar year. One is left to wonder whether other designs or timeframes could reduce moral hazard and apply incentives more consistently—such as, the same cost share regardless of where the price falls (along the current my money-their money continuum). Or perhaps long term policies without a sudden "reset" button on New Year's Day—regardless of how recently you spent your money.

This discovery brings up questions about health plan design changes and healthcare spending. Many of us resist the idea that rules about health insurance alter how much healthcare consumers will seek. There is a general assumption that healthcare delivery is a simple equation: a system responding, necessarily and efficiently, when people get sick. We rarely hear about the degree of discretion consumers have in their treatment options. Yet, this phenomenon is one example of how plan design does (and could) alter patterns of healthcare consumption.

In the meantime, if you are a patient who must face an illness, have your episode in January so that you have more time to receive additional services at a lower cost. If you are health plan sponsor and some of your people will get ill, hope their illnesses all occur in December.

Some analysis detail

Total expenditures in the twelve months following the day a person reached their deductible was the dependent variable. Multivariate regression included age, gender, health status (Charlson Index), salary, and region of the country. The day between start of year and achieving the deductible was a predictor, as well as the square and cube of that variable. Because the analysis controlled for costs the month before the deductible was reached, only individuals reaching their deductible in February or later were included.

As in any non-randomized, empirical study, sample selection may also have some influence on the pattern we observe since the outcome (total expenses) is partially a function of health events (and their expenses that drive us over the deductible) that influence the beginning of each individual's "sample" experiment. We partially mitigate against this by examining the expenditures for the following twelve months after the deductible is reached, while controlling for other factors in our multivariate regression analysis.

July 11, 2006

Blog 3.10   Proof that consumers can and do make logical, economic choices in healthcare: they bypass poorly priced "consumer" plans

We find irony in some recent suggestions that "consumer" plans are not gaining traction. Some argue that consumers are not capable of making wise choices based on financial parameters. In truth, consumers have been doing exactly that. We have witnessed several large employers offer a high-deductible health plan (HDHP) in combination with savings accounts (either HSAs or HRAs). When this HDHP-savings combination is offered as one option among more traditional plans, very few employees have signed up. Skeptics might conclude that these plans are too complicated or risky to be desirable. Or, perhaps they would think HDHPs are just a bad idea.

Another explanation—ironically—demonstrates consumers are making a logical choice. In examples from HCMS datasets, HDHP premium contributions for employees were not attractive. Even though premium costs were lower than other choices, they were not low enough to offset the increased risk of a higher deductible. As an illustration, the table below shows some actual rates for a company. The premium difference between the lowest ($350) and highest ($2,500) deductibles was only $800 per year, while the increased size of the deductible—a possibility of three times the out-of-pocket expense—was $2,150 (see the two cells colored dark gray).

TABLE 3.1   HDHP PREMIUM PRICING, EXAMPLE

	Deductible	Annual total premium	Employer pays 85% annually	Employee pays 15% annually
Plan 1	$350	$5,330	$4,530	$800
Plan 2	$2,500	$4,530	$3,850	$680
Difference in cost if switching from $350 to $2,500 deductible	$2,150	-$800	-$680	-$120

HHCF 2006

At this company, *very* few employees chose the HDHP option (only about 2%). Looking at the price, one understands why. Because employees pay only 15% of the premium cost, the employee would take on the risk of a possible $2,150 deductible and receive a premium discount of only $120. The combined premium and deductible of the HDHP would be $3,180, versus $1,150 for the traditional plan. Is $10 per month out-of-pocket worth the risk? Evidently not.

This is not atypical of the differences in premiums for "regular" and HDHPs, as shown in table 3.2. Nationally the patterns are similar: the consumer is offered the option to pay $6 to $12 less per month in return for taking on the possibility of an additional $1,200 to $1,300 of out-of-pocket expense.[1]

Further, the difference in premium cost for the employer (in our example, $680 less) falls well short of the amount needed to cover the possibility of higher out-of-pocket costs through deposits in a health savings account. So, to make it attractive under these circumstances, an employer would have to pay *more* in total for the HDHP (plus savings) than for typical low-deductible plans, which is not a desirable option either.

Given the difference in premiums, it makes sense why employees, even when premiums are subsidized, don't choose HDHPs and why employers do not fund savings accounts at the level that would make this option more attractive.

TABLE 3.2   HDHP PREMIUM PRICING, NATIONAL

	Deductible	Annual total premium	Employer pays 85% annually	Employee pays 15% annually
HMO	$352	$3,899	$3,314	$585
PPO	$473	$4,385	$3,727	$658
HDHP	$1,715	$3,405	$2,894	$511
Difference in cost if switching from HMO to HDHP	$1,363	-$494	-$420	-$74
Difference in cost if switching from PPO to HDHP	$1,242	-$980	-$833	-$147

HHCF 2006

Who says consumers don't make rational choices?

In another entry,* we will explore some reasons why HDHPs aren't priced lower.

November 12, 2006

References

1 Kaiser Family Foundation Employer Health Benefits 2006 Annual Survey http:// www.kff.org/insurance/7527/upload/7527.pdf (accessed November 10, 2006).

---

* See Blog 2.8 Why don't high deductible plans have low premiums?

Blog 3.11 Patient costs should and do matter in healthcare choices: our reinterpretation of a recent study

When patients spend their own money on healthcare, instead of someone else's money, do they pay more attention to how much they spend? Of course they do (see a previous blog about the RAND Health Insurance Experiment*). However, authors of a recent study advise against more patient cost sharing for an interesting reason: doctors don't consider patient costs important.

The study, published in the *Archives of Internal Medicine*,[1] found that a majority of doctors surveyed (78%) considered out-of-pocket (OOP) costs for patients when prescribing medication, but 51% or fewer considered OOP costs in their recommendation of diagnostic tests, or their choice of setting in which a procedure would occur (e.g., inpatient or outpatient). Over 6,500 doctors, representative of practicing doctors across the nation, participated in this telephone survey.

FIGURE 3.10 PERCENT OF DOCTORS CONSIDERING PATIENT COSTS IN THEIR RECOMMENDATIONS

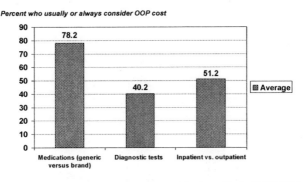

Pham, H.H., Alexander, G.C., O'Malley, A.S. *Arch of Internal Medicine* 2007;167(7):663-668.

As shown in figure 3.10, only two of five doctors consider what a diagnostic test would cost their patients, and only half consider patient cost when recommending outpatient versus inpatient procedures. These

---

* See Blog 3.1 Remembering the RAND Health Insurance Experiment.

rates indicate that doctors generally do not consider patient costs an important factor in these decisions. One might wonder whether this is because patient OOP costs are, in fact, low enough that neither doctors nor patients care about them. Or whether doctors just believe that other factors are more important in their decisions. The dramatically greater consideration doctors give patients for cost for medication choices (four out of five doctors did consider patient cost in this case) is striking and requires some explanation. Why was this so different?

The study authors used traditional medical perspectives to explain their findings, including points such as the following:

1) Interestingly, all decisions were described as doctor's decisions, not shared decisions with patients.

2) The high rate of considering OOP costs for generic versus brand medications was attributed to such decisions being more "straightforward," while the other, "more complex," decisions required a higher level of clinical decision making.

3) The lack of greater attention to cost was attributed in part to a lack of available price information.

4) Because "doctors are responsible for making decisions that affect 90% of each medical dollar spent," they are the primary influencers on spending.

5) Thus, since doctors don't pay attention to OOP cost, changing patient incentives will have "limited" potential to influence healthcare spending.

We might interpret their findings in a different way.

While the authors attributed the large difference between medication decisions (80% considered cost) and procedure decisions (40% considered cost) to clinical simplicity of the former, we might suggest that the difference is partly due to differences in economic pressures *because* of consumer involvement.

Consider these aspects of medication decisions:

1) They are the most commonly made decisions of those in the study.

2) Drug costs are more familiar to patients.

3) Drug formularies and prices are more likely to be discussed as a detail of enrollment.

4) Thus, it is plausible that patients may initiate discussions about price for medications more than tests and procedures.

Also worth noting is that when a patient consumes significant healthcare services, they reach an OOP maximum (often around $3,000 to $5,000). After that time, doctors are aware that the individual no longer has financial responsibility for the bill and may consider it less important.

Suppose discussions about price are most often initiated by the patient. If so, one would expect that patients who have more of a concern about cost would be most likely to have such discussions. Indeed, the study showed that doctors were most likely to consider OOP cost when they had low income patients (with greatest economic need); see figure 3.11.

Further, when the study compared doctors who worked in a group-

FIGURE 3.11   PERCENT OF DOCTORS CONSIDERING PATIENT COSTS IN THEIR RECOMMENDATIONS BY PATIENT INCOME

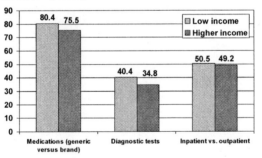

Pham, H.H., Alexander, G.C., O'Malley, A.S. *Arch of Internal Medicine* 2007;167(7):663-668.

model HMO (where the patient often does not pay a portion of the treatment cost, but does have a copayment for medications) to those who worked in solo fee-for-service practices, the HMO doctors were far less likely to consider costs in their decisions (fig. 3.12). Although doctors were not asked *why* they did or did not consider costs, both of these findings suggest that when their patients had a higher relative cost burden, doctors were more likely to take that into account and consider price.

FIGURE 3.12 PERCENT OF DOCTORS CONSIDERING PATIENT COSTS IN
THEIR RECOMMENDATIONS BY HMO OR SOLO PRACTICE

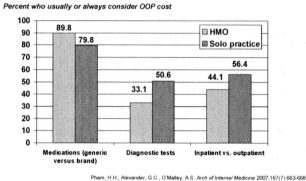

Pham, H.H., Alexander, G.C., O'Malley, A.S. *Arch of Internal Medicine* 2007;167(7):663-668.

It seems to us that the authors ignored a very plausible conclusion: doctors do not consider patient OOP cost when it is not very important to the patient.

This article suggests that *because* doctors ignore cost to the patient the system should not ask patients to share costs. However, economic theory would suggest the reverse: by asking patients to have active control of healthcare spending, they would, in turn, ask doctors to consider costs more often.

Thus, we would suggest a completely opposite course of action—put more economic responsibility on patients, so that they become active participants in care decisions. Patients are the true purchasers, who deserve transparency in the quality and price of their options. Perpetuating a belief system that implies that doctors have sole responsibility for choosing "90% of all services" that patients receive moves us further away from, rather than closer to, the levels of transparency and participation required to transform our current system.

April 22, 2007

References:

1 Pham, H.H., Alexander, G.C., O'Malley, A.S. Physician consideration of patients' out-of-pocket costs in making common clinical decisions. *Arch of Internal Medicine* 2007; 167(7):663-8.

Chapter 4
Nothing Is Free:
Everything Is a Tradeoff

Acknowledging that there are some rare things in life that are so plentiful and available that we can consider them free (economists like to point out things like air and sunlight), virtually all other goods and services come at a cost to someone. Consumption that seems to occur at little or no cost to the consumer must be paid for in other ways by other parties.

Costs of wasted items in the all-you-eat-buffet must be covered in the overall price of the meal, spread across all big and small eaters. When a person can see a doctor for $5, the remaining costs of the service are paid for through other business arrangements. Part of the fees may be paid for through a prepaid insurance premium, which has similarities to the all-you-can-eat prepaid buffet. Although the services are "covered" by insurance and the out-of-pocket price to the insured person may be zero, the full costs of the service will have to be paid for by those in the insurance pool, or the insurance company will go broke in the long run.

Insurance premiums may appear to be paid for or subsidized by an employer or government program. Although this may reduce the direct cost to the consumer, indirectly the remaining cost of the premium must be covered in other ways. Because the amount of resources an employer can devote to compensating employees is roughly limited to the value of their productivity, employees may experience the cost of health insurance indirectly through a concept known to economists as *opportunity cost.* That is, employees may not pay for insurance directly, but instead will have fewer total dollars paid out to them for wages, raises, training, bonuses, and other benefits. If healthcare is subsidized by the government, taxpayers—consciously or not—pay directly and also experience the opportunity loss of having to use dollars for healthcare that could have been applied to other government services.

When a consumer receives products or services "for free," either because someone else pays or through a prepaid insurance arrangement, there may be other consequences in addition to excess consumption resulting from moral hazard. One is a lack of awareness of the price of specific healthcare services and the parallel lack of attention given to what is actually being done. Another is a lack of engagement in usual consumerism behaviors such as shopping for better quality and price, or asking for performance guarantees. Further, when consumers anticipate that future needs will be met at low cost, there is less incentive to take proactive steps to avoid future problems.

Similar to the opportunity cost of insurance premiums, costs for paid-time-off benefits affect employees in other ways. As with health insurance premiums, spending on paid time-off reduces available funds for other sorts of compensation and benefits. Additionally, when employees are absent from work, especially for extended periods, there may be personal opportunity costs of fewer resources for training, advancement, and bonuses. Absent workers also lose contact with what is going on in the workplace and become less valuable to employers when they return to work, resulting in lower future wages and benefits.

The following examples illustrate how things we think are free (or really cheap) just cost us in other ways.

Blog 4.1   The wage-benefit tradeoff: who actually benefits?

Total compensation for employees is determined by labor market forces in the private sector. However, employers vary in the proportion of the compensation that they provide in the form of benefits (versus wages). More spending in one category will decrease what is available for the other.[1] When we hear that only 60% of companies offered health insurance to their employees in 2005, down from 69% in 2000,[2] it confirms that employers face tough decisions. For the first time, the average annual cost of healthcare for a family now exceeds the annual salary of a person making minimum wage at a full-time job. So, every full health insurance policy a small employer covers is equivalent to one more job. An employer must choose: two workers with no insurance, or one worker with full coverage?

FIGURE 4.1   THE BENEFITS VERSUS WAGES TRADEOFF

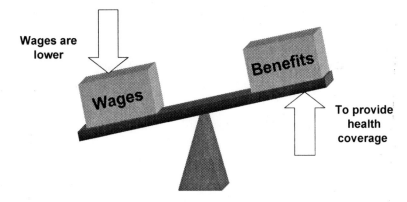

Miller, R.D., Jr. *Int J Health Care Finance Econ* 2004;4(1):27-41.

The current trend toward health savings accounts is a step toward allowing the worker to choose between benefits and wages. This happens because monies *not* used in the accounts accumulate as additional wages that can be used for medical expenses in the future, or as supplemental retirement income. In addition to this option between benefits now and income in the future, lower projected premium costs (from higher deductibles) can shift some of the health-benefit spending back to workers to be used at their discretion.

Paid time-off (PTO) is also a compensation tradeoff. As a faculty member at a university, I received 22 days of paid vacation per year and 15 sick days per year, for a total of almost eight weeks of paid time-off. This was in addition to all national and state holidays. I could accumulate and roll over unlimited sick time and up to nine weeks of vacation. This is not uncommon for jobs in public agencies. From a 'total comp' perspective, this implies that the university could afford to have me work only 80 to 85% of the time, or that—if I wasn't interested in all that time off (which, a majority of people did not use)—I could have been making a 15% higher salary. But the option offered to me was time off, not additional pay.

The incentives generated by such a scheme are interesting. As I became accustomed to the rapid accumulation of days, it became important to try and use them. In December, many of us realized we had to use 8, 10, 12, days before the end of the year or "lose them." This presented a personal dilemma of balancing work we needed to finish and personal loss of benefits we wouldn't choose. I would gladly have traded in the days for pay to continue working. Instead, I had an incentive *not* to apply my human capital on those final days. Despite this counterproductive tradeoff, when I faced a limited PTO bank (15 days of vacation and sick time lumped together) in a subsequent corporate job, I was appalled by its lack of "compassion." I still had not made the connection between what I could earn and benefits that I did not fully value (for what they cost me).

Self-employment was a great lesson. How in the world did my previous employers afford to pay me, give me paid vacation, and pay benefits? When I wasn't working, the company was losing money…but they paid me anyway. As an employer and an employee, I had to choose which, and how much benefits I wanted to trade for less income. I learned that these benefits had opportunity costs, directly for the firm and indirectly for me.

I also experienced the phenomenon of "job-lock,"[3] where individuals are less likely to leave a job because they are afraid that health benefits will not be available. The professional considerations for starting a business (which is what *should* matter) were balanced against concerns about whether health coverage would be available. That consideration was a much bigger issue than I had anticipated.

Is providing more benefits rather than paying higher wages (or employing more people) truly beneficial? Do most employees actually benefit from the tradeoffs resulting from 'better' benefits? And at what level is the tradeoff worth it? Further, are employees stuck in jobs they don't like because they want to keep their benefits?

When the design of employee benefits encourages employees to value them more than the primary compensation for their work, it is detrimental to work and a counterproductive reward. The health as human capital philosophy would say that giving workers more control over their

110

compensation—in the form of dollars they spend directly—and tying it directly to productive work, will align employee incentives with the firm's survivability. Pay people more for the work they do, and less for not working. Let people earn more for the time off they do not use, rather than scramble to miss work to avoid losing benefits. And strive to retain people with rewarding work, rather than with benefits too good to lose.

February 6, 2006

References

1 Miller, R.D., Jr. Estimating the compensating differential for employer-provided health insurance. *Int J Health Care Finance Econ* 2004;4(1):27-41.

2 The Kaiser Family Foundation. Employer Health Benefits 2005 Survey, September 2005, http://www.kff.org/insurance/7315.cfm (accessed February 4, 2006).

3 Cooper, P.F., Monheit, A.C. Does employment-related health insurance inhibit job mobility? *Inquiry* 1993;30(4):400-16.

Blog 4.2   A reminder that everything is a tradeoff

According to the Bureau of Labor Statistics, average total compensation for workers in private industry in the third quarter of 2006 was $25.52 per hour. [1] If we apply this to full-time workers (and assume 40 hour weeks and 48 weeks of work = 1,920 hours), this is a total package of almost $49,000 per year. Of this, $34,640 was salary and $14,361 was benefits ($3,380 of which is for healthcare).[2] These numbers are not truly averages, because they represent all workers (including part time) and many workers who are not eligible for or do not select certain types of benefits. But, in aggregate, this is the picture of employer spending in the U.S.

Over the past two years, total compensation in private industry has increased from $23.29 to $25.52 per hour. But employer costs for benefits have increased faster than the increase in wages. As we see in the two graphs in figure 4.2, the percent of compensation awarded in wages declined from 71.5% to 70.7% (with an even bigger decline for

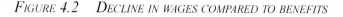

FIGURE 4.2   DECLINE IN WAGES COMPARED TO BENEFITS

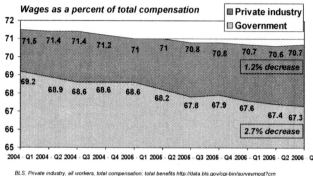

government workers in salary[3] and benefits[4]). Conversely, the cost of benefits increased from 28.5% to 29.3%.

These appear to be small changes, which may lead some readers to wonder why they are worthy of attention. Well, even tiny numbers add up. As recently as 1999, compensation was comprised of 73% wages and 27% benefits.

FIGURE 4.3   INCREASE IN BENEFITS COSTS COMPARED TO WAGES

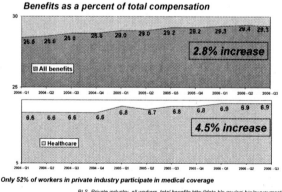

This means that in 1999, for every dollar in wages the employer spent:
$0.37 on benefits
$0.07 on medical insurance

112

By the end of 2006, for each dollar in wages, the employer spent:

$0.42 on benefits

$0.10 on medical insurance

Because benefits grew at a faster rate than wages, employers are essentially spending five cents more on benefits for every dollar spent on wages; three of those cents are for medical insurance.

If we believe that an additional dollar spent on medical insurance has become more valuable to workers than an additional dollar spent on wages—and more importantly, if workers believe this is true—then the tradeoff of more benefits for less wages will enhance workers' interests. However, in the larger scheme, one must wonder if a majority of workers would choose to forgo an increasingly greater amount of their wages to retain a steady amount of healthcare coverage.

We find that these tradeoffs rarely come to workers' direct attention in discussions about rewards. Employees may grumble about increases in cost share for medical insurance, but not realize how the rise in healthcare costs also restricts pay raises. What would happen if employees could choose? One example where employees were told about the tradeoff was Whole Foods. Whole Foods implemented a high-deductible, consumer-directed plan and many employees were unhappy. So the CEO, John Mackey, decided that employees should vote on what benefits would be provided, including the choice of one type of health plan for all employees.[5] The options were a high-deductible, consumer-directed plan or a traditional plan that had a higher overall cost. Employees were provided the list of benefits and what they cost. Once employees understood the tradeoff, the votes were counted. Eighty-three percent of employees chose the lower-cost, consumer-directed plan.

Would all employees, in all industries, make the same choice? Nobody knows. But it does make us wonder about how much employees know about the tradeoffs being made on their behalf.

January 15, 2007

References

1 Employer costs for employee compensation (sic): private industry, all workers, total compensation 2004-2007 - CMU2010000000000D. Compensation and Working

Conditions, Bureau of Labor Statistics, http://data.bls.gov/cgi-bin/surveymost?cm (accessed January 12, 2007).

2 Employer costs for employee compensation (sic): private industry, all workers, total benefits 2004-2007 - CMU2030000000000D. Compensation and Working Conditions, Bureau of Labor Statistics, http://data.bls.gov/cgi-bin/surveymost?cm (accessed January 12, 2007).

3 Employer costs for employee compensation (sic): state and local government, all workers, total compensation 2004-2007- CMU3010000000000D. Compensation and Working Conditions, Bureau of Labor Statistics, http://data.bls.gov/cgi-bin/surveymost?cm (accessed January 12, 2007).

4 Employer costs for employee compensation (sic): state and local government, all workers, total benefits - CMU3030000000000D. Compensation and Working Conditions, Bureau of Labor Statistics, http://data.bls.gov/cgi-bin/surveymost?cm (accessed January 12, 2007).

5 Mackey, J. Whole Foods Market's consumer-driven health plan. State Policy Network 12th Annual Meeting, October 2004, http://www.worldcongress.com/news/Mackey_Transcript.pdf (accessed January 12, 2007).

Blog 4.3   Knowing how parts affect the whole. Example 1: Do changes in healthcare cost sharing affect use of workers' compensation?

This entry presents the first of two examples showing how changes in the design of one type of employee benefit program can affect another. In this entry, we examine the relationship between changes in a medical insurance benefit and changes in incurred medical costs in the workers' compensation system.

First we will distinguish between the two types of benefits. When companies provide health insurance for their employees, the "benefit" comes as a subsidized premium for a health insurance policy. Essentially, the employee exchanges a portion of his or her wages for an employer's sponsorship of a policy and payment, usually a majority of a premium. Employers can choose to pay greater or lesser amounts of the premium. Employers can also choose to modify—or eliminate—the type of health insurance policies available to employees.

Another benefit provided by employers and mandated by law (in almost every state) is insurance against personal losses due to accidents or injuries at work. This coverage falls under the workers' compensation (WC) system. This insurance covers three types of losses that could occur due to accidents or injuries while on the job: all medical costs associated with the injury; lost income during treatment of and recovery from injury; and lost income or lost future opportunity due to permanent disabling effects of an injury. This system was designed to protect the current and future livelihood of workers and their families when injured on the job. Because this system covers occupational injuries (i.e., injuries due to one's work), the medical aspect of this type of insurance pays 100% of all costs—with no cost sharing by the injured worker. The direct cost of providing this type of insurance is paid entirely by the employer.

Of course, some illnesses and injuries have a gradual onset or an unknown cause and could be as easily attributed to work-related activities as to other activities. As such, there is some discretion in whether a medical problem is classified as occupational or not. Thus, we wondered if changes in the non-occupational health policy would change the likelihood that care would be received in one system versus another.

Our research team studied a population of about 100,000 employees from multiple companies and found that about 1.5% of all medical costs were spent in the WC system. The remaining 98.5% of costs were incurred under the healthcare insurance system. Obviously, this portion will vary by type of company and type of job, but in general most illnesses are treated outside of the WC system.

So, if these two benefit programs cover different events—injuries and illnesses that occur on-the-job versus those that occur elsewhere—how would their design affect each other? Using the same population of 100,000 people (all of whom had both workers' compensation and health insurance coverage), across many companies and health plans, we tracked the change in the portion of medical treatment costs that were spent under the WC system. Specifically, the analysis looked at whether a change in the overall cost sharing in an employee's health insurance policy from year 1 to year 2 would alter the portion of spending that occurred in the WC system in the second year. Figure 4.4 shows the results.

FIGURE 4.4   IMPACT OF CHANGES IN HEALTHCARE COINSURANCE ON COST
MIGRATION TO WORKERS' COMPENSATION

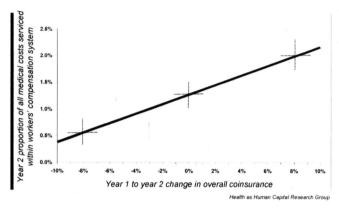

Health as Human Capital Research Group

The graph indicates that individuals whose companies did not change the cost-sharing rules of their health insurance policies could be expected to spend 1.3% of their healthcare costs in the WC system in the following year. Individuals who worked for companies whose health insurance policies changed to increase the employee cost share could be expected to spend a higher portion of services from WC. For example, the cross on the top right shows that individuals whose cost share increased by 8 percentage points could be expected to spend 2% of all medical care dollars in the WC system. Individuals whose cost share decreased by 8 percentage points could be expected to spend only 0.5% of all medical care dollars in the WC system.[*]

Literally, increasing the cost share on healthcare services resulted in more reported accidents at work. Why? Not because the workplace

---

[*] The analysis controlled for salary and year-one health insurance cost. The team also looked at the possibility that the increase in WC percentage could be attributed to the change in overall spending that one might expect when cost share increases. In other words, the overall spending went down, so the same WC spending would now look bigger due to the smaller total. However, the change in overall spending required to produce this change in WC portion (from 1.3% to 2.0%) was too dramatic to be plausible. As an example, if $13,000 (1.3%) of $1,000,000 is spent in WC, then the remainder ($987,000) is spent in the medical system. In order for that same $13,000 to be 2.2% of all spending, medical costs would have to decline from $987,000 to $578,000, which is not likely to occur with a 10% increase in cost share. This left us to conclude that cost shifting is occurring.

became less safe. Instead, the increase in cost share in health insurance provides more incentive to classify one's health conditions as compensable in the other (WC) system. Behavior changes as one system becomes more advantageous.

As we have pointed out before, these behaviors are not necessarily an indication of deception or cheating, but rather an indication of discretion and choice in the face of changed economic incentives. A sore shoulder can be attributed to an incident at work or an incident at home, or a combination of both. If treatment can be received for free by classifying its cause as work-related, there is incentive to classify the injury to one's financial advantage.

This study provides an example of some of the complex interactions among the many ways employees are compensated and insured. Each affects the others. The example also reminds us of a fundamental aspect of human nature: given a choice, we will act in ways that maximize our own best interests.

While this analysis focused on incentives of workers, the same sort of substitution has been found with respect to incentives for providers of healthcare coverage. We find those employees with HMO medical expense coverage are more likely to file workers' compensation claims than those employees covered by fee-for-service policies.[1] The reason is financial: since workers' compensation pays fee-for-service regardless of the form of group health reimbursement, HMOs increase their revenue by classifying as many health conditions as possible as work related, thereby capturing the workers' compensation fee-for-service payments in addition to the capitated fees that they have already contracted for with the employer.

July 23, 2006

References

1 Butler, R.J., Hartwig, R.P., Gardner, H. HMOs, moral hazard and cost shifting in workers' compensation. *J Health Econ*, 1997;16(2):191-206.

Blog 4.4   Knowing how parts affect the whole. Example 2: How is the rate of LTD claims affected by changes in other benefits and compensation?

This is a continuation of examples showing how changes in the design of one type of employee benefit program can affect another. In this entry we examine the relationship between various benefit design choices and the expected rate of long-term-disability (LTD) claims.

Long-term-disability insurance pays a portion of an employee's salary (most commonly, about 60% of salary up to a maximum, but this can vary) during an extended illness/injury. These salary-replacement payments begin after a period of continuous disability (such as 90 days or 6 months) and continue for an extended duration (e.g., five years or until a person is 65 years old), depending on the policy. If an employer provides short-term-disability (STD) and long-term-disability insurance, employees receive salary replacement through STD first, followed by LTD after the STD timeframe is exceeded.

Qualification rules regarding whether the person is unable to perform his or her specific job or unable to perform any job also apply. A person receiving long-term-disability payments is classified by a health professional as incapable of performing work due to medical reasons.

In this project, our research team looked at over 100,000 employees. The outcome of interest was the rate of LTD claims and, specifically, the direction and magnitude of expected change in LTD claims rate in the year following changes in other factors. The analysis controlled for age, gender, exempt status, region of the country, sick leave usage, STD claims, STD wait period, workers' compensation claims, workers' compensation wait period, medical insurance costs, medical plan type, number of suspensions from work, and performance score.

Figure 4.5 shows the expected change in rate of LTD claims if other factors change. Specifically, each bar shows the predicted change in rate of LTD claims if the other indicated factors increased by 10%. As a general rule, a bigger bar in the graph (in either direction) indicates that LTD claims rates are more sensitive to this factor. Economists refer to this type of sensitivity as elasticity.

FIGURE 4.5   CORRELATES OF CHANGE IN LONG TERM DISABILITY RATES

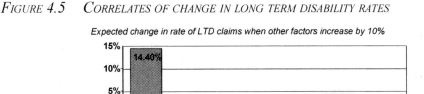

Expected change in rate of LTD claims when other factors increase by 10%

Health as Human Capital Research Group

As one might expect, older employees can be expected to have more LTD claims. A ten percent increase in average age would produce an expected increase in LTD claims of 14%.* Interestingly, LTD claims were not very sensitive to increases in medical costs or shorter episodes of disability. A ten percent increase in either medical costs or STD claims only produced small (less than one percent) positive effects on the LTD claims rate.

Two interesting factors that seemed to influence the rate of LTD claims were the duration of waiting periods for other (interim) salary replacement programs. A ten percent longer waiting period before one is eligible for salary replacement under a STD policy, results in a 5.5% lowered rate of eventual LTD claims. Essentially, it appears that longer waiting for eligibility for salary replacement in the STD system lowers the risk of subsequent LTD claims. Conversely, a ten percent longer waiting period under the workers' compensation system (WC) resulted in an expected 4.1% increase in LTD claims.

---

* Note that these are relative increases. For example, if a population has an average age 40 years and a rate of LTD claims of 2%, a ten percent increase in age is from 40 to 44 years and a fourteen percent increase in rate is from 2.0% to 2.28%. It is not simply equivalent to an increase of 14 percentage points which would imply an increase from 2% to 16%.

Lastly, a ten percent increase in job performance could be expected to decrease the rate of LTD claims by 13.2%. In other words, a person who performs well on the job has a reduced likelihood of LTD.

As was discussed in the last blog entry,[†] there are several ways one might interpret these correlations. If the classification of disability was a "perfect" science—such that every case would be uniformly classified (or not) as a disability by every physician, in every circumstance, for every job, and if worker and attending physician always deferred to the perfectly informed scientific result despite their economic incentives to do otherwise   it is likely that relationships among benefit program designs would not exist.

Improvements in job performance and extended STD waiting periods probably do not improve health status to reduce the medical need for disability pay. Neither do WC waiting periods damage employee health resulting in extended disability. But these changes do seem to shift incentives in ways that alter the likelihood of future LTD claims. If I experience more "personal cost" for filing a LTD claim, it will decrease my likelihood. If I experience barriers in other systems (e.g., WC), it will increase my likelihood of using the LTD system.

Employment is a set of contracts made in the human capital marketplace. Workers exchange their efforts for compensation, benefits and opportunity. The relationships among multiple benefit programs, performance and work are complex. What we see in these examples is that each part will affect the whole. Changes in benefit programs—and the incentives they create—will have consequences in other aspects of employment.

August 6, 2006

---

† See Blog 4.3 Knowing how parts affect the whole. Example 1: Do changes in healthcare cost sharing affect use of workers' compensation?

Blog 4.5   Obesity: two perspectives

We all see the world through our own lenses; our experiences and education give us a specific perspective. One illustration of the importance of perspective is how different professionals view the topic of obesity and what to do about it.

A medical view

In health professions the prevailing perspective is that obesity is a medical issue. As such, a person should have the same access to medical treatments for this problem as any other medical condition. Expensive treatments, such as bariatric surgery, are considered medical breakthroughs to treat this severe problem.

There have been considerable recent efforts to legally classify obesity as a disease, for which those afflicted are entitled to certain protections and services. Because discrimination against obese people has been well documented,[1] the Americans with Disabilities Act (ADA) has established certain criteria under which a morbidly obese person must be protected in the work setting.[2] Further, the IRS has rules where a person diagnosed by a doctor as obese can claim deductions for certain types of programs that are otherwise not deductible.[3]

Medical costs and absence rates for obese workers are significantly higher than for their normal-weight colleagues. But this is no different than pointing out that people who have cancer or multiple sclerosis cost more too. Suggestions that obesity is different, because an individual has the ability to alter this condition, are not welcomed in the medical paradigm—provoking some reactions that such suggestions are at least mean-spirited and uninformed, and at worst perpetuate harmful discrimination. Often one hears that obese workers need to be protected from consequences: social, financial and otherwise.

An economic view

Two recent contributions by economists, one a published study and the other a television episode provide another perspective.

After documenting the additional costs of obese workers, a National Bureau of Economic Research (NBER) paper published in April 2005

121

contends that insurance premiums are not adjusted to fairly reflect the known differences in costs for obese and non-obese employees.[4] Even though obese employees have higher costs and a higher number of co-morbid conditions,[5] insurers apply an average premium, which makes the quantity of health insurance purchased by all consumers less efficient (in the economic sense). Essentially, high-risk (obese) individuals purchase too much health insurance because the premium is low relative to their actuarially fair premium, while low-risk (not obese) individuals purchase too little because their premium is higher than it should be for their level of expected need. Essentially, normal weight workers are subsidizing obese workers.

Because premiums are not higher for obese enrollees, it can lead to moral hazard—people are more likely to engage in risky behaviors that affect health expenditures. When premiums reflect risk, individuals have incentives to expend resources on self-protection. A lack of risk rating (i.e., charging more for known risks) will reduce incentives to take better care of one's self (i.e., lose weight). In other words, the failure of the obese to pay for their higher medical care expenditures through higher health insurance premiums reduces incentives for individuals to maintain a normal weight. So, the system that charges equal amounts for both groups yields inefficient outcomes for both the obese and the non-obese. The non-obese pay more than they should, and the obese are protected from incentives that might help them improve their health. Which leads us to a question: should we protect ourselves from incentives that make us more likely to help ourselves?

Another interesting part of this study was the authors' hypothesis that employers who sponsor health insurance find other ways to lower the costs of employing obese workers, namely, reducing their wages. Sure enough, obese workers who worked for companies that provided health insurance made significantly less money per hour (equating to almost $5,000 per year), thus, covering their additional medical and absence costs. The same difference was not evident *for employers that did not supply health insurance*—meaning that discrimination did not occur, but wage differentials reflect a tradeoff for higher benefits costs. From an economic perspective, the obese worker received similar compensation, but a larger portion went to cover additional healthcare rather than wages.

Credible threats

In an episode of "Primetime Live" on ABC last March, Barry Nalebuff, an economics professor from Yale used Game Theory (an idea that won a Nobel Prize) to demonstrate how he could get five out of five volunteers to lose 15 pounds in two months.[6] All volunteers wanted to lose weight, but all tried previously and failed.

The aspect of Game Theory that Dr. Nalebuff used is the notion of a non-credible threat. Essentially, since the consequences of being overweight are not immediate, people have low motivation to act on them. "You can always start your diet tomorrow." For a threat to be credible, one must be absolutely certain it will happen.

Skipping to the end of the two-month period: he was successful. Four out of five lost over 15 pounds and the remaining one lost 14 pounds. Dr. Nalebuff did not provide a program, or diet advice, or exercise equipment. In fact, all the participants admitted they knew what to do: eat less, exercise more, and substitute high fat foods, sweets, and alcohol with more vegetables, whole grains, and water. The episode followed the volunteers, who used quite rational approaches on their own.

How did the professor do it? He provided immediate consequences—a credible threat—of shame and humiliation. The volunteers agreed to pose for pictures wearing tiny "string" bathing suits. If they lost 15 pounds in two months, "Primetime" agreed not to show the embarrassing photos. But if they failed to lose the weight, the photos would be shown on national TV and the internet. The volunteers saw how awful they looked in tiny swim suits and were motivated to keep those photos private.

In his view, the obesity problem is partly a problem of insufficient incentives to change. People are capable, they just need appropriate motivation to change.

Can we learn from both perspectives?

Obesity is a complex personal, social, economic, and health issue that has neither a simple cause nor an easy solution. But these differing perspectives warrant consideration when designing the right balance of protection, incentives, and responsibility. Must one be completely protected from all health consequences regardless of cause? The health as human capital approach would suggest otherwise. Sharing the burden of poor health (between employer and employee or between individual and society) is not for the purpose of assigning blame or creating hardship, but for the purpose of aligning incentives.

To keep us *all* moving toward optimal human capital and functionality, there should be shared incentives for good health. When an individual receives additional tax deductions, greater access to expensive treatments, and a better relative deal on health premiums because of his or her health issue, there is less incentive to improve. How much should a person be protected from consequence, versus rewarded for improvement? Since the bikini approach can't be broadly implemented, what combination of incentives will work?

August 22, 2006

References

1 Puhl, R., Brownell, K.D. Bias, Discrimination, and Obesity. *Obesity Research* 2001;9(12):788-805, . http://www.obesityresearch.org/cgi/content/full/9/12/788 (accessed August 20, 2006).

2 National Council on Disability. The Americans with Disabilities Act Policy Brief Series: Righting the ADA, No. 5: Negative Media Portrayals of the ADA. February 20, 2003, http://www.ncd.gov/newsroom/publications/pdf/negativemedia.pdf (accessed August 20, 2006).

3 NAASO, The Obesity Society, http://www.obesity.org/subs/tax/irsruling.shtml (accessed August 20, 2006).

4 Bhattacharya, J., Bundorf, M.K. The incidence of the healthcare costs of obesity. NBER Working Paper No. 11303, May 2005, http://www.nber.org/papers/w11303 (accessed August 20, 2006).

5 Finkelstein, E.A. Ruhm, C.J. Kosa, K.M. Economic causes and consequences of obesity. *Annual Review of Public Health* 2005;26:239-57.

6 Lose the weight, or wear the bikini on tv. *ABC News*, March 15, 2006, http://abcnews.go.com/GMA/Diet/story?id=1725982&page=1 (accessed August 20, 2006).

Blog 4.6 The importance of human capital as a national crisis looms

We have all heard it: Social Security and Medicare are in big trouble. Perhaps huge trouble.

The latest projections* by the U.S. treasury department indicate that ten years from now, in 2017, we will be taking more money *out* of the fund that pays Social Security than we put in—for the first time since it was created in 1935.† The yearly deficit for Social Security will increase steadily, and by 2041 the fund will be empty.[1] Medicare funds will run out sooner, in 2020.[2]

Our current financial commitments to these two programs are immense. With no changes, costs are estimated to grow to almost 20% of GDP, with a projected shortfall of over $35 trillion between now and 2080.[3] Unless things change significantly, the country in which our next generation lives and works could collapse under the weight of these unfunded commitments.

How did we get here? Mostly by becoming an older, longer-living, more affluent society and not adjusting our expectations about government entitlements.

Consider that in 1940, the average life expectancy was 64 (less than the age where one would begin earning social security), 6% of the population was over 65 years of age, and there were seven working-age people for every person over 65 (see figure 4.6). Now, the average life expectancy is 77, 12% of the population is over 65 years old, and there are five working-age people for every person over 65. Most sobering, experts predict that by 2040, life expectancy will increase to 81, one-fifth of us

---

    * Projections are always uncertain, but anything close to these numbers warrants concern.

    † For detail about Social Security and how it works:
United States House of Representatives, Committee on Ways and Means (2004). "Section 1: Social Security: The Old Age, Survivors, and Disability Insurance Programs." In "Background Material and Data on the Programs within the Jurisdiction of the Committee on Ways and Means," informally known as the Green Book (WMCP 108-6);. http://waysandmeans.house.gov/media/pdf/greenbook2003/Section1.pdf (accessed March 6, 2007).

will be over 65, and the ratio of working age to elderly will be 2.5 to one.[4]

*FIGURE 4.6   CHANGES IN LIFE EXPECTANCY AND ELIGIBILITY FOR FULL
SOCIAL SECURITY BENEFITS*

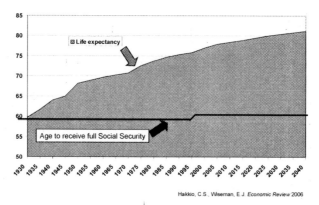

Hakkio, C.S., Wiseman, E.J. *Economic Review* 2006

A desperate but inevitable situation looms. The landscape has changed dramatically, but we cling to the benefits promised to our fathers and grandfathers in another time and situation. Logically, if we kept up with societal changes, citizens would not qualify for Social Security or Medicare until their mid-seventies. Further, as budgets got tighter, it would have made sense to base some of the programs on need, rather than providing equal benefit to millionaires and struggling families.

Politicians avoid difficult subjects like taking away benefits. This explains why few historical adjustments to Social Security or Medicare programs have reduced benefits or adjusted them to account for demographic trends.[‡] Individual voters, even if they know they will live 10 to 15 years longer than their parents, do not vote in favor of delaying retirement benefits or getting less money. Thus, we postpone difficult choices and further mortgage our children's future. As it stands, to cover the shortfall, we need to make significant, immediate modifications (probably more than one)—all of them painful.

Option A) Increase revenues to the trust fund. For example, fully funding the trust funds would require a permanent increase in payroll tax for both Social Security (from 12.4% to 14.3%) and

---

‡ In 1983, legislation was passed to increase the age (eventually) for receiving full Social Security benefits to 67 (see Hakkio).

Medicare (from 2.9% to 5.9%). The longer we wait, the more of a tax increase we will need. Another possibility is to raise the cap on taxable payroll, which currently does not tax earnings above $90,000 per year.

Option B) Earn more interest on the money already in the trust fund. Currently, all money in these trust funds are invested in Treasury Bonds, which make low interest (around 2%). Whether one believes that the money should be placed in individual accounts or kept by the government, it could be earning higher interest. Some of the funds could earn greater interest in indexed funds.

Option C) Decrease benefits. This can occur by raising the retirement age. A retirement age of 70 would reduce the projected shortfall by one-third. Benefits can also be reduced in amount or weighted according to need or other factors.

Option D) Add market pressures to health care spending. By far, Medicare will cost more over the next half-century than Social Security. Because someone else pays the bill for health care, people consume more care (moral hazard). Rational consumer involvement in health care will be just as important after 65 as it is when people are younger.

How does this topic relate to our concept of health as human capital? In several ways:

1) **We will (and already do) need more older workers.** If one in five members of our population is over 65 by 2040, our workforce will become increasingly grey. As such, human capital assets— skills, motivation, and health—will become even more valuable to us. Those who stay healthy and update their skills later in life will have significant opportunity in a short-handed job market.

2) **Illness will cost individuals more, longer.** Regardless of when or how policies change, health benefits will have to be scaled back or delayed to avoid bankrupting the country. Managing and protecting one's own health will pay off in dollars, independence and quality of life.

3) **Workplaces that facilitate and reward human capital growth will win the battle for workers.** Motivated workers who feel rewarded are more likely to protect their health and continue working when others retire. Workers who receive skills training throughout their careers can more successfully transition to other productive jobs as they age.

127

4) **Protecting and contributing our human capital becomes our responsibility to future generations.** We are headed toward an inter-generational showdown. Caring for our elderly will require increased taxes and/or a sacrifice of funds for education and other youth-focused programs. Each additional year of good health and productive work we contribute lessens the collective burden on younger citizens in the next half century.

The longer we wait, the worse the situation gets. Perhaps it's time to adjust our expectations and consider meaningful solutions, even if they are difficult or politically unpopular. Choices will only get harder, not easier.

March 11, 2007

References

1 Hakkio, C.S., Wiseman, E.J. "Social Security and Medicare: the impending fiscal challenge." Federal Reserve Bank of Kansas City *Economic Review* First quarter, 2006;7-41, http://www.kc.frb.org/publicat/econrev/PDF/1q06hakk.pdf (accessed March 6, 2007).

2 Duggan, J., Soares, C., Warshawsky, M. Social Security and Medicare trust funds and the federal budget. Office of Economic Policy, U.S. Department of Treasury; March 2004, http://www.treas.gov/offices/economic-policy/reports/budget_trust_fund_3_23.pdf (accessed March 6, 2007).

3 Hakkio.

4 Palmer, J.L., Saving, T.R. A summary of the 2006 annual Social Security and Medicare trust fund reports. Office of the Chief Actuary, Social Security Administration. http://www.ssa.gov/OACT/TRSUM/tr06summary.pdf (accessed March 9, 2007).

Blog 4.7 Should you pay less for healthcare if you are sicker? Opening a can of incentive worms

In the January 2006 issue of the *American Journal of Managed Care*, a group of reputable researchers suggested a novel health payment strategy.[1] To get the most from our investments in pharmaceuticals (in this case treatments for high cholesterol), the authors reason that it is most beneficial to encourage high compliance from the sickest people. First, they provide analysis showing that high medication compliance by people who have the highest risk of hospitalization or emergency visits results in better cost savings and more avoided health events than high medication compliance by people at lower risk of medical events.

In economic terms, this demonstration shows that the marginal utility of a dollar spent on medication for the high-risk people is greater than the marginal utility of a dollar spent on medication for those at lower risk. This conclusion probably makes sense in the short term. Low-risk people won't get sick soon enough to demonstrate cost savings. To get the best "bang for the buck" this year, pick the cases where one has the best chance to avoid big expenditures.

The next step in their proposed strategy—a seemingly simple restructuring of benefits—suggests applying an incentive based on clinical risk. The authors note that patients are sensitive, naturally, to the price of their medication. Thus, they propose eliminating any out-of-pocket cost for medication for moderate- and high-risk patients and doubling the cost of medications for low-risk patients to cover the difference.* From a clinical perspective, where the goal is to increase compliance by those who would achieve the greatest gains, the authors make a convincing case. Their analysis projects a high return on investment in the short term and an avoidance of 80,000 hospitalizations nationally every year.

While the proposed strategy is intended to provide economic

---

* The authors of the article do recognize some of the problems associated with their proposed design. And they suggest that some other sorts of rewards should be made available for low-risk patients. However, it is not the primary focus of their discussion.

incentives that encourage a desired behavior in those who can achieve maximum benefit, let's look at its other potential effects. Remember that incentives create a behavioral pull—like gravity or low tide—in the direction of what is paid for (and away from what is not paid for). Giving the sickest people free medications does encourage higher compliance in that group. However, it also makes being high risk a criterion for something desirable. So this pulls behavior toward the following:

1) A high-risk patient finds it less desirable to reduce risks (because he will be punished economically for doing so).

2) A low-risk patient becomes less likely to stay compliant (price is now double).

3) A low-risk patient finds it more desirable to have a doctor label him as sicker.

4) A high-risk patient finds it more desirable to choose this plan (one that provides medication for free).

5) A low-risk patient finds it less desirable to choose this plan (one that charges him double for medication).

6) A high-risk patient is less likely to ask for less expensive or generic alternatives (because they are all "free").

7) A high-risk patient may be more likely to ask for (and doctor more likely to prescribe) more expensive medications (because they are perceived as free).

8) A doctor feels more pressure to label a person as higher risk, to help her get her medication for free.

9) A low-risk person has one less reason to stay low risk.

I'm not suggesting that most patients will make a conscious effort to become ill to qualify for free medications. But it is not hard to imagine low- to moderate-risk patients asking their doctor how to qualify for the discount. In the world of incentives and rewards, making an undesirable thing (high risk for heart disease) more desirable (now we get free medications) does not serve us well in the long run. And making a desirable thing (staying low risk) less desirable (we have to pay double) creates a subtle pull in the wrong direction. The bottom line is that in this proposal, the price incentives run in the direction of encouraging higher risks for low-risk people and not lowering risks for high-risk people.

Consider this true story about an employee who wanted gastric bypass surgery. The employee was told that her insurance only covered this surgery in the case of extreme obesity (defined as 100 lbs. overweight). At 60 lbs. above ideal weight, the employee did not qualify, but could attend weight management classes at no charge. Four months later, the employee returned to the clinic and announced that she had gained the required 40 lbs. She received her surgery, fully covered, and qualified for eight weeks of disability pay. When we make an undesirable thing (gaining extreme weight) more desirable (free surgery and paid time-off), behaviors are pulled in that direction. Be careful what you pay for; you just might get it.

In the health as human capital framework, better health should align with rewards. For example, healthy people with health savings accounts will retain more of their assets than unhealthy people. Appropriate management of illness should be rewarded regardless of clinical level of risk, even when the short-term return on investment makes it tempting to treat bad outcomes preferentially. Aligned incentives make desirable behavior and desirable outcomes even *more* desirable, rather than pulling a person in opposite directions.

March 19, 2006

References
1 Goldman, D.P., Joyce, G.F., Karaca-Mandic, P. Varying pharmacy benefits with clinical status: the case of cholesterol-lowering therapy. *Am J Manag Care* 2006;12(1):21-28.

Blog 4.8   It would be so much easier if there were a true villain

In a recent conversation about healthcare, it became clear that the person I was speaking with, "Bob", (who does not work in a health-related field) was asking me to name "the villain." He wanted a clear enemy to blame for the healthcare mess. Surely, he implied, one entity is *most* at fault for high prices, less-than-ideal quality, and lack of access. Bob wanted someone held responsible, someone at which he could direct his frustration.

My realization that Bob (and probably most of us) wanted our problem to be *someone's fault* got me thinking about all of our blame-assigning options. If we look for *the* culpable party, there are many to choose from. For starters, it would be easy to point fingers (and many do) at greedy capitalists. Many of the largest U.S. health plans and pharmaceutical firms had double-digit profit increases just this past quarter. One health plan CEO resigned last month when it was revealed that he may have illegally inflated the value of his $1 billion of stock options. The healthcare industry employs thousands of lobbyists to influence policy makers. So, some may decide companies are to blame for profiting on the misery and misfortune of others.

One could also blame government for either doing too little or too much. Some think government needs to take over the entire process; others believe it should completely get out of the way. The problem with blaming *the* government is that *the* government is really a cumbersome bureaucracy created in part by us. It is a process by which our money, our votes, and our opinions are reshuffled and reallocated across "the public" and over time. Rather than blaming *the* government, we can also choose to blame a single political party, usually the one to which we don't belong. Depending on which side we support, politicians (whom *we* are to blame for electing) either allocate too much to the sick, poor, and less fortunate through inefficient entitlements, or unfairly place burdens upon them in favor of lowering taxes for the rich.

We can also blame a long list of others…

- Lawyers—for making malpractice litigation resemble a high-stakes reality show;
- Physicians—for not adopting technology quickly enough and hiding safety information in the name of professional privacy;
- Vendors (of all types)—for promising cost-cutting, disease-curing, symptom-relieving products and services at higher and higher cost, with uncertain return; or
- Consumers—for denying our mortality, doing and consuming things we know are harmful, and staying blissfully uninformed and

unaware of the tradeoffs we make for life-at-any-cost.

My conversation with Bob demonstrated to me how much energy we create by identifying a specific enemy or scapegoat. Blame simplifies a problem by assigning responsibility elsewhere and limiting our own. Bob was less interested in understanding the messy complexity of healthcare financing than in identifying "the real villain." He seemed energized by a possible enemy (especially one that fit his world view), and deflated by the suggestion that we have all, collectively, participated in creating the current, dysfunctional system.

The lesson for me in this conversation was not a lack of villains to choose from—there are plenty. Instead, the lesson was how natural it is for us to *want* a villain. A *single one* would be best. Most of us are like Bob, hoping for a culpable adversary even though we know that answers to huge social issues are never as simple as any one perspective might suggest.

In the health as human capital approach, we believe that rational solutions will not evolve from rigid adherence to (or blanket opposition of) a specific ideology. There is no single enemy to defeat. Rational solutions can only result when we all acknowledge some difficult truths. These include:

a) We now spend 16% of Gross Domestic Product on healthcare. There are estimates that we will reach 20% of GDP by 2015.[1] We must acknowledge the constraints this places on our national economy. The growth is unsustainable. We sacrifice investments in wages and other services. Placing limits on spending will require difficult decisions.

b) There are many levels of decisions that will be required, none of which are easy or politically popular:

- Deciding how to structure a more efficient and effective delivery system,
- Deciding who will pay whom in the business transaction of healthcare,
- Deciding what services will be paid for (or *not* paid).

c) To improve the system overall, virtually every stakeholder will have to give up something. That's the reality of optimizing resource allocation.

The entire structure needs to change such that consumers become more responsible and realistic, providers become more prudent, imperfect and incomplete markets become more efficient to produce better quality and lower prices, old systems become obsolete, law suits become less common (and less costly), and insurance becomes less regulated.

Certainly, it is human nature to assign fault (usually elsewhere!). But the perverse or inefficient outcomes in the healthcare industry do not result from "bad" or even "blameworthy" people. "People" are citizens who try to do the best they can by responding to real situations in a rational way. The true villains are not people at all, but failures of systems and institutions to provide incentives in the form of information, rules, regulations, and prices that produce positive outcomes in the interests of all. In other words, if we could get the information, rules, and prices right, the medical care industry could and would produce a win-win situation that could benefit all: providers, insurers, employers, and especially consumers.

My conversation with Bob reminded me to spend less time pointing fingers at others and more time looking honestly at the system as a whole and at how we can each contribute to constructive solutions.

December 4, 2006

References

1 National Coalition on Health Care, "Health Insurance Cost." http://www.nchc.org/facts/cost.shtml (accessed December 1, 2006).

Chapter 5
What Gets Paid for Gets Done

How we structure payments dictates what gets accomplished. Like the teams in our hypothetical reality show, walkers paid by the step will likely travel a different distance than walkers paid by the hour. Likewise, businesses may create priorities based on how and for what workers are rewarded.

In medicine, payments are based on transactions, not outcomes or satisfaction. Providers are not usually compensated for cure rates, functional status of patients, or short waiting times in their offices. In fee-for-service arrangements, compensation is based on the number of visits and transactions achieved. Consequently, it is natural that visits will be tightly booked, supported by technicians (to draw blood or do tests) with little time (unpaid) devoted to patient follow-up by phone. In essence, our system pays medical professionals for doing more to patients. We do not pay them for successfully helping patients feel better. And in truth, medical providers have economic incentives inversely related to improved health. If a patient returns for repeat treatments, because previous attempts have failed, the system will make more money. From a purely financial perspective, quick relief is bad for business.

In end-of-life circumstances, insurance covers highly technical interventions that may prolong life, but may not cover comfort-based or counseling services. This financial structure leads to the usual end-of-life experience, which is more technical and less comforting.

In each business arrangement, we can predict how the system prioritizes its efforts by knowing the payment structure. If someone is compensated only for quantity of services, there will be a tendency to provide more, lower-quality services than if someone is compensated for both quantity and quality. If someone is compensated for hours spent rather than tasks completed, he will maximize time over outcomes. When a higher fee is applied to a prescription medication, patients will refill the prescription less often.

If providers were paid for having constructive conversations and compensated for measurable health outcomes, the form of medicine would change. The following examples illustrate how the structure of payments influences behavior of various actors in the healthcare and employment dramas.

Blog 5.1   RAND Health Insurance Experiment: provider incentives

Let's continue our look at the RAND Health Insurance Experiment (HIE).[*]

The HIE also looked at whether patients in an HMO used the same amount of care as patients in a fee-for-service (FFS) plan. Researchers compared families who had similar cost-sharing requirements (small or free), but received their care either in a plan that paid providers for each service (FFS), or paid providers a set amount for each patient regardless of the amount of care given (HMO).[1] While a previous blog entry[*] about the HIE dealt with how cost affects patient behavior, this entry is about how payments affect provider behavior.

Not surprisingly, providers who stand to be paid more for providing more services will provide more services than those who stand to lose money when they provide more services. Figure 5.1 shows that hospitalizations were dramatically lower in the HMO group (42% lower). Similarly, for every 100 persons in their plan, HMOs had 38 hospital days per year and free FFS plans had 83 hospital days per year—more than double. A follow-up chart review of hospitalizations found that admissions in the FFS plans had a significantly higher rate of inappropriateness than HMOs. (Inappropriateness was determined using a standard protocol with three general levels: certainly appropriate and efficacious, possibly appropriate and efficacious, and inappropriate and non-efficacious. The FFS plan had significantly higher rates of admissions rated as inappropriate and as possibly appropriate compared to the HMO.)

---

* See Blog 3.1 Remembering the RAND Health Insurance Experiment.

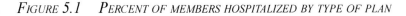

FIGURE 5.1   PERCENT OF MEMBERS HOSPITALIZED BY TYPE OF PLAN

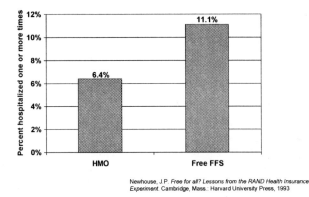

Newhouse, J.P. *Free for all? Lessons from the RAND Health Insurance Experiment.* Cambridge, Mass.: Harvard University Press, 1993

Again, we should emphasize that out of 46 different physiologic outcome measures, only two were significantly different between HMO and free FFS groups (care for varicose veins and urine cultures). No major differences in health status could be found. Of note, HMOs did not seem to provide less of all types of care. HMO enrollees actually received more preventive care (60 visits for every 100 people) than FFS enrollees (41 visits for every 100 people).

If you have wondered whether incentives matter…wonder no more.

October 10, 2005

References
   1 Newhouse, J.P. *Free for all? Lessons from the RAND Health Insurance Experiment.* Cambridge, Mass.: Harvard University Press, 1993.

Blog 5.2   Getting paid more for doing worse… only in healthcare

Imagine paying your lawyer more for losing a case than winning it. Imagine paying your realtor a higher commission for not selling your house than he or she might earn when it sells. Imagine returning a new bicycle that doesn't work and being charged extra for its flaws. Such a system would seem objectionable, unfair, and perhaps even criminal.

Yet, that is essentially how the medical payment system works.

If you enter a hospital to have a procedure, the hospital charges one fee. But if you experience complications, need to stay longer, or need to return to repair a problem, the hospital will receive higher fees. The "fee-for-service" (FFS) system is pay-as-you-go, offers no refunds, and allows no discounts for poor quality (although health plans do get discounts based on quantity). How is it that the system we most rely upon to deliver health services makes more money when we stay sick?

One reason patients accept such a contrary arrangement is a general perception that medicine is a very technical, complex field and medical expertise is infallible. We assign such high regard to trained physicians as the people who "know best" that, when something does go wrong, it cannot be their fault. Another reason is that once a problem becomes expensive, the insurance company pays the bill rather than the patient. At that point, cost is no longer the patient's problem.* Whatever the reasons, our healthcare delivery system has evolved with little (and sometimes an inverse!) connection between size of payment and effectiveness of treatment. Essentially, poor outcomes will likely cost more than good outcomes.

Should we expect more? Here is an example that suggests we can, when the payment system rewards positive outcomes.

A hospital system in Pennsylvania[1] tested the consequences of providing heart surgery plus 90 days of follow up care for a set price.† To support their efforts, the surgeons implemented a quality process called "ProvenCare," which consists of 40 specific policies and procedures known to improve outcomes. The ProvenCare process includes pre-surgery preparation, surgical standards, and post-operation care.

---

* Indeed, a hospital billing representative I spoke to about a large, uninterpretable bill said, "Ma'am, you don't need to question this bill, you aren't the one who has to pay it."

† The price included the average surgery price plus the historical "average" cost for care over the following 3 months. We will point out that, based on our research, the average cost may still be an inflated number, since it will likely be higher than 80% of all cases. However, it is better than having no price ceiling. See Blog 2.2 What the mean does and doesn't mean: when average isn't normal.

The result: better outcomes, drastically fewer complications, fewer readmissions, and an impressive rise in adherence to quality standards from 60% to almost 100%.[1] In fact, surgeons reported that their approach became much more uniform—rather than each following a different method of providing care as was the case prior to implementing the new process.[2]

In this example, the facility devised a system that, instead of rewarding the number of services, rewarded the healthy recovery of the patient, which led to better outcomes, lower overall cost, and a demonstration of unusual consistency in delivery of care. It proves first, that many potential problems associated with a serious procedure *are* avoidable and second, that methods for doing so can be identified. Finally, it reinforces the economic reality that aligned financial incentives influence behavior.

Perhaps the most promising part of this experiment is that it was developed and implemented proactively by the health system, rather than being imposed by purchasers, as are so many pay-for-performance initiatives. Further, it rewards the health system if—and only if—the person does well, rather than rewarding them for following guidelines (regardless of whether the person does poorly or dies).

What about procedures that are not covered by insurance and completely subject to the discretion of the patient? These types of arrangements can shed light on how a direct patient and provider exchange can influence both cost and quality. A facility called the 20/20 Institute in Denver offers a full money-back guarantee if Lasik surgery fails to provide 20-20 vision or better.[3] When we talked to their business manager, he said that historically they know 95% of these procedures achieve 20-20 or better, and patients should expect nothing less. He pointed out that this is more of a shift in philosophy than anything else: "We had to start to think like the Ritz. Customer satisfaction needs to be our primary goal."

What if consumers had to pay directly for the full price of all services? Wouldn't we demand better care, at a guaranteed price, with no extra fees if something unexpected went wrong? Yes, we probably would, especially for common procedures like knee replacement, hip replacement, gallbladder removal, and many more. Perhaps we would consider asking for a refund if the problem isn't fixed.

Since the money for healthcare comes from us anyway (either as taxes or lower wages)…perhaps we should demand the same deal for price and quality *right now*.

July 15, 2007

References

1 Casale, A.S., et. al. 'ProvenCareSM': A Provider Driven Pay For Performance Program for Acute Episodic Cardiac Surgical Care. American Surgical Association 127th Annual Meeting, April 26-28, 2007, Colorado Springs, Co. http://www.americansurgical.info/abstracts/2007/20.cgi (accessed July 10, 2007).

2 Abelson, R. In Bid for Better Care, Surgery with a Warranty. New York Times, May 17, 2007, http://www.nytimes.com/2007/05/17/business/17quality.html?ei=5088&en=3d8a549fa8ccb22c&ex=1337054400&pagewanted=print (accessed July 10, 2007).

3 20/20 Institute. 20/20 Institute Lasik guarantee, http://www.2020institute.com/guarantee.htm (accessed July 10, 2007).

Blog 5.3 Using stockbrokers or healthcare brokers: either way, you want a *win-win*

A quick quiz: Look at figure 5.2 and guess what characteristic results in Group 2 getting three to seven times more MRI and ultrasound tests than Group 1. Are those people older, sicker, poorer, more rural, or higher risk?

FIGURE 5.2 WHY ARE THEY GETTING MORE TESTS?

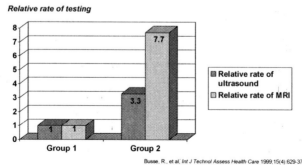

Relative rate of testing

Relative rate of ultrasound
Relative rate of MRI

Group 1   Group 2

Busse, R., et al; *Int J Technol Assess Health Care* 1999;15(4):629-37.
Kouri, B.E., et al, *AJR Am J Roentgenol* 2002;179(4):843-50.

To get the answer, read on. *Hint: none of the mentioned factors is the reason*

Sometime we need support

As consumers, when we have assets to protect, we often want advice from experts. We seek someone who will be on our side, someone whose goals are aligned with ours. In a practical sense, we can tell if their goals align with our goals by how much we both gain from the transaction.

Financial assets

The first couple of times I invested money in stocks and mutual funds, I didn't understand how the brokers made their living. I went to brokers recommended by friends and chose some (seemingly) wise investments based on my age and investment goals. While it was a positive step overall to save and invest, I learned later that I could have done much better in selecting my broker, from the standpoint of how the arrangement worked. The relationships were not necessarily win-win.

1) One of the arrangements was with a broker who only made money if he sold the mutual funds run by his own company. This isn't necessarily bad, except the funds in his company had lower returns than those run by some other companies. So, the broker had incentive to tell me only about his options. I paid a fee to invest in his funds, and was then locked into my choices and would pay a penalty (to them) if I moved the money. I was losing potential gains in their under-performing funds, and I would be penalized for leaving.

2) Another arrangement allowed stock trading, where the broker made money on each transaction. Her incentive was to maximize the number of trades I made, rather than how much money I earned. Consequently, the advice I received was more often related to how many trades I made, rather than a smart overall strategy.

Neither broker charged me for his time advising me, and neither gave horrible advice or acted unethically. However, in the big scheme of things, I might have been better off paying an independent expert for his or her time to advise me about *all* my options and *all* the pros and cons of various arrangements. However, even in that scenario, the advisor has an incentive to spend as much time with me as possible, so I may not have received information efficiently.

Ideally, I need an advisor who gets paid in proportion to how much money I earn in the long run. Not unlike a lawyer who wins a portion of a successful settlement, I want someone who has the same goals as I do, and the same incentive to achieve a positive outcome. I learned the hard way, and paid the penalties, when I eventually moved to a situation more beneficial for me.

Are heath assets any different? Not really

Similar to financial assets, I have health assets to protect and sometimes I need expert support on how I might improve or manage my health. Who is best aligned to give me objective guidance and information? A physician whose top priority is to help me stay healthy. Once again, incentives will influence how medical experts will give advice.

Traditional health insurance pays medical experts a lot less to share their expertise and provide objective advice than to "do something" to me. It makes perfect sense that if we don't pay providers well for simply talking to us, providers will be inclined to provide services other than expertise. Further, a provider has an incentive to consider treatment options that are not exclusively in my best interest, but may also be in his.

Like a broker who makes money on each stock trade, healthcare providers in our system make more money by increasing the number and intensity of services they render. Certain services will do more to maximize their incomes rather than improve your health. Here is the answer to the quiz at the start of this blog entry: the difference in the group receiving three to seven times more ultrasound and MRI tests is that their healthcare providers owned the ultrasound or MRI equipment (fig. 5.3).[1,2]

These higher rates of tests occur without evidence that the additional tests contributed to better care. Indeed, tests are one of the most over-used procedures in the medical care system.[3,4]

FIGURE 5.3   FINANCIAL INCENTIVES IN HEALTHCARE

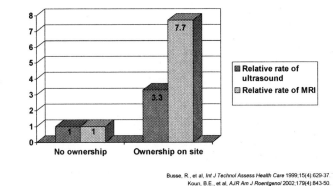

Busse, R., et al, *Int J Technol Assess Health Care* 1999;15(4):629-37.
Kouri, B.E., et al, *AJR Am J Roentgenol* 2002;179(4):843-50.

A few examples demonstrate that the healthcare system is shaped by how we pay and what we pay for:

Q: Why has the duration of office visits become so short?

A: Partly because providers are paid by the number of patients they see, so revenue will increase as visit time decreases.

Q: Why do only 24% of doctors communicate with patients via email,[5] even though emails improve clinical efficiency,[6] and 75% of consumers would like the ability to do so?[7]

A: Because most insurance plans do not pay for a doctor to send emails to patients,[8] even if those emails are as helpful as a visit.

Q: Does a doctor actually earn more from bad outcomes than good outcomes?

A: Until late 2008, when Medicare rules change, providers actually receive additional fees for extra services, even those resulting from avoidable medical errors.[9]

While society often thinks about healthcare differently than other professions, it is still a business. There is an exchange of services for pay. Suppliers' decisions will be influenced by potential revenues. Consumers will only reject an unreasonable exchange (paying more for a bad outcome, or paying for unnecessary services) when they have to pay the bill. As long as someone else pays (an issue we have addressed before), we are less likely to object.

Aligning incentives

I learned from my early investment experiences to ask how a broker gets paid. I am satisfied paying my broker a portion (bonus) for high-performance earnings. But I object to paying more for activities (like trades) that do not grow my assets.

Similarly, I have learned that medical providers are both experts as well as business-people. I would rather purchase objective time and expertise rather than get advice from someone who has a financial stake in a specific treatment choice. Now, if only we could arrange for payments that are proportionate with health improvement…it could truly be a win-win situation.

November 5, 2007

References

1 Busse, R., Hoopmann, M., Schwartz, F.W. Which factors determine the use of diagnostic imaging technologies for gastrointestinal complaints in general medical practice? *Int J Technol Assess Health Care* 1999;15(4):629-37.

2 Kouri, B.E., Parsons R.G., Alpert H.R. Physician self-referral for diagnostic imaging: review of the empiric literature. *AJR Am J Roentgenol* 2002 Oct;179(4):843-50, http://www.ajronline.org/cgi/content/full/179/4/843 (accessed November 1, 2007).

3 Consumer Reports: Ten overused medical tests and treatments. FindLaw.com, http://news.corporate.findlaw.com/prnewswire/20071001/01oct20071927.html (accessed November 2, 2007).

4 Brownlee, S. *Overtreated: Why Too Much Medicine Is Making Us Sicker and Poorer*. New York: Bloomsbury USA, 2007, 200.

5 Physicians reluctant to provide care via email. iHealthBeat.org, October 3, 2006, http://www.ihealthbeat.org/articles/2006/10/3/Physicians-Reluctant-To-Provide-Care-Via-EMail.aspx?topicID=55 (accessed November 2, 2007).

6 Bergmo, T.S., Kummervold, P.E., Gammon, D., Dahl, L.B. Electronic patient-provider communication: will it offset office visits and telephone consultations in primary care? *Int J Med Inform* 2005;74:705-10.

7 Stone, J.H. Communication between physicians and patients in the era of e-medicine. N Engl J Med 2007;356:2451-4, http://content.nejm.org/cgi/content/full/356/24/2451?ijkey=eEQmrEWRXfxUU&keytype=ref&siteid=nejm (accessed November 2, 2007).

8 Patt, M.R., Houston, T.K., Jenckes, M.W., Sands, D.Z., Ford, D.E. Doctors who are using e-mail with their patients: a qualitative exploration. *J Med Internet Res* 2003;5: e9, http://www.jmir.org/2003/2/e9/ (accessed November 2, 2007).

9 Medicare will not pay for preventable conditions acquired at hospitals. Senior Journal.com, August 20, 2007, http://64.23.76.120/NEWS/Medicare/2007/7-08-20-MedicareWillNot.htm (accessed November 2, 2007).

Blog 5.4   Medical service coding and billing: a complicated system in need of nosy consumers

Corporations often use health claims data to describe and understand the important health issues faced by their workforce. This presumes that health claims are primarily a record of health problems and treatments. But medical services coding and billing primarily have a business purpose: how doctors and hospitals get paid. We also recognize that claims data are powerful indicators of how reimbursement policies affect consumer and provider behavior. Depending on who pays, and what is paid for, the behavior of both consumers and providers changes, regardless of the actual health issues being treated.

My first lesson on this subject came during a review of health claims data for a large company in the early 1990s. Our analysis revealed that the most expensive service (in total cost) for the entire population was an obscure code labeled "other ill-defined dislocations of the cervical vertebra." To translate, this implies treatment provided for an uncommon spinal injury in the neck.

Though many workers at this company did physical and manufacturing work, our team was perplexed by what could possibly cause so many serious (and expensive) spinal injuries. Physicians we consulted about the code guessed that it was likely a severe type of whiplash, however, since our investigations revealed that almost 25% of the workforce was receiving the treatment at a rate of over 20 times per year there would clearly have to be a whiplash epidemic if this explanation were valid.

With a little more digging, we discovered that this code was only applied by a type of provider whose identifier was labeled "other," as opposed to orthopedic or physical therapy, which made the fees even more confusing.

So what was this mysterious ailment?

Lo and behold, the mysterious and frequent "spinal adjustments," were being provided as a regular service by chiropractors. Evidently, the corporate CEO was a fan of chiropractic treatment and wanted regular adjustments where the cost was covered by insurance. At his request, there were no limits on coverage for this service. Once workers and the chiropractic community became aware of this feature—and which code to use—this category of service became the greatest expenditure of all.

The following year, not surprisingly (with the blessing of the CEO), the company limited how many chiropractic treatments were covered by their health plan.

When voluntary chiropractic treatments exceed the cost of cancer and diabetes in a health plan, it's a clear example of the power of policy-induced consumption. In this case, where chiropractic services were quite specific, the company's policy about coverage could easily be modified. But in most cases, coding peculiarities are not as evident and can be much more difficult to remedy; the same providers can deliver so many different services. (What actually was done? How sick was the patient? Is a specific provider rating services differently than another?)

Payments and coding: a significant issue

While our chiropractic discovery proved slightly humorous, the business of coding is no laughing matter. Provider reimbursements involve an extremely complex system of codes that places differing monetary values on the activities doctors report having delivered to a patient. Two doctors who do the exact same thing, but report it differently, will receive a different payment. The system tends to value complicated things over simple things and actions (like tests or procedures) over discussions. It is natural that a doctor will want to code his or her services in the way that maximizes payment. A Google search produces a list of numerous vendors who can help hospitals and doctors maximize their legal reimbursements from Medicare, Medicaid, and other insurers. This is a direct sort of coding and "revenue-maximizing" assistance, and such strategies are within the rules.

Outside the rules, the National Health Care Anti-Fraud Association reports the cost of miscoding, extra coding and "up-coding" (indicating that a service or a condition was more severe than actual) is somewhere between $50 and $170 billion per year—an estimated three to ten percent of costs. Further, anyone who has received a hospital bill detailed with service and treatment codes knows how difficult and time consuming they are to decipher. Though mistakes are common, they often require significant investigation to verify. How many mistakes are there? No one really knows. And consumers rarely have an incentive to endure the headache required to figure it out.

What should we do? Within the current system, efforts usually focus on more detailed coding regulations[1] and computer programs that identify suspicious coding patterns.[2] But these solutions focus on tightening rules and detecting inaccuracies after-the-fact, rather than addressing their root causes. Some doctors are opting-out of insurance entirely and going to a cash-only system.[3]

Consumer involvement might be a far more affordable and effective solution.

All of the examples cited here involve services provided by doctors and services received by patients that were paid for by someone else. When a third party (our employer) pays for a service, we consume more of it (chiropractic care). Also, when someone else pays, we have little to no incentive to ask about price (or negotiate a better price), or to make certain we get our money's worth. If I have a choice between purchasing two different services that provide the same outcome, I would choose the less expensive option. However, if I do not pay directly with my money, these issues are someone else's problem—and I seek the most I can get.

Economic principles suggest that involving a consumer in direct payment changes the system in profound ways. The person becomes more aware of price, appropriateness, and quality of services he or she receives. The provider provides services of higher value to the patient, who has chosen a doctor with greater understanding. And the system gains more fraud safeguards inherent in direct transactions (I have incentive to review the bill). No one in an insurance company or working for Medicare knows as much about what services a patient needs or receives than the patient himself. A patient with incentive to scrutinize the charges has a greater chance of finding problems than an outside party. And, a patient interested in the costs and options ahead of time has a better chance of making the most appropriate choice.

Consumers with dollars to spend will decide which items they value and how many services they want. Whether these dollars are sitting in an employer-funded health account, or in a consumer's own savings account, individual spending changes the equation. Simple questions like, "How much will that cost?" "How effective is that?" "What value do I get from those other services?" and "What are my choices?" alter the dynamic.

These are samples of the simple questions that could reform a broken system—probably faster than more rules or sophisticated software.

September 9, 2007

References

1 Centers for Medicare and Medicaid Services. Physician Fee Schedule. U.S. Department of Health and Human Services, February 2, 2007, http://www.cms.hhs.gov/PhysicianFeeSched/01_overview.asp (accessed August 31, 2007).

2 Appleby, J. Computer programs help flag insurance fraud before payment. *USA Today*, November 7, 2006, http://www.usatoday.com/tech/news/computersecurity/2006-11-07-medicare-side-usat_x.htm (accessed August 31, 2007).

3 Forrest, B.R. Breaking even on 4 visits per day. *Family Practice Management* 2007;14 (6):19-24 http://www.aafp.org/fpm/20070600/19brea.html (accessed August 31, 2007).

Blog 5.5 Annual physicals and patient sensitivity to copayments

Until recently, I wasn't aware that most medical organizations recommend against getting annual physicals. The American Medical Association (AMA)[1] and the U.S. Preventive Services Task Force (USPSTF),[2] among others, have taken the position that annual physicals provide insufficient value to justify the burden they place on the system. If a person is not in need of a recommended test (such as a mammogram after age 50) or facing a specific problem, there simply is little value in a check-up. Ironically, however, almost two-thirds of doctors surveyed recently reported that they do recommend annual physicals to their patients.[3] The authors reporting the survey results indicated that physicians recommend physicals partly because their patients expect annual check-ups[4] and partly because insurance will usually pay for this service, providing physicians with steady, certain revenue.

My economics colleagues remind me that all of these behaviors reflect the costs and benefits to each stakeholder. From a societal perspective of healthcare delivery, the AMA and the USPSTF recommend against annual physicals because the benefits are less than the costs overall. But practicing physicians get paid to do physicals and recommend them because the benefits to their practice generally exceed the costs. Patients will favor physical exams if their benefits exceed costs, and this will depend on the patients' insurance coverage and their copayments. These are all rational economic decisions.

This made us wonder if we could calculate the association between insurance copayments and patients' likelihood of getting annual physicals. To estimate the answer to this question, our analysts extracted data from tens of thousands of check-ups, across hundreds of plans with varying copayments for an annual check-up office visit. Through regression modeling, they estimated how differences in copayment correlated with the rates of annual check-ups.

FIGURE 5.4   LIKELIHOOD OF ANNUAL PHYSICALS BY COPAYMENT

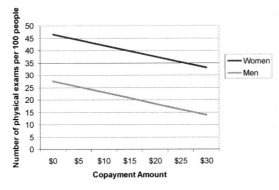

Health as Human Capital Research Group, 2005

Correcting for age, we find that the likelihood of having a physical declines with higher copayments. Although women get check-ups more frequently than men overall, both genders respond similarly to copayment size. Figure 5.4 shows that at a zero copayment (free visits), we would expect 27.5 check-ups per 100 men and 46.6 check-ups for 100 women, annually. If patients had to pay $30, we would expect 13 fewer check-ups for each gender. A higher copayment for a physical increases the patient's marginal cost of the physical, resulting in fewer visits. Part of this effect may be the result of people selecting a specific low copayment because they like getting check-ups. However, it is unlikely that such selection is so strong that it can explain the size of the response.

October 2, 2005

References

1 Medical evaluations of healthy persons. Council on Scientific Affairs. *JAMA* 1983;249(12):1626-33.

2 U.S. Preventive Services Task Force. *Guide to Clinical Preventive Services: Report of the U.S. Preventive Services Task Force*. 2nd Edition. Baltimore: Williams and Wilkins; 1996.

3 Prochazka, A.V., Lundahl, K., Pearson, W., Oboler, S.K., Anderson, R.J. Support of evidence-based guidelines for the annual physical examination: a survey of primary care providers. *Arch Intern Med* 2005 27;165(12):1347-52.

4 Oboler, S.K., Prochazka, A.V., Gonzales, R., Xu, S., Anderson, R.J. Public expectations and attitudes for annual physical examinations and testing. *Ann Intern Med* 2002;136(9):652-9.

Blog 5.6   Interpreting attrition rates in disease management through a lens of market efficiency—who is paid, by whom, to do what?

This entry will interpret findings from a recent article describing rates of attrition from a disease management (DM) program.[1] The study looked at a DM program offered to employees and families of a large employer.

Over 23% of employees and spouses were identified as eligible for DM across four illnesses, but only one-quarter of those identified (5.8% out of 23.5%) for the program had any participation. After 12 months, only 1.7% of the employee population (7% of those identified) continued participating. This means that 93% of those identified (21.8% out of the 23.5% identified) were lost between identification and the end of the first year—more than 9 out of 10.

Figure 5.5 shows the percent reduction in each step (black arrows are the percent reduction at that step, not overall). Attrition occurs for several reasons: some people were excluded by the vendor, some could not be contacted, half of those contacted declined to participate, and two-thirds of those who enrolled dropped out over time. Such rates of attrition are worrisome, and add to persistent questions about the value that such large-scale third-party DM programs provide.[2]

FIGURE 5.5   SELECTION AND PARTICIPATION RATES IN DISEASE MANAGEMENT PROGRAMS

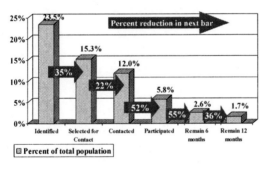

Lynch, W.D. et al. JOEM 2006;48(5):447-54.

Perhaps even more of a concern was the finding that the program was least successful in enrolling those who had the poorest rates of compliance with recommended tests and services.

There are many possible explanations for why the program failed to attract and retain most employees who had chronic illnesses. Behavioral scientists might point to an employee's "readiness to change" as a barrier to enrollment. Vendors might blame the inaccuracy of contact information or insufficient promotion. Patients might further contend that they already have sufficient help and do not need "managing." While these and many other reasons are plausible, today's discussion will explore some economic concepts that one rarely hears in reference to disease management.

Namely, we will ask the question: "who is being paid, by whom, to do what?"

To start, let's back up. Ultimately, the goal in disease management is to reduce the future cost of treating illness. The more immediate goal is to help persons with chronic illness to take appropriate actions under their control to feel well, avoid problems, and slow progression of illness. Desired actions may include monitoring their illness, getting appropriate tests, taking their medication, and changing their lifestyle. Studies confirm that when people do these things, they will cost less and function better in the long run.

If we focus on the most concrete aspects of disease management for this discussion (rather than lifestyle), we might simplify by describing the desired business transaction as the doctor prescribing appropriate tests and medications, and the patient following the prescribed regimen. The more direct the business transaction (in terms of the buyer/seller relationship) the more effective and efficient the exchange will be. Efficiency (in the market sense) is highest when the person getting a service pays directly for it. Direct payment makes it more likely that a person is invested in getting maximum utility for the price. Direct exchanges also put market pressures on providers to compete for customers who shop for high quality at a good price. So, a direct exchange between consumer and provider increases the likelihood that the market for similar services achieves an equilibrium: what people want at a price they will pay.

Effectiveness (in the sense of achieving a desired outcome) is highest when the person pays for the outcome, rather than paying for the effort to achieve the outcome. For example, if I pay a real estate agent a commission for selling my house, I am assured of paying for the desired outcome. If I pay, instead, for an agent's time, I might have to pay without achieving my goal. Essentially, I want to pay her for selling my house, not for trying hard to sell my house.

Applying these rules of thumb to disease management services, we would hypothesize that maximum effectiveness and efficiency would occur when a patient purchases services directly from a provider, and pays specifically for the service (even better, for long-term health, but we will start with services).

Now back to the original question: in this DM example, who is being paid, by whom, to do what? How far is this transaction from our ideal?

Who is paid by whom: A DM services nurse (not the same nurse the patient would go to for a test) is paid by a DM company, who is paid by a health plan, who is paid by an employer (who actually provides the service to employees in lieu of higher wages). So, the transaction is anything but direct. In addition, this service is supplemental to payments to the patient's own doctor. So the two parties whose behavior most needs influencing (patient and doctor) are not part of the transaction.

What is paid for: DM vendors are usually paid to identify individuals who have chronic illness, and paid for attempts to contact both employees and providers of medical services to remind them of the necessity of certain services. In this instance, the DM company was not paid for achieving clinical outcomes, but instead for attempts to deliver information. The transaction does not reward the desired outcome, but instead pays for indirect efforts to try to make the desired outcome more likely. Again, far from ideal.

The next time you hear that a program has questionable effectiveness, ask yourself who is paid by whom to do what. It will help you understand, from a market economics perspective, how close the transactions and rewards are to an ideal, direct transaction. Certainly there is more to this story than who is paid for what, but hopefully this will make you wonder about how to create the shortest distance between a patient and good care.

May 30, 2006

References

1 Lynch,W.D., Chen, C.Y., Bender, J., Edington, D.W. Documenting participation in an employer-sponsored disease management program: selection, exclusion, attrition, and active engagement as possible metrics. *J Occup Environ Med* 2006;48:447-54.

2 Congressional Budget Office. An analysis of the literature on disease management programs. October 13, 2004, http://www.cbo.gov/ftpdocs/59xx/doc5909/10-13-DiseaseMngmnt.pdf (accessed September 6, 2005).

Blog 5.7   When the most expensive option isn't the best option

We often hear people express how the healthcare Americans receive is the "best" in the world. From the standpoint of scientific advancement, it is true: the level of technology and types of interventions available are amazing.

Today we can detect and "fix" problems that were a mystery a generation ago. Surgeons can operate from thousands of miles away using robotics, women in their sixties can bear children, genetic abnormalities can be detected before birth, devices can be implanted to do everything from medication delivery, to heart rhythm regulation, to diagnostic photography. Evening news programs frequently feature new technologies and treatments that have saved lives using recent scientific advancements. In short, we are proud of our medical miracles.

Perhaps it is this pride, or our desire to have everything readily fixable, that leads us to disparage messages that question the value of technical intervention. Are we so biased toward aggressive intervention that we ignore the risks and costs associated with it? One recent example was a study published in the *New England Journal of Medicine*.[1] The study compared two interventions for patients who were stable following a heart attack. It showed that angioplasty (a standard intervention in which a balloon is inserted in blocked vessels to open blood flow) was not better than medication in preventing another attack or death. In fact, rates of death and repeat heart attack in the angioplasty group were actually worse over 4 years (see fig. 5.6).

Bias among doctors in favor of intervention was so strong that many doctors refused to enter patients in the study because they felt it was unethical to place patients into the control group that would receive only medication. Now it appears that *half* of the 100,000 angioplasty procedures done in the U.S. annually could, and perhaps should, be replaced with a less invasive alternative. Further, the cost of these now-questionable procedures exceeds $500 million per year. Interestingly, despite its $5 billion implication over the past decade, news media gave

FIGURE 5.6   *HIGH-COST INTERVENTION WAS NOT BETTER AT*
PREVENTING SERIOUS OUTCOMES

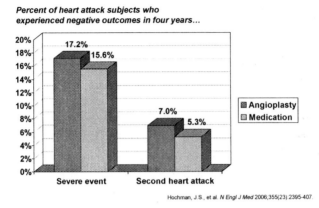

**Percent of heart attack subjects who
experienced negative outcomes in four years...**

Hochman, J.S., et al. *N Engl J Med* 2006;355(23):2395-407.

the topic limited coverage.

It's not as dramatic or interesting to tell the public that taking a medication regularly will provide better outcomes than an operation in which doctors use tools to unblock your arteries for you. And certainly, it is not as dramatic or interesting to tell the public that maintaining a healthy weight and exercising regularly will help you avoid the problem in the first place. However, it is worrisome when information about what procedures you don't need (and perhaps shouldn't have) receives such limited coverage.

More disturbing, given the low degree of adherence to "best practice guidelines" in medicine, it is likely that the healthcare industry will be slow to adopt this new quality "standard" regarding care after heart attack. In our non-competitive healthcare system, it is not surprising that cost-saving technologies are only slowly adopted, which means that there are few incentives to cut back on the number of angioplasties.

As long as cardiovascular care centers make (a lot) more money doing angioplasties than giving medications—and as long as patients do not pay a portion of the excess cost of a more expensive option—it will be difficult to move medical practice to optimal rates of angioplasty, or any other high-tech procedure.

January 28, 2007

155

References

1 Hochman, J.S., et al. Coronary intervention for persistent occlusion after myocardial infarction. *N Engl J Med* 2006;355(23):2395-407.

Chapter 6
Incentives Always Exist, Influencing the Direction of Behavior

Incentives are like gravity—always there and easier to work with than against.

In all social systems, there are rules and arrangements that create an environment of underlying incentives. These incentives operate in ways that pull behaviors in a particular direction. When we are unaware of existing incentives, we may find ourselves baffled by the behaviors of others. Employers may wonder why employees are not accomplishing the desired amount of work, and doctors may wonder why patients are not complying with recommendations. When systems are not functioning the way we want them to, it is helpful to examine underlying incentives.

In economics, the process of delegating responsibilities to another person (a patient to a doctor or an employer to an employee) is referred to as a *principal* contracting for someone to act as an *agent* on his behalf. The *principal-agent* arrangement naturally involves several levels of uncertainty: the principal does not know if the agent has the skills to perform the activities, if the agent is giving a high level of effort, or whether she will make decisions exactly as the principal would like. In short, does the agent always act in the best interest of the principal? The agent may have incomplete information about what the principal really wants him to do, and the principal may have incomplete information about opportunities for the agent to act in his own interest rather than that of the principal.

This uncertainty is sometimes referred to as *information asymmetry*, where one party has knowledge or takes actions that are hidden from the other party. Information asymmetry is problematic when the two parties have different objectives as they almost always do. When considering the multitude of necessary contacts in an organization—shareholders with executives; supervisors with workers; managers with consultants—it is easy to imagine a large number of different objectives. Shareholders want returns on their investments; workers want rewarding work for a fair salary; consultants want to be paid well for their expertise. Because there is information asymmetry in each of these relationships, there is significant potential for inefficient and ineffective actions by the various actors.

While information asymmetry may not lead the agent to behave in ways that intentionally harm the principal (i.e., doctors causing intentional harm to the patient), there is still a tendency to behave in ways that benefit the agent. For example, the doctor would like to earn money for his or her services, while the patient wants to feel better. Medical reimbursement, except in managed care, is based on visits and procedures. Add to that a fear of being sued and the *tendency* is to *induce demand* for more visits and services known as practicing defensive medicine. The patient is not equipped with sufficient knowledge to question the need for these services. And, since she is not paying, is unlikely to query whether such services could be provided over the phone or through less expensive means.

Employment agreements have similar degrees of information asymmetry, especially in jobs where the actual work activity is difficult to track or observe. This problem is especially acute when work is done by teams of workers and the contribution of each employee to the bottom line is difficult to determine. Naturally, the employer (principal) would like the employee (agent) to behave in ways that maximize profit for the principal's organization. While most employees understand their job involves advancing the goals (profits, products) of the organization, economics tell us that employees can be expected to serve their own best interests as well, which will be a balance of pleasing the employer for a high salary, taking leisure, and perhaps other personal objectives. If work is paid on a straight salary, with no bonus, the employee may experience little penalty for lapses in effort. The risk from shirking is borne by the employer, who cannot easily verify level of effort, whereas any benefits are captured by the employee. Further, if an employee has paid sick-leave, there is no penalty for periods of no work.

Economic theory provides models for designing aligned incentives that mitigate the costs of the principal-agent and information-asymmetry circumstances. In general, the goal is to align the incentives of both principal and agent such that there is a win-win when the principal's objectives are met. In addition, to whatever degree possible, agents should bear some of the costs of periods of low or no output. Of course, these incentives and disincentives must be measurable, fair, and obvious to both parties. Certainly economists acknowledge the influence of other incentives like approval, community, learning, positive culture, etc., but focus on the underlying tendency for individuals to maximize their own gains.

One way to think about aligned incentives is in noting that a partnership is usually a mutually beneficial financial relationship. This is especially true when there are fewer parties (rather than many), and clear definitions of accountability between the parties. Do both (all) parties gain when goals are achieved?

In its simplest form, the self-employment arrangement (with no disability insurance) is perfectly aligned. One has to work to be paid. There are more earnings for more work output, or for a greater quality of output, and, therefore, a strong incentive to increase one's earning power and remain healthy. In a self-employed situation, the same person (who is both principal and agent) experiences all rewards and losses.

The forthcoming examples demonstrate how a policy implemented for one purpose can have unintended consequences upon the incentives it creates in other areas.

Blog 6.1   Getting value from health benefits: use them or lose them

Sometimes people object to our position that when a third party pays for health benefits, individuals tend to consume more. But it's true: misaligned economic incentives increase the cost and reduce the quality of care. Because of this, we believe consumers should be more aware of the cost of healthcare and pay more (and directly for) their health benefits. People become more engaged in consumer decisions when they have incentives to do so—like paying more of the cost of the commodity being purchased.

Protestations we hear usually involve such statements as: "no one would choose to be sick (have surgery/be injured) if they do not have to," or "making health issues about money is blaming the victim," or "you imply that anyone unfortunate enough to get sick is cheating." Such arguments miss the point. The health as human capital paradigm does not apply a value judgment on any decision or choice. Rather, it simply acknowledges that human choices are influenced by incentives inherent in social systems (like businesses, government services, and families). Simply, we each act in ways that we perceive to be in our own best interest.

Policies governing how services are paid for will change the likelihood of certain choices. That's all.

For example, take two people with the exact same circumstances (same illness, same family responsibilities, same boss, same bank account balance, etc.) considering whether to take a day off from work. If one works for a company offering five sick days, and one works for a company that offers a combined paid-time-off bank of days for vacation and sick time, the time-off policy changes the overall likelihood of an absence. The person who has to "pay" more for a sick day (losing a future vacation day) is more likely to attend work that day. Our discussion does not focus on whether the choice of absence versus attendance is right or wrong. We argue that policies alter a human's assessment of pros and cons in ways that make a choice more or less likely. Besides, "sickness" is not an objective, single dimension, but a broad continuum of degrees of discomfort and impairment. Our analysis of these issues is not normative, centered on the question of what "ought to be," but is predictive, centering on understanding the reality of "what actually happens."

By acknowledging human nature and recognizing existing incentives, decision makers can make conscious decisions about future strategy regarding health benefits. As examples, we have already seen data showing that paying less than 100% of pay reduces the *likelihood*[*] and the *duration*[†] of disability. We have also seen that the size and timing of

---

[*] See Blog 3.2 Money matters in decisions about disability.
[†] See Blog 3.3 Hoping for absolutes in a subjective world.

deductibles[‡] and copayments[§] affect use of medical services. These are policy-design decisions.

The use-it-or-lose-it phenomenon

The following is another example of how economic incentives influence benefits utilization. In most large organizations, employer-sponsored health and paid-time-off benefits are substituted for wages. While these benefits are considered "insurance" against misfortune, in most cases the only way to get value from one's investment (lost wages) is to use services. (The exception is Health Savings Accounts or payment for unused sick time.)

When we examine most health issues, we find that a majority include choice—how, when, and from whom one will receive care. Take for example an older employee with chronic, degenerative knee pain. He will have many options regarding what, when, and how to treat this condition. Options may range from over-the-counter pain medication to knee replacement surgery.

Imagine that the same older person has generous, employer-sponsored benefits and decides to leave his job in the next year. To get value from benefits before leaving employment, it is not illogical for him to make choices about the timing, type, and cost of treatment for his knee pain with his already-paid-for benefits in mind.

FIGURE 6.1   MEDICAL COSTS AND WORKER TRANSITION

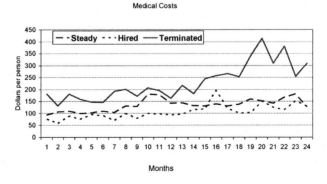

Health as Human Capital Research Group

---

‡ See Blog 3.9 Moral hazard and the New Year's effect.
§ See Blog 3.1 Remembering the RAND Health Insurance Experiment.

Does this scenario occur? *Absolutely.* Figures 6.1 and 6.2 compare similar populations of people who were recently hired (six months before the period shown), terminated soon after the period shown, or steadily employed before and after the period shown. Controlling for differences in age, gender, job type, and other factors, figure 6.1 shows the differences in monthly medical spending. As we see, the employees who will soon leave have significantly higher spending.

In figure 6.2, we see that those who terminate also take more combined time off (sick leave, disability, and workers' compensation days). The scale on the left represents the dollars spent in salary-equivalent lost time. Thus, the combined utilization of medical care and time off amounts to thousands of dollars per terminated worker. Our analysts did extensive research and found that this relationship holds true *regardless of other health factors* (chronic illnesses, previously very low cost, previously very high cost, etc.).[¶] In all cases, those who were preparing to leave spent more and those newly hired spent less. These observations reflect logical choices made by individuals facing health issues, along with a transition in their working status and potential loss of value in unused benefits.

FIGURE 6.2   TIME OFF AND WORKER TRANSITION

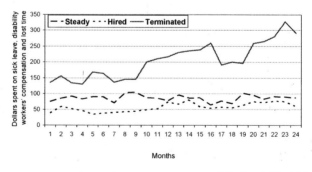

Health as Human Capital Research Group

[¶] On an analytical note, our team has done extensive analysis to dissect the chicken-and-egg aspect of medical costs prior to job termination. On the one hand, poor health could lead to a higher likelihood of quitting. On the other, intention to quit can lead to higher utilization of healthcare services prior to departure. By our calculations, both phenomena are present. However, the majority of the cost differences result from the latter. Given two people with similar health and health costs, the one intending to leave spends more than the one intending to stay.

The phenomenon does not suggest a choice "to be sick" or "to cheat," but to make use of services given important considerations of timing and cost. (For another similar example, see the spike in procedures** prior to introduction of a high deductible.)

In our view, recognizing underlying incentives and the discretionary nature of many medical decisions is ultimately respectful to individuals. Instead of dismissing all medical care as an uncontrollable misfortune that happens *to* people, we would rather acknowledge and encourage the degree to which individuals *make active decisions* about all aspects of their care—what, when, and how.

Saying that economic incentives do and should influence choice does not imply mistrust or a character judgment. On the contrary, ignoring economic incentives oversimplifies health issues as separate from, rather than imbedded in, the broader context of life decisions.

August 26, 2007

** See Blog 3.6 The challenge of insuring discretionary events.

Blog 6.2 There are wellness incentives, and then there are incentives that increase the importance of being well

Anyone who has implemented wellness programs knows that offering cash and prizes can increase participation. It has become commonplace to offer money or premium discounts (a financial "wellness incentive") to employees to encourage participation in questionnaires and behavior-change programs. While we wish everyone would *want* to participate without a financial carrot, most employees seem to need a little extra encouragement.

Interestingly, the presence or absence of a wellness incentive is not universally predictive of participation. Some companies can achieve a

63% response rate with *no* incentive,[1] while others might only achieve a 5%-10% participation rate with a modest incentive. These differences must be explained by something other than offering a specific carrot for a specific action.

In the health as human capital paradigm, health is a human capital asset owned by the person. Like investments in his other human capital assets (such as skills), an employee can invest in his health to increase his worth in the labor market. Earnings potential is influenced directly by growth in all human capital assets.

Economic evidence demonstrates that performance-based pay increases productivity.[2] When higher productivity results in a greater direct payoff (increased earnings), it also increases the perceived value of a worker's own human capital. So, in essence, bonuses give workers—theoretically—an added incentive to become better at their jobs and to protect their well-being.

We tested this premise in our recent Health as Human Capital Survey. Respondents were asked to rate their agreement with this statement: "Staying healthy is really important for me to be successful in my career."

As shown in figure 6.3, a majority agreed with the statement. Of respondents whose health status was excellent or very good, almost three-quarters agreed. Of those rating themselves as less healthy, 57% agreed. Interestingly, 27% to 43% either disagreed or were neutral.[*]

My economist colleagues were not surprised to learn that about one-third of employees do not consider health important to their careers. First of all, many jobs are not physically demanding. Also, employees may believe that (if covered by paid time off and health benefits, and little performance-based pay) the financial consequences of poor health will be borne by someone else.

However, we were interested in understanding what factors made

---

[*] For those with a greater interest in the detail: Another question was asked regarding whether "improving my health would make me more successful in my job." Those in poorer health were more likely to agree with this statement than those in very good/excellent health. When we tested whether agreement with this statement had a similar relationship to bonuses, results were similar to those reported here regarding "staying healthy."

FIGURE 6.3   WHAT MAKES HEALTH IMPORTANT?

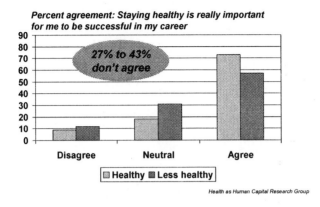

Percent agreement: Staying healthy is really important for me to be successful in my career

27% to 43% don't agree

Disagree   Neutral   Agree

☐ Healthy ▩ Less healthy

Health as Human Capital Research Group

workers rate their health as more important. Although the survey does not allow us to conclude that one factor truly causes another, we could test to see what worker characteristics were associated with a higher rating of importance. Specifically, we were interested in aspects of how people were paid. (Other correlations are noted at the end of this entry and in our overall report.[†])

In addition to wages or salary, about half of respondents were eligible for bonuses at their job. Those eligible were asked about how much bonus they could earn and also what they knew about how their bonus was determined. About one-third of those eligible for a bonus had little or no idea how their bonus was determined. One-third knew exactly how to get a bonus. The rest knew "in general" how the bonus was to be calculated. Thus, only a small fraction of employees could earn bonuses and knew exactly what they needed to do to earn a bonus.

Our hypothesis? Holding other things constant, higher performance-based rewards make health more important. Two specific assumptions were tested:

1) A person who is eligible for a higher bonus will consider health

---

† Gender was not an important predictor, nor was company size. Salary was positively correlated with health importance (controlling for age, gender and company size), meaning that higher paid workers rated it more important. We also looked for associations between health importance and job characteristics. For example, having more health-related benefits was not correlated with level of rated importance of health.

more important than someone eligible for a smaller bonus, and

2) A person who knows with certainty that he will be rewarded for better performance will value his own human capital—including health—more than someone who is unclear about how to earn a bonus.

Both assumptions held true. Most telling, there was a positive association between size of bonus and importance of health. Further, figure 6.4 demonstrates the association between bonus certainty and the importance of health. As shown, we controlled for many other important factors and found that the more precisely a person knew how to earn a bonus, the more likely they were to rate health as highly important. This reveals that two people of equal age, gender, salary, company size, and health status rated the importance of health differently depending on how

FIGURE 6.4   WHAT MAKES HEALTH MORE IMPORTANT? CLEAR GUIDELINES ABOUT BONUSES

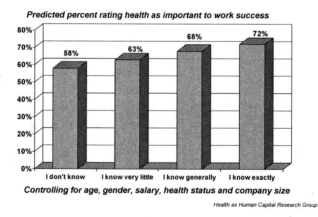

Predicted percent rating health as important to work success

Controlling for age, gender, salary, health status and company size

Health as Human Capital Research Group

much they knew about their bonuses.

As mentioned before, we cannot conclude that one factor (well-defined bonuses) entirely predicted the other (importance of health). Perhaps people who value their health also choose jobs with well-defined bonuses. But, our collective research findings from this survey and other sources continue to convince us that compensation and health are connected in important ways.

A dose of aligned rewards for performance may just have a side-effect of improving health. Next time you are deciding how much to increase the reward for completing a health questionnaire, consider reallocating that wellness incentive budget to your CFO to be used as a broader human capital incentive, such as bonus pay. It appears that a high certainty of greater rewards for good work will make *both* work performance and health more important.

June 17, 2007

References

1 Turpin, R.S., Ozminkowski, R.J., Sharda, C.E., Collins, J.J., Berger, M.L., Billotti, G.M., Baase, C.M., Olson, M.J., Nicholson, S. Reliability and validity of the Stanford Presenteeism Scale. *J Occup Environ Med* 2004 Nov;46(11):1123-33. Note: Dr. Baase has discussed their approach, without incentives, at several conferences.

2 Lazear, E.P. Performance pay and productivity. *American Economic Review* 2000;90(5):1346-61.

Blog 6.3   Pay and use of paid time-off: they are related

Did you know that the higher your salary, the lower your likelihood of filing a disability claim? Figure 6.5 shows results from an analysis of disability claims for exempt (salaried) workers* from the HHC research database—a population of over 200,000 employees from multiple employers and a variety of paid-time-off (PTO) plans.

Individuals with a salary of $30,000 filed short-term-disability (STD) claims at a rate about five times higher than those who make $150,000 or more, and twice the rate of those who make $70,000. This trend applies to both longer (dark) and shorter (lighter) STD episodes and remains significant after controlling for age and gender. Thus, it cannot be

---

* Exempt and non-exempt are classifications of workers that we often simplify as salaried and hourly workers, respectively. In actuality, the classification involves many regulations, including how people are paid and whether they are eligible to be paid for overtime. In general, exempt workers are salaried and not paid for overtime. The highest paid workers also tend to be in an exempt category, though not always. See the Fair Labor Standards Act (FLSA) home page for details: http://www.flsa.com/coverage.html (accessed December 15, 2005).

FIGURE 6.5   PERCENT HAVING A SHORT-TERM-DISABILITY CLAIM
             BY ANNUAL SALARY

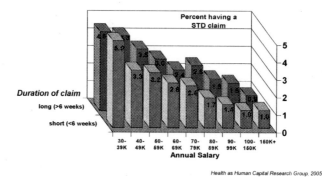

Health as Human Capital Research Group, 2005

explained by having more women or older people in lower paying jobs. This relationship between STD and salary was only significant for exempt (salaried) workers.

Before you decide that this relationship is related to health, you should know that the trend also remains significant when we control for the person's healthcare costs that year. Therefore, we cannot explain the relationship by assuming that employees with lower salaries had more serious illnesses. Further, even though there are studies showing that health status is related to income, it is unlikely that individuals making $70,000 are twice as likely to be seriously ill as those making $100,000, or that those making $50,000 are three times as likely to be seriously ill as those making $100,000. If differences in short-term-disability rates reflect simple differences in health status, we would expect to see little difference among the higher salary levels.

Related analyses also indicate that the rate of disability is over twice as high for non-exempt workers than for exempt workers, regardless of salary.

What does this relationship mean? We can't say for sure, but it implies that there is more incentive for lower-paid workers to use paid-time-off benefits. This could be because higher paid workers have more control and flexibility in their jobs when they are ill. Or it could be that the opportunity cost of going on a disability claim for those with higher wages is higher (better paid workers give up more wages and opportunities when they are out on a disability claim). Or it could be that the incentive to use paid-time-off benefits is more powerful, and possibly more acceptable, for those who are paid less. Another possible explanation is that higher-paid individuals like their work more and want to avoid missing work that they enjoy. Whatever the reasons, the pattern seems to have less to do with illness, and more to do with economics.

As a reminder, economic incentives influence disability rates in other ways. In an earlier entry,[†] we learned that the level of salary reimbursement a company provides during disability affects the rate of disability claims as well.

December 18, 2005

---

† See Blog 3.2 Money matters in decisions about disability.

Blog 6.4   Do anticipated health events affect the choice of health plan?

When consumers know ahead of time that they will need significant medical care, do they behave differently than when the need for care is less certain? It would make sense that in times when care is highly probable, families may choose insurance coverage that minimizes out-of-pocket expenditure.

We decided to look in our own dataset for evidence of this phenomenon. A few of my colleagues in the Health as Human Capital Research Group ran an analysis. They identified employees from a large corporation who were employed continuously over a two-year period. More than 4,100 of these employees were in PPO plans that included either a $200 or a $400 deductible. Controlling for a variety of other variables (including age, gender, salary, ethnicity, and region) we tested to see if those employees who added a new baby to their family in the first eight months of year 2 were more likely to switch to a zero-deductible plan at the end of year 1.

FIGURE 6.6 *PLAN-SWITCHING IN ANTICIPATION OF MATERNITY COSTS*

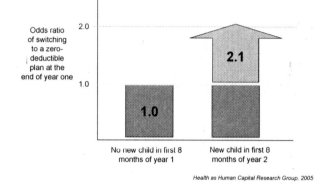

Odds ratio of switching to a zero-deductible plan at the end of year one

2.0

1.0

2.1

1.0

No new child in first 8 months of year 1

New child in first 8 months of year 2

Health as Human Capital Research Group, 2005

The answer? Yes they were. As you see in figure 6.6, the odds of switching to a zero-deductible plan in year 2 were *2.1 times higher* for families adding a child than for similar families who did not have a child in that time period.

This behavior demonstrates that, where possible, consumers will choose those insurance options that minimize the costs to themselves of accessing and consuming medical care. When patients suspect they might need care they will shop for advantageous coverage—as we would expect.

October 23, 2005

Blog 6.5 Kids, paychecks, and healthcare deductibles

Besides health issues, what other factors influence a person's likelihood of choosing a high-deductible health plan (HDHP)? We studied many factors in our recent analysis of employees choosing health plans with deductibles at or above $1,000.[1]

If we assume that individuals will weigh the personal costs and benefits of different plan options, we would expect that any factor increasing one's likelihood of an out-of-pocket expense would make a high deductible less attractive. One such factor is family size because, all other things being equal, the larger the number of people covered in a policy, the higher the probability of an insurance claim.

We tested how the choice of a HDHP differed for employees who had children, using an odds ratio where the rate of choosing a HDHP in each group is compared to the rate for those with no children. The analysis controlled for differences in demographics, health status, benefits use and a few other issues. As shown in figure 6.7, given the choice of a high-deductible health plan or a low-deductible health plan, those with more dependent children had a lower rate of choosing a high deductible. We see here that employees with four or more children were only one-third as likely to choose a HDHP. Larger families can expect more costs and thus have a higher likelihood of expenses. Consequently, few take on the additional, expected out-of-pocket expense.

FIGURE 6.7   ODDS RATIOS FOR CHOOSING A HIGH-DEDUCTIBLE HEALTH PLAN BY NUMBER OF DEPENDENT CHILDREN

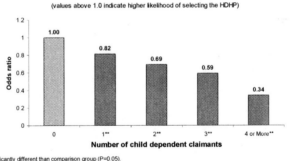

(values above 1.0 indicate higher likelihood of selecting the HDHP)

** Significantly different than comparison group (P=0.05).
Odds ratio adjusted for differences in age, tenure, salary, number of child claimants, exempt status, race, prior sick leave, disability, workers' compensation costs, and prior highest Charlson co-morbidity index in family.

Health as Human Capital Research Group, 2006

On the other end of the spectrum, we would expect that factors that mitigate the relative burden of an unanticipated expense will increase the likelihood of selecting a HDHP. The best example is income. We see in figure 6.8 that individuals with higher salaries are significantly more likely than those with lower salaries to choose a HDHP (even correcting for differences in age, family size, and other factors). Some early studies from consumer-driven health initiatives suggest that more high-paid employees than low-paid employees participate voluntarily in consumer-directed health plans (CDHPs).[2]

FIGURE 6.8   ODDS RATIOS FOR CHOOSING A HIGH-DEDUCTIBLE HEALTH
PLAN BY SALARY GROUP

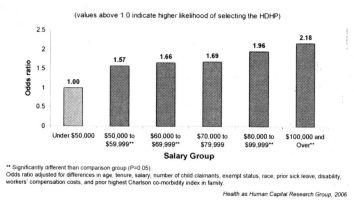

(values above 1.0 indicate higher likelihood of selecting the HDHP)

** Significantly different than comparison group (P=0.05).
Odds ratio adjusted for differences in age, tenure, salary, number of child claimants, exempt status, race, prior sick leave, disability,
workers' compensation costs, and prior highest Charlson co-morbidity index in family.

Health as Human Capital Research Group, 2006

So, who will choose a HDHP? Those who believe that its benefits outweigh its personal risk for additional costs. Many factors other than health status will influence this choice. And this has implications for adoption of both high-deductible plans as well as consumer-directed plans. For a more detailed discussion of factors influencing adoption of HDHP, see our white paper[1] on the Health as Human Capital Foundation website.

February 19, 2006

References

1 Lynch, W.D., Gardner, H.H., Kleinman, N.L., Health as Human Capital Research Group. "Selection of high-deductible health plans: Attributes, influencing likelihood and implications for consumer-driven approaches, February 2006, http://www.hhcfoundation.org/hhcf/pdf/adverseselection_2_13_06.pdf (accessed February 13, 2006).

2 Parente, S.T., Feldman, R., Christianson, J.B. Employee choice of consumer-driven health insurance in a multiplan, multiproduct setting. *Health Serv Res* 2004;39:(4 Pt 2)1091-112.

Blog 6.6   The effects of passive and active choosing on HDHP enrollment

When given multiple options that include a reasonably priced lower-deductible health plan, only a small percentage of employees chose a plan with a deductible over $1,000. We have seen in past blog entries and in our white paper[1] that those who do choose a high deductible tend to be healthier, higher paid, and have smaller families. Because the high-deductible plan carries more risk of out-of-pocket costs, we also found that a higher portion (14%) *switched away* from a high-deductible option over a four-year period than *switched to* a high-deductible option (fewer than one percent in the low-deductible plan).[*]

Since a smaller portion of those in a low-deductible plan chose to switch to a plan that had higher risk, we wondered how behaviors differed depending on whether a person was forced to make an active choice, compared to individuals who could maintain their current plan through passive re-enrollment. For a population of over 35,000 employees, we tested whether, in a given year, new employees signing up for benefits for the first time were more likely to choose a high deductible than existing employees, who were not required to change their plan choice.

As we see in figure 6.9, in all but the oldest age group, the new employees were far more likely to choose the high-deductible plan than the existing employees. We controlled for salary and a few other demographic characteristics, but not the previous year's medical expenditures (which are not available for new employees). These are relative rates compared to others in the same age category. The younger groups (with more child dependents and lower salary) did have lower absolute rates in the HDHP. However, continuously employed employees were far less likely to enroll in a HDHP than new employees of the same age.

---

[*] Because so few select the HDHP, in raw numbers, more people actually switched to the HDHP. But as a percentage, far more switch away from rather than to the HDHP.

FIGURE 6.9   RELATIVE ODDS OF NEW EMPLOYEES VS. EXISTING EMPLOYEES
CHOOSING A HIGH-DEDUCTIBLE HEALTH PLAN BY AGE GROUP

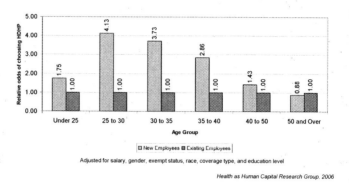

Adjusted for salary, gender, exempt status, race, coverage type, and education level

Health as Human Capital Research Group, 2006

This finding has implications about how employees will participate in new benefit options. There are personal investments required in making a new choice—time, hassle, cognitive energy—and many individuals will choose *not* to invest in making a choice if it is not required. And among the continuing employees, those who do bother to consider changes are the select group who do so in order to reduce risk (possibly as they develop a health condition or increase the size of their family), not to take on additional risk.

There is no way to eliminate all other explanations, such as the possibility that people who switch jobs may also be willing to take on greater risks than those who are not switching jobs. Or that the new employees—of all ages—are healthier. However, this analysis controlled for several other factors (age, family, education, salary), suggesting that people who have recently decided to take a new job—and have to choose a plan—are more willing to choose the high-deductible plan.

Not making a choice when you don't have to is certainly a rational behavior. Staying in a low-deductible health plan may also be a prudent decision. However, other things being equal, it appears that requiring an active choice results in different behaviors than passive re-enrollment. Thus, if employers want employees to consider their options carefully, they may need to ask their employees to make an active choice.

March 5, 2006

174

References

1 Lynch, W.D., Gardner, H.H., Kleinman, N.L., Health as Human Capital Research Group. "Selection of high-deductible health plans: Attributes, influencing likelihood and implications for consumer-driven approaches, February 2006, http://www.hhcfoundation.org/hhcf/pdf/adverseselection_2_13_06.pdf (accessed February 13, 2006).

Chapter 7
Consumers Make Choices—
Whether We Inform Them or Not

In many aspects of life, policy makers question whether citizen agents can make sound decisions about finances, health, or politics. Over the past few decades, a majority of companies have changed from corporate-run pension plans to 401(k) plans controlled by employees. There was great resistance, however, to the notion that individuals could manage this responsibility. Many argued that investments should be made on their behalf.

Today, similar arguments are made regarding healthcare. Some argue that placing control of healthcare decisions (part of the movement known as consumer-directed healthcare) in the hands of consumers is dangerous, because healthcare is too scientifically technical and complex. Further, critics argue, consumers have insufficient information on which to make good decisions.

What is often overlooked in such debates is the reality: consumers already make decisions in the current healthcare system. Thus, arguments about whether individuals *should* make decisions are moot. Our position is that better aligned incentives between providers and patients—for quality and efficiency at a market-determined price—would improve all aspects of the system. Rather than protecting consumers from active involvement, the system needs the exact market pressures and transparency that true consumerism would bring.

The following examples discuss misinformation about consumer involvement and the advantages that consumer pressure might bring.

Blog 7.1   In case you hadn't noticed, Pandora went digital a while back

Question: Is it irresponsible to encourage consumers to jump into the ocean of health information?

Answer: Too late, consumers started swimming years ago.

While some would like to debate whether consumers *should* be encouraged to investigate and make their own health decisions, we contend that the discussion is moot; consumers navigate oceans of information every day. Even for those who fear it's a Pandora's box with potential for more harm than good, it's too late to take it back.

Let's consider the size of the information ocean today:

- Over seven million new pages of information appear on the World Wide Web each day.[1]
- There are over 61,000 scholarly/academic journals in print in the U.S. alone.[2]
- We broadcast 132 million hours of television and 320 million hours of radio programming each year.[3]
- We send over 50 billion emails every day (plus 120 billion more as spam),[4] over 30 million instant messages,[5] and conduct over 200 million internet searches daily.[6]

Experts trying to quantify the amount of information we generate and transmit in today's world estimate it's about five exabytes (in 2002). That's five times 10 to the 18th power bytes, and is more written, optical, and digital information than could fit in 500,000 Libraries of Congress, more than thirty books of information for each of the 6.3 billion persons on the planet, and more words than every word spoken by all humans in all of history.[7]

Compared to a generation ago, there are few items a determined consumer can't find or learn about today. The web is amazing, wonderful, and frightening all at the same time.

> *Note: Pandora's box opened a while ago, and its contents have been scanned, digitized, and posted on YouTube.*

My economist friends remind me that we can explain this explosion of information using the laws of supply and demand, where the product being exchanged is information itself. Consumers, physicians, or any other rational decision makers will invest in more information acquisition as long as the marginal benefits exceed the marginal costs to them. In today's electronic age, tremendous growth in the supply of information has caused the price of getting information (over the web for instance) to plummet. Relative to the same level of marginal benefit, the cost is lower. Thus, as information technologies deliver more information at lower cost, consumers (and providers alike) will naturally demand more information. Bigger ocean, more swimmers.

Medical information is no different

The explosion and availability of medical information is no different. Like the good and bad in Pandora's box, it contains all levels of accuracy, quality, and understandability. Consumers can find credible sources alongside quackery, unbiased alongside blatantly commercial, and fear-driven opinion alongside well-documented research. We are actively exploring the information ocean. As examples:

- The National Institutes of Health websites receive over six million unique visitors a month.[8]
- WebMD has 20 million visitors a month.[9]

Don't kid yourself into imagining that consumers rely primarily on doctors for their important health information. And don't assume doctors are exempt from their own professional information overload. One study estimated that a physician would need to spend over 627 hours per month reading new research findings simply to stay current in primary care topics.[10] Family doctors are expected to follow an estimated 800 different medical practice guidelines, which may each be updated at any time.[1] It is unlikely that any professional can stay current in any field without new technologies and navigational tools to support good decision making.

Keeping up with new research knowledge is only part of the

information challenge. A 2000 report from the Institute of Medicine estimated the human cost of safety and quality problems amounts to 98,000 avoidable deaths per year.[11] Many of these are attributed to doctors' reluctance to adopt computerized systems. Yet, by 2005, only 23% of primary care practices used electronic records and only 5% of hospitals used computer order entry for medications—despite proven effectiveness in reducing avoidable medication errors.[12] For whatever reason (expense, risk, inconvenience) adoption has been slow.

Along with limited information technology, the realities of medical visits make meaningful communication challenging. The pressures of medical practice are many. An average medical consultation, including the exam, is under 20 minutes. And studies indicate that it only takes a doctor between 18 and 23 seconds to interrupt a patient's opening explanation of what is wrong.[13] One has to be realistic about the limits of the traditional doctor-patient relationship as the ideal source for complete, up-to-date information.[14]

So, let's move on to the real question:

Yesterday's Question: Is it irresponsible to encourage consumers to jump into the ocean of health information?

Today's Question: How do we best support millions of people, of varying skill, already swimming (some drowning) in information?

When policy makers resist consumer-directed care, a primary reason is their belief that consumers are not capable of participating constructively in their own care. We would argue that most consumers have been participating in some way, and this trend will continue to expand along with the broader information explosion. Consumers made the leap, and they didn't ask for our permission.

Consumers (and providers alike!) will need new sorts of support, both electronic and human, to better select and apply the information they get. But we think it's time to stop pretending that consumers are "not ready to get in the water," and get on with helping them stay afloat.

September 24, 2007

References

1 Hall, A., Walton, G. Information overload within the healthcare system: a literature review. *Health Information & Libraries Journal* 2004;21:102-8, http://www.blackwell-synergy.com/doi/pdf/10.1111/j.1471-1842.2004.00506.x (accessed September 18, 2007).

2 Lyman, P., Varain, H.R. How much information? 2003. School of Information Management and Systems, University of California at Berkeley, http://www2.sims.berkeley.edu/research/projects/how-much-info-2003/ (accessed September 18, 2007).

3 Lyman.

4 Tschabitscher, H. How many emails are sent every day? About.com, http://email.about.com/od/emailtrivia/f/emails_per_day.htm (accessed September 18, 2007).

5 Kerner, S.M. IM accounts to number in the billions. July 19, 2005, Internetnews.com, http://www.internetnews.com/xSP/article.php/3521456 (accessed September 18, 2007).

6 Sullivan, D. Searches per day. SearchEngineWatch.com, April 20, 2006, http://searchenginewatch.com/showPage.html?page=2156461 (accessed September 18, 2007).

7 Lyman.

8 Iakovidis, I., Wilson, P., Healy, J.C. E-Health: Current Situation and Examples of Implemented and Beneficial E-Health Application. Washington, D.C.: IOS Press, 2004.

9 Web search gateway, Center for Health Policy Law and Management, Duke University, http://www.hpolicy.duke.edu/cyberexchange/intelligence/lit/web.htm (accessed September 18, 2007).

10 Alper, B.S., Hand, J.A., Elliott, S.G., et al. How much effort is needed to keep up with the literature relevant for primary care? *J Med Libr Assoc* 2004;92:429-37, http://www.pubmedcentral.nih.gov/articlerender.fcgi?artid=521514 (accessed September 18, 2007).

11 Kohn, L.T., Corrigan, J.M., Donaldson, M. S., eds. *To Err Is Human: Building a Safer Health System.* Committee on Quality of Health Care in America, Institute of Medicine. Washington, D.C.: National Academy Press, 2000, http://www.nap.edu/openbook.php?isbn=0309068371 (accessed September 18, 2007).

12 Jha, A.K., Ferris, T.G., Donelan, K., et al. How common are electronic health records in the United States? A summary of the evidence. *Health Aff (Millwood)* 2006;25:w496-507, http://content.healthaffairs.org/cgi/content/abstract/hlthaff.25.w496 (accessed September 18, 2007).

13 Lussier, M.T., Richard, C. Doctor-patient communication. Time to talk. *Can Fam Physician* 2006;52:1401-2, http://www.pubmedcentral.nih.gov/articlerender.fcgi?artid=1783704 (accessed September 18, 2007).

14 Seaman, B. Charting the doctor-patient relationship. *The Spiral Notebook: Short Takes on Carnitine Palmitoyl Transferase Deficiency* 1999;2:Supplement, http://www.spiralnotebook.org/chartingthedoctorpatientrelationship/index.html (accessed September 18, 2007).

Blog 7.2 Big-screen TVs, crack cocaine, and wolves

In an earlier blog entry* we discussed an alternative for how healthcare could be purchased in the U.S.—provide funds directly to individuals (rather than government or employer-sponsored insurance) and let them create a competitive market with their individual healthcare choices. These funds could come in the form of higher wages or accounts designated specifically for healthcare expenses.

This suggestion often provokes some doubt. Despite our acceptance of individual participation in choices for virtually every market of life-necessities—housing, food, clothing, transportation, financial investing, etc.—the same does not apply to healthcare.

Negative reactions usually reflect a preference for giving individuals health services, rather than money to spend on services. Statements also reflect a judgment about choices our fellow citizens would actually make. The two responses I have heard most often are: *"How do you know some people won't just go spend the money on crack instead?"* and the same comment substituting *"big-screen TV"* instead of crack. These comments presume that people—because of ignorance, irresponsibility, or untrustworthiness—cannot choose for themselves. If the conversation can progress beyond beliefs about blatant misuse of funds, it usually turns to generalizations about how "most people" wouldn't be capable of making the "right" choices, couldn't understand something so complicated, and would inevitably spend their funds unwisely.

While certainly there are people in our society who need others to make financial and health decisions for them, such as children and severely disabled individuals, generalizing this need to "most" adults in our society seems extreme. Most Americans have allowed their medical decisions to be made by others (doctors, insurers, and payers) because these parties pay for and provide medical services, *not* because people are *incapable* of participating constructively in such decisions. A useful metaphor is that of purchasing an automobile—consumers need not possess the technical expertise to build or repair automobiles, but

---

* See Blog 1.5 An option rarely mentioned in the current healthcare debate.

rather must possess enough information to select which automobile and accessories are "worth the price" for their needs.

Our medical system evolved due to many influences, including powerful economic, professional, and governmental pressures. It was not created because citizens asked for less involvement in important decisions. Are we really incapable of making choices among alternatives that are fundamental to our state of health and well-being? Or have we been trained to think this way?

Two considerations may have lead to these conclusions:

1) **We have been taught to believe that medical expertise is beyond question.**

Evidence shows that except in the case of traumatic injury, basic hygiene, public health measures, genetics, and personal behaviors have far greater influence on our eventual health than medical treatment. Yet, we tend to put medical expertise on a pedestal as *the* solution. We are a society that smokes, overeats, and under-exercises, yet believes open-heart surgery can and will save us. How did this evolve? Not by accident.

One hundred and fifty years ago doctors were not well-respected or well-paid. To become a powerful, respected profession, medicine had to develop significant authority—which means that individuals surrendered private judgment and relied on an expert.[1] Through social, institutional, and legal reforms, physicians became exclusive providers in the medical domain. Whether through intentional manipulation or as a side-effect of standardization, citizens were convinced that relying on one's own judgment was not only unwise, it was dangerous. Care moved from homes to hospitals. Care-giving moved from families to support professionals. Laws made treatments from non-physicians illegal. Licensing became more elite and restricted. The profession convinced us that new science about illness—invisible to the naked eye—was far too complex for an ordinary person to understand.

While exclusive licensing provides the public some reassurance about higher quality, economists (including Milton Friedman) have argued that, in general, licensing is really more about restricting entry, thus creating monopoly power and increasing incomes, than it is about enhancing service quality.[2] Such cultural dependency has yielded great economic and political power[†] for medicine.[‡]

So, when we make statements about "most people" being unable to make "good" decisions, how much of our opinion evolved from cultural traditions regarding medical authority? How much reflects an unfair generalization about individual ability?

At the Health as Human Capital Foundation, our basic assumption is that most people *can* and *do* make important decisions about their health already. Furthermore, the individual is the *only* person truly qualified to weigh the benefits and risks of their own care. While treatments can be based on science, their value to a specific individual is entirely subjective and unknowable by anybody else.

2) If we wait until there is "enough" good information, individuals will never participate meaningfully in healthcare decisions.

Once a conversation progresses past a point where my companion acknowledges that an individual can (sometimes) decide about (some of) his or her own care, the next objection points to the system. Even if people *can* decide, the system provides insufficient information to do so. Releasing the public into the current system is "throwing them to the wolves."

Certainly, they say, we must wait for full transparency of cost and quality information and access to credible interpreters before allowing individuals to wander alone in a dangerous medical wilderness. Indeed, many employers—with good intention—delay or avoid implementation of consumer-directed health plans in part because of this concern.

To be clear: we AGREE that better (probably not more) information is needed.[3] We DISAGREE about the forces that will cause this to happen.

The current system allows great inefficiency and variability (in both quality and cost). Health plans negotiate with large networks of providers,

---

† This is not intended to be a condemnation of people who practice medicine, just a commentary regarding the historical evolution of the profession into a powerful system of social and business arrangements.

‡ For a discussion of how this occurred, see *The Social Transformation of American Medicine* by Paul Starr, winner of the 1984 Pulitzer Prize.

within which, some are better than others and some are cheaper than others.

Facilities and providers who suspect their services are lower-quality or higher-priced than most have no incentive to share information. And consumers who do not pay directly for care have little incentive to demand information. As long as providers continue to get paid without revealing price or performance, and consumers continue to get services without paying the bill, information will remain limited.

More useable information will appear (quickly) when consumers demand it. But consumers will not demand it until they shop. Consumers will not shop until they own the transaction. Ownership comes from holding the purse. Without millions of new purse-holders, entrepreneurs have little incentive to package new forms of information.

If we continue to wait for better information before giving consumers ownership, the system remains in an endless loop of waiting, with no incentive to behave differently.

Do we, as a society, underestimate "most people?"

Before falling into a knee-jerk response about "most people" buying big-screen TVs instead of healthcare or becoming wolf-bait, question where these opinions came from. Are we truly safer in a system where someone else decides and we remain unaware of disparities? What if wolves hidden in our current system are just as ferocious as those we fear in a consumer-directed one?

It took several generations to convince us that only medical authorities have sufficient expertise to guide us through health decisions. Simultaneously, we have allowed medicine to conceal important information for decades. Hopefully it won't take us that long to decide to have "most people" take an active role.

April 8, 2007

References

1 Starr, P. *The Social Transformation of American Medicine*. New York: Basic Books, 1982, 10.

2 Friedman, M. *Capitalism and Freedom*. Chicago: University of Chicago Press, 1962. Excerpted in "A Freedom Daily Classic Reprint: Medical Licensure," Freedom

Daily (The Future of Freedom Foundation, January 1994), http://www.fff.org/freedom/
0194e.asp (accessed April 5, 2007).
    3 Hoffman, J. Awash in information, patients face a lonely, uncertain road. *New York Times*, August 14, 2005, http://www.nytimes.com/2005/08/14/health/14patient.
html?ex=1175918400&en=c54c780008451807&ei=5070 (accessed April 5, 2007).

Blog 7.3   An online Rx shopping trip shows that consumers can save a lot

How much of a difference in price would you find if you were to actually shop for healthcare?

People with insurance and a low deductible have little incentive to compare prices for healthcare services. Take medications as an example. If there is a relatively small copayment on medications, or a differential of $10 to $25 on brand-name versus generic medication, why spend much time comparing? Even if we do find an inexpensive alternative, some health plans limit their coverage to "approved" pharmacies—further discouraging efforts to save money. Because most of us do not think of shopping, we may assume that the price difference would be minimal.
Think again.

Because of controversy about the legality and authenticity of medications obtained from sources outside the U.S., we limit comparisons in this blog entry to U.S. sources. Also, all pharmacies required a doctor's prescription. We searched a few online lists to compare prices and chose some large, chain-store options as examples.[*]

The online shopping trip detailed below focuses on two frequently-prescribed medications whose patents expired in 2006. These are Zocor, a cholesterol-reducing medication and Zoloft, an antidepressant. After almost a year off patent, pharmacies have had time to add the generic

---

    [*] These certainly do not represent all alternatives. While these prices were listed when we searched, they may or may not remain the same. Prices are those found the week of May 21, 2007 at the following sites.
    www.cvs.com
    www.walgreens.com
    www.costco.com

versions of these products to their lists.

As shown in table 7.1, Walgreens and CVS (large, chain-store pharmacies) websites list prices for both the brand and generic versions of these medications. Comparing prices, one sees the significant effect of a medication going off patent. The difference between brand and generic prices was as much as $3 per pill, or $90 per month. Differences in price for the same exact medication between the two stores were not as great ($0.06 to $0.33 per pill).

TABLE 7.1   ONLINE PRICES FOR BRAND AND GENERIC MEDICATIONS AT WALGREENS AND CVS

Medication	Walgreens			CVS		
	Price for 30	Price per pill	Annual difference*	Price for 30	Price per pill	Annual difference*
Zocor (brand) Simvastatin (generic)	$149.99 $89.96	$5.00 $3.00		$154.99 $64.99	$5.17 $2.17	
Difference	$60.03	$2.00	$730.00	$90.00	$3.00	$1,095.00
Zoloft (brand) Sertraline (generic)	$93.99 $69.99	$3.13 $2.33		$95.59 $59.99	$3.19 $2.00	
Difference	$24.00	$0.80	$292.00	$35.60	$1.19	$434.35

*Based on price per pill

The lesson in this comparison is *to ask* for a generic equivalent, or make sure that the doctor indicates that a generic version is an acceptable alternative when he or she is writing the prescription. While there may be reasons why a person would not choose the generic option, this choice should be made based on full information – including price.

However, the shopping trip does not end here. Knowing that Wal-Mart[1] and Target[2] offer many generic prescriptions for $4 per 30 day supply, we searched their sites for generic drug availability. These specific medications were not listed online in the $4 category, although there were other cholesterol and depression treatments listed. Whether they are available, but not yet on the website, is unknown.

We did look at another price comparison site and found that Costco lists brand and generic prices side-by-side, as shown in table 7.2

TABLE 7.2   ONLINE PRICES FOR BRAND AND GENERIC MEDICATIONS AT COSTCO

Medication	Costco			
	Price for 30	Price per pill	Annual difference*	
Zocor (brand)	$147.52	$4.92		
Simvastatin (generic)	$8.04	$0.27		
Difference	$139.48	$4.65	$1,697.25	
Zoloft (brand)	$84.17	$2.81		For both medications
Sertraline (generic)	$6.32	$0.21		
Difference	$77.85	$2.60	$949.00	$2,646

*Based on price per pill

Brand prices at Costco were not much lower than other stores. However, generic versions were substantially lower than any other website we found (so low in fact that we called to make sure it was not an error). The 30-day price for a generic prescription was actually lower than many insurance copayments.

Projecting the difference between the highest cost per pill for brand pills and the lowest cost generic pills across 365 days (one pill per day), the difference is a staggering $2,644 for a year's supply of these two medications. Because economic analyses indicate that patient cost affects compliance, we can also assume that the lower-cost option may result in better clinical management.

These findings are not intended to be an advertisement for any particular store, treatment, brand, or generic alternative. However, they do indicate that, even without crossing borders to Mexico, Canada, or India, prices vary and potential savings exist. How many of us really investigate price options—unless we are "encouraged" by high deductibles or health savings accounts?

Imagine the price pressures if we all had incentive to compare! There are certainly better bargains available if we look.

June 3, 2007

References

1 Wal-Mart Pharmacy $4 prescriptions, http://www.walmart.com/catalog/catalog.gsp?cat=546834 (accessed May 30, 2007).

2 Target Pharmacy $4 Program, http://sites.target.com/images/pharmacy/4dollar_program_list_111706.pdf (accessed May 30, 2007).

Blog 7.4   Healthcare price and quality information for consumers

One goal of consumer-centric health strategies is to engage users in a true healthcare marketplace. Instead of simply using care, consumers would investigate, shop, compare, and choose their care based on information—the same way consumers choose most goods and services.

A shift toward true consumerism will require two behavioral drivers. First, and most important, consumers must spend their own money on care. Meaning that what is *not* spent is, and remains, their money.* Second, consumers must have sufficient information about price and quality to make sound decisions. Even without information, early results suggest that consumers try to find less expensive treatment alternatives.[1] However, without readily-available and reliable information, consumers will be inefficient and inconsistent in applying the type of market pressure that can improve price and quality in the long run.

Evidence suggests that most healthcare consumers do not engage in typical consumer-like behaviors. For example, two-thirds (67%) of consumers spend at least eight hours researching automobiles before buying a car, but only about half as many spend this amount of time researching a doctor (38%) or health plan (34%). Further, when asked about prices, consumers are able to predict the price of a Honda Accord within $300 on average, but were off by $8,100 on a four-day hospital stay.[2] This survey report concluded that, clearly, consumers are uninformed about prices of healthcare services.

Yet, while we agree that most consumers lack awareness of price, it

---

* See Blog 3.1 Remembering the RAND Health Insurance Experiment.

appears that even if consumers were aware, their price estimates might not improve. Unlike a Honda Accord, there is no MSRP for a medical procedure and one "actual" price may not exist. The State of Wisconsin has developed a set of websites called Healthclick Wisconsin[†] that provides consumers with information about the variation in both price and quality of care.[3] The Pricepoint[4] site compares the price of hospital procedures for specific hospitals, within regions, and statewide.

One extract seen in figure 7.1 is the variation between a Milwaukee hospital and other hospitals in the region and state. The price of a joint replacement varies significantly depending on the facility, from a high of $42,000 to a low of $28,000. Appendectomies vary in price from $12,000 to $19,000. Information about each facility also helps consumers understand why prices and services may vary. With this information, consumers may still not know what the "actual" price should be. But they do know that the price may vary by 50% or more depending on the facility they choose.

FIGURE 7.1   VARIATION IN AVERAGE PROCEDURE PRICE

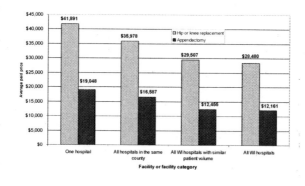

Wisconsin CheckPoint www.wicheckpoint.org

While quality can be harder to define, Wisconsin's Checkpoint[5] site does an admirable job of showing how medical groups and facilities compare with regard to safety practices, timeliness, and efficacy in the delivery of recommended care, and even some outcomes. Figure

---

† Since this blog was posted, the service has been renamed to Wisconsin Health Reports.

7.2 shows the results of a query comparing medical groups in their management of HbA1c levels (a blood test that measures how well a diabetic patient's blood glucose is controlled). A diabetic patient can see here that only one third of patients in medical group C have optimal control, while over half the patients treated by medical group D have optimal control.

FIGURE 7.2   VARIATION IN QUALITY METRICS

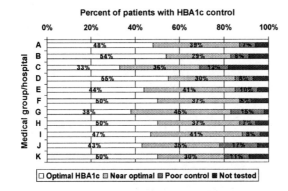

Wisconsin Collaborative for Healthcare Quality http://www.wisconsinhealthreports.org

Some believe that medicine is so complex and technical that consumers can never make efficient decisions; the present state of ignorance is inevitable. From the health as human capital perspective, we believe that consumers don't have the required knowledge because they have no incentive to acquire it and information suppliers have no incentive to supply it. Someone else pays for care, so the relevance of price and quality information is minimal. If consumers paid out of their own pockets, they would have an incentive to acquire information and an information industry would develop to supply what was needed to direct efficient decisions.

Putting control of spending in the hands of patients will create huge demand for good information along with price pressures that drive gains in healthcare efficiency and choice. When we add good information about price and provider performance, it creates pressures that drive improvement in quality and delivery of care. Wisconsin provides an example of what, hopefully, is only a first step toward improvements in all of these.

April 3, 2006

References

1 Agrawal, V., Ehrbeck, T., O'Neill Packard, K., Mango, P. Consumer-directed health plan report: Early evidence is promising. North American Payor/Provider Practice, McKinsey & Company; June 2005 http://www.mckinsey.com/clientservice/ payorprovider/Health_Plan_Report.pdf (accessed March 30, 2006).

2 Great-West Healthcare. Consumer healthcare survey reveals mixed bag of results. July 28, 2005, http://www.harrisinteractive.com/news/newsletters/clientnews/ Great-WestHealthcare.pdf (accessed March 30, 2006).

3 Wisconsin Health Reports. http://www.wisconsinhealthreports.org/ (accessed November 16, 2007).

4 Wisconsin Pricepoint. http://www.wipricepoint.org/ (accessed March 30, 2006).

5 Wisconsin Checkpoint. http://www.wisconsinhealthreports.org/ (accessed March 30, 2006).

Blog 7.5   Consumer choice in healthcare. Part 1: Who chooses a high deductible

Consumer-driven health plans—plans that combine medical savings accounts with large deductibles—are designed to provide protection from large losses while allowing the consumer to face the economic consequences for smaller, marginal outlays on healthcare. In other words, under a consumer-driven health plan, each individual is more likely to consider whether she would rather spend that additional $100 on higher quality food or recreation rather than an additional lab test. Observing how consumers respond to the incentives created by high-deductible health plans is instructive.

One of the issues often mentioned with consumer-driven plans is the topic of "adverse selection," the possibility that only healthy people will sign up for a voluntary consumer-driven plan, while "sicker people" choose other plan options. As such, the other plans would experience a higher rate of premium increases, due to the "adverse" profile of its members.

Adverse selection occurs when some consumers perceive (correctly) that their risk of high out-of-pocket costs is low, and shop for health plans on the basis of their lowered expected risk. Do consumers really perceive their risks accurately and engage in "adverse selection?" The answer to this can be shown with data from over 150,000 employees who had the option of enrolling in health plans with varying levels of deductibles.* Did those who enrolled in the high-deductible plans have lower rates of most illnesses? Yes.

As figure 7.3 shows, people who signed up for the high deductible had the lowest rates of chronic illnesses, such as hypertension, high cholesterol, and back pain. We also see that those in the highest deductible group have the lowest rate of a sprain and strain diagnosis. Whether healthier people choose a high-deductible/lower-premium plan because of their good health (adverse selection), or *having* the high deductible causes all individuals (regardless of their self-perceived risk) to seek less care in order to minimize expenses, is not clear.

FIGURE 7.3   RATE OF ILLNESS BY DEDUCTIBLE AMOUNT

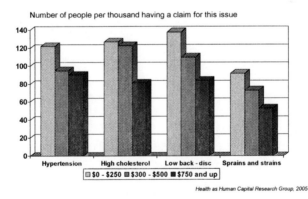

Number of people per thousand having a claim for this issue

$0 - $250 $300 - $500 $750 and up

Health as Human Capital Research Group, 2005

---

*   Data are from multiple businesses in the HCMS research reference database. Over 6,000 of the approximately 150,000 employees were enrolled in high-deductible plans. Because these plans were offered to employees from a number of companies, we won't present exact details of the premium differential between the low-deductible and high-deductible plans. In general, the high-deductible plan required less of a contribution by the employee, but that difference varied. I acknowledge that this is not a minor factor, and studies have shown the specific migration from plan to plan for every dollar difference in premium. However, we're trying to keep things simple here, and only intend to demonstrate general trends.

The rates of these diagnoses are lowest in the high-deductible group. Across all 261 diagnostic categories (defined by AHRQ, the Agency for Healthcare Research and Quality) we found a 10% lower incidence in the $300 to $500 deductible plan and a 30% lower average incidence in the $750+ plan, compared to the low-deductible plan.

This suggests that people take health into account when choosing a deductible. Other things being equal, if you give people an option that saves money up front with lower premiums—but carries a risk of a high out-of-pocket expense if serious issues arise—healthier people will choose that option. If one's anticipated need for care is high, higher deductibles are not an attractive choice. Of course, people vary in their tolerance of risk, and even many healthy people may choose a low deductible "just in case." The point is that people will make choices according to what suits them.

What does this tell us about consumer-driven plans? Well, since consumer-driven plans require large deductibles, we must be aware that healthier people will find them the most attractive. To mitigate the natural selection of only healthy employees, sponsors will need to consider:

- offering consumer-driven plans as the only option,
- mitigating the risk through high levels of funding of savings accounts, or
- making the cost of the plan attractive.

It also tells us that we cannot underestimate consumers' ability to make choices that serve their own best interest and minimize financial risk.

In the next entry[†] we will talk about strategies that consumers do, and don't, use to control their costs.

January 8, 2006

---

† See Blog 7.6 Consumer choice in healthcare. Part 2: Voting with their feet.

Blog 7.6   Consumer choice in healthcare. Part 2: Voting with their feet

In the previous entry* we demonstrated how consumers self-select into low- and high-deductible health plans, based in part on their anticipated need for care. In this entry, we look at how deductible levels influence consumption of health services.

Theoretically, one would expect that a consumer who has to spend his or her own money would "shop" for services to minimize expenses. Shopping might include considerations of price, quality, convenience, and becoming better informed about all of these. There are three behaviors that a consumer can use to manage the cost of care: 1) She can not seek care at all; 2) She can seek care less often; or 3) She can seek care at a lower cost. Let's look at each of these choices.

Not seeking care (indicated by prevalence of diagnoses)

In our example, it is difficult to measure the number of people who choose not to seek care due to cost. This is because, as we discussed in the last entry,* we don't know precisely if healthier people chose the high-deductible plan in the first place, or if, after choosing the plan, those people just don't seek medical care when they are mildly sick. However, we saw last time that the rate of sprain and strain diagnoses was much lower for members of the highest-deductible plan. Actually, the highest-deductible group had the lowest rate of almost every diagnosis. The few exceptions include appendectomy, ectopic pregnancy, and fractures, all of which require immediate care and will be less sensitive to price (a characteristic my economist colleagues refer to as price inelasticity). Of note, the highest-deductible group had 40% fewer people with a diagnosis of upper respiratory infection, for which care-seeking is very discretionary. Acknowledging that adverse selection and risk adverseness are also involved, *fewer people in high-deductible plans seek care for most illnesses.* It is not proof, but suggests that these people may choose not to

---

* See Blog 7.5 Consumer choice in healthcare. Part 1: Who chooses a high deductible?

receive care for some illnesses.[†]

Seeking care less often (indicated by number of services within a diagnosis)

The second behavior is an interesting one. Do consumers with a high deductible seek care less frequently? Yes, most of the time.

On average, those in the highest-deductible group sought fewer services across *all 261 conditions,* compared to the lowest-deductible group. But it varies for specific illnesses. Figure 7.4 shows how the high-deductible group received fewer services for back pain and sprains. However, for chronic illness, the behavior was not as evident. In economic terms, the price elasticity for musculoskeletal issues is greater than the price elasticity for hypertension or high cholesterol. Once again, we cannot rule out the possibility that those who selected the high-deductible plan needed fewer services. Thus, *we cannot say why we see this trend,* we can only state that, on average, they sought fewer services than individuals who had lower deductibles.

FIGURE 7.4   SERVICES SOUGHT PER PERSON BY DEDUCTIBLE AMOUNT

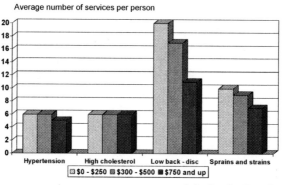

Health as Human Capital Research Group, 2006

---

† For proof of similar behavior, see Blog 3.1 Remembering the RAND Health Insurance Experiment.

Shopping for a lower price (indicated by the price of services within a diagnosis)

The last behavior a consumer might choose to manage costs is "shopping" for a lower price per service. Unlike the other two behaviors, this did not seem to occur in our study population. As seen in figure 7.5, those in the highest-deductible plans actually had a higher average price[‡] per service for these conditions. People in the highest-deductible plan paid a higher average price in 19 of the top 30 most costly conditions, and for services in over half of all conditions.

FIGURE 7.5   AVERAGE PRICE OF SERVICE BY DEDUCTIBLE AMOUNT

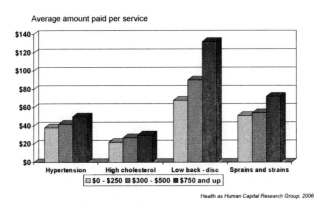

Average amount paid per service

$0 - $250 $300 - $500 $750 and up

Health as Human Capital Research Group, 2006

Thus we cannot verify any evident consumer "shopping" based on lower price. And it appears that for some conditions the reverse actually occurs. Consumers seem to either select more expensive services, or avoid some of the less expensive ones. Given that our patterns for incidence and frequency of services suggest that the high-deductible group is healthier, it is difficult to conclude that the same individuals require more expensive care. Rather, it seems more plausible, that some of the lower cost services are being avoided.

Realistically, because most prices are "fixed" by contracting in the medical system, consumers may not have the option to truly "shop" for lower prices.

---

‡ Price here is the combined amount paid by the patient and the insurer for a service.

What do these findings imply? That when patients spend their own money, they choose services more carefully. But they appear to manage cost by "voting with their feet." In other words, they manage cost by choosing a specific plan, or the type and number of services, not necessarily by choosing lower-priced services.

This is quite different from other consumer markets where price shopping is common, as with cars or electronics, which leaves us to wonder what type of information and plan design will be necessary to introduce price considerations into patient decision making.

January 20, 2006

Blog 7.7   Statistics help, but only you can decide if the odds are worth it

There's been much in the news confirming that virtually no medical treatment or drug comes without risk. A few that caught our attention:

1) A study reports that children who take Ritalin for Attention Deficit Hyperactivity Disorder (ADHD) will not grow as quickly as other children, averaging a height one inch shorter than similar children not taking the medication.[1]

2) Amid controversy, a review panel recommended to the Food and Drug Administration (FDA) to keep a diabetes drug on the market even though it increases the rate of heart disease. Their reviewers believed that in some cases the benefits may outweigh the risk.[2]

3) Reviewers for the FDA recommended against U.S. release of a new medication to target obesity and cardiometabolic syndrome because of increased risk of mood changes, including depression. The same medication is available in a number of European countries.[3]

In each case above, scientists are working hard to quantify risk, but only the consumers involved will be able to decide what is best for them.

Take an aggressive form of chemotherapy used to fight cancer, which also produces significant side effects (nausea, hair loss, confusion, nerve damage). For a given type and stage of cancer, scientific studies can estimate the increased likelihood of remission and survival due to chemotherapy. The same studies often report the likelihood of uncomfortable or serious side effects. Depending on one's assessment of value and cost of treatment, the same statistics may lead to different decisions. One oncologist I spoke with said she has had patients choose to undergo lengthy, difficult chemotherapy treatments based on statistics showing a 3% improvement in survival rate, and others who decided chemotherapy was not worth pursuing despite a predicted 50% improvement in survival rate. The same treatment carried a different value for each patient.

Opinions vary about whether there should be more oversight of the drug approval process, and who should take responsibility for deciding if a treatment has *too* much risk to allow it on the market. Does potential harm outweigh potential benefit for everyone, or just some? If a product is someone's last chance at treatment, can the individual decide to take the risk, or should a regulatory agency protect him from it? Who should decide what constitutes enough risk or enough benefit? And if the FDA does approve a product, should consumers presume it has low risk and high benefit for everyone? Furthermore, how does an agency possibly test for potentially harmful effects of all possible medication and treatment combinations for people with multiple medical conditions and medications?

Figure 7.6 shows data from our large, multi-employer database illustrating the likelihood of a medical "misadventure," as they are called.* We used the same list of codes defined by an expert panel[4] and measured whether a person had experienced a harmful reaction to medication or a mistake during a procedure. As we see, the more unique medications that a

---

* The analysis shown here is based on a single year of data for over 50,000 individuals. The "misadventures" were defined according to a published list (see note 4), which includes both serious and minor problems due to medical treatment. According to our statistical analysis, the likelihood of adverse effects accelerates at about 10 or 11 medications. Once people reach 28 medications, they are almost certain to have had at least one treatment-produced problem.

person has taken in the past 12 months, the more likely it is that something goes wrong. Someone taking 12 different medications in a year, which is more common than one might think, has a one in three chance of an adverse medical event.

FIGURE 7.6   *LIKELIHOOD OF AN ADVERSE MEDICAL EVENT BY NUMBER OF MEDICATIONS*

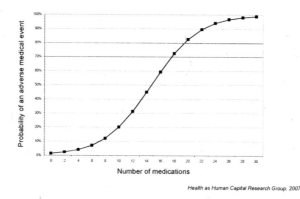

Health as Human Capital Research Group, 2007

In our opinion, because no treatment is completely risk-free, and because each person assesses value differently, consumers need to be at the helm when it's time to decide. Only the individual and his or her family and caregivers can make a decision about net value. What consumers need is assurance of high-quality, objective information with which to make informed decisions. Further, they need qualified, independent professionals committed to helping each person make the best decision for their unique situation. As much as society might wish for (or expect) protection, we doubt that any agency can decide whether a treatment is "right" or completely safe in every case.

When the government, the scientists, the hospital, and medical manufacturers all finish making decisions without you, the potential misadventure will not be theirs; it will be yours. Perhaps the decision should be, too.

August 12, 2007

References

1 DeNoon, D.J. ADHD Drug Does Stunt Growth: After 3 Years on Ritalin, Kids Are Shorter, Lighter Than Peers, WebMD Medical News, July 20, 2007, http://www.webmd.com/add-adhd/news/10101/adhd-drug-does-stunt-growth (accessed August 8, 2007).

2 FDA Advisory Committees Vote to Keep Avandia Available, Wolters-Kluwer Health, August 1, 2007, http://factsandcomparisons.com/News/ArticlePage.aspx?id=7752 (accessed August 8, 2007).

3 Goldstein, S., Letzing, J. Sanofi-Aventis Shares Stumble on Drug's Rejection: Weight-loss Drug Acomplia Raises Too Many Risks, FDA Panel Finds, MarketWatch, June 14, 2007, http://www.marketwatch.com/news/story/sanofi-aventis-shares-drop-fda-panel/story.aspx?guid=%7B2E311C6B-D5EB-4EB4-9892-AF962C00703A%7D (accessed August 8, 2007).

4 Expert Panel for Classification of Adverse Event ICD-9-CM Codes. The 2002 report on the findings of rating the Utah/Missouri ICD-9-CM adverse event codes, March 25, 2002, http://health.utah.gov/psi/pubs/Expertpanel.pdf (accessed August 12, 2007).

Chapter 8
Employment is a Human Capital Marketplace

Although most employees may not recognize it, every job is a dynamic, perpetual business transaction. Employees exchange valuable resources that they own for rewards from their employers. Those resources consist of personal human capital. Individuals can influence their human capital value in three ways: gaining skills and expertise, improving attitude and motivation, and maintaining good health.

The first five principles that have guided our analysis and discussion are:

1) Your own time and money matter more to you than someone else's;
2) Nothing is free—everything is a tradeoff;
3) What gets paid for gets done;
4) Incentives always exist, influencing the direction of behavior; and
5) Consumers make choices—whether we inform them or not.

These principles provide a framework for understanding why the typical employee-employer relationship is burdened by misaligned incentives that have unproductive consequences for both parties. A general lack of awareness about the human capital consequences of poor health, for the employer and the employee, has led to a widespread misconception that there is little career or earnings risk to becoming ill. And because most medical costs and all of salary are generally paid during a period of illness, there is little incentive to think proactively about health. Further, because employees do not connect higher costs for healthcare and paid absence with lower salaries, they do not realize the association between health and career.

Incentives (intentional or not) that eliminate any earnings risk for health-related lost time create an environment for increased moral hazard. While in the short term an individual may gain from the ability to be paid while not working, a lack of incentives for quick return to work and quick return to high performance inevitably harms both parties. The employee loses growth opportunities, and the employer loses work output.

Until employees and employers both understand how illness jeopardizes human capital and how current systems lead to competing objectives, efforts to add more medical—rather than economically rational—solutions are unlikely to improve the current cost situation.

Blog 8.1   Our people are our greatest asset...but no, we don't track their performance or attendance

A key element in the health as human capital paradigm is a clear employment contract. In this contract, an employer and an employee agree that a day's pay will be provided in return for a day's work. In a perfectly efficient employment market, each worker would be paid the value of his work, and would contribute work effort equivalent to his pay. However, in most organizations, employers pay people based generally on time at work—not based on productivity or output—with a set salary or an hourly rate.

The practice of paying people to "be there," rather than paying people by the amount of work they do, began in the industrial era. Factories needed a steady shift of workers on the assembly line and it became important to fill positions at all times. Also, in this new, complex, team-oriented type of production, it was difficult for employers to tell who actually did what—so a time-based contract made sense. This was different than traditional payment for each product produced or each service completed.

In today's workforce, there are exempt and non-exempt types of jobs.

By definition, non-exempt jobs are paid by the hour and employers almost always track work (or absence) by the hour for workers in these jobs. For exempt jobs, salary is based—at least theoretically—on responsibilities a worker agrees to achieve, rather than the exact time spent achieving them. (The label exempt, which covers numerous regulations, refers to a person not being eligible for overtime pay. Hence, one does what is necessary to get the job done.) Despite this official definition, in many white collar jobs, there is an implicit understanding that a person is expected to spend his work week engaged in work activities. If this was not the case, there would not be designated allotments of holidays, vacation days, and sick days. Thus, while some may argue that not *all* salaried workers are actually being paid based on time, in a great majority of white collar jobs, time is probably the best proxy we have as a measurement of "working."

It is ironic, given that time is the unit exchanged for pay in most settings, that most companies do a poor job of tracking time at work and time away from work for salaried workers. According to a 2004 survey, only one-third of companies track absences formally, and only 20 percent calculate the cost of lost time.[1] From 2005 to 2006, the estimated rate of unscheduled absence nationally increased from 2.3% to 2.5% of all workers on any given day, and two-thirds of those absences were for reasons other than personal illness. In 2005, absence costs were estimated at $660 per employee per year, or $55 per month.[2]

Anecdotally, it seems that we have a cultural distaste for monitoring salaried workers. I spoke with the human resources director of a small company recently who was reluctant to implement an absence and vacation tracking system. She said, "We have been running on the honor system and we're afraid that employees will think we don't trust them." Yet, the same company is quite worried about the cost of healthcare premiums, travel expenses, and overhead. It is not uncommon for companies to track their equipment carefully and require receipts for small travel expenses, yet not know if a highly paid employee is actually working that day.

While we understand the morale (distrust) argument, our experience has been that there is also a morale risk when responsible and dependable workers see a few workers abusing a poorly monitored system. Rather than rewarding positive worker behavior, it creates a culture where good workers are not appreciated and frequent absence (by a few) is tolerated.

Other companies insist that although absenteeism is not tracked in a centralized system, it is monitored at the manager level. In other words, there is no overall knowledge of absence patterns across the workforce, but a belief that if there *were* a problem, individual managers would handle those specific instances. Yet without data, a company has no way to assess whether that assumption is true.

From a human capital perspective, if a company is exchanging a day's pay for a day's work, it is important to know if workers are engaged in the tasks for which they are being paid. Far from distrustful, this is simply part of the business arrangement. The vast majority of compensation is pay. Presumably, pay reflects the approximate value a worker brings to the employer. Ideally, one could be paid for work output or achievement of performance goals. Because work performance can be difficult to measure for some jobs, it is understandable that employers may not be able to base pay solely on performance. However, effective engagement in work often requires a worker's presence and that presence is straightforward to measure.

Another reason to measure absence is its distribution. Similar to medical costs, absences are skewed. As an example, figure 8.1 shows typical absence days in a population whose annual average is five days per employee. Four percent of employees are using over 50% of all illness

FIGURE 8.1   A SAMPLE DISTRIBUTION OF ILLNESS ABSENCES

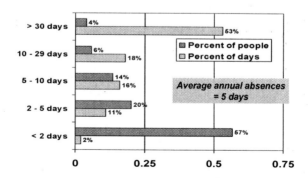

Health as Human Capital Research Group, 2006

absence days. Conversely, the lowest 77% of employees are generating fewer than 15% of all absence days. Knowing more about what factors are contributing to the high-absence group could be quite valuable. A week of absence is about 2% to 3% of annual time which, for moderate- to highly-paid workers, can amount to thousands of dollars in salary paid for time where no services could have been rendered. The value of lost time may be even higher if the worker is part of a team or involved in a sequential production process.

Figure 8.2 below is an illustration of total compensation. In this population, the average salary was about $40,000 and accounted for over three-quarters of compensation. Medical care costs accounted for about 10% of compensation. Even when we examine subsets of low-paid workers (under $20,000), medical care (in terms of actual amount spent for medical services) for employees and families accounts for no more than 25% of all compensation, on average. In either case, salary is the bulk of compensation. If we think of salary and bonuses as the reward tied most directly to work performance, it warrants far greater energy and resources to track people and performance than medical benefits utilization.

FIGURE 8.2   A SAMPLE ILLUSTRATION OF TOTAL COMPENSATION

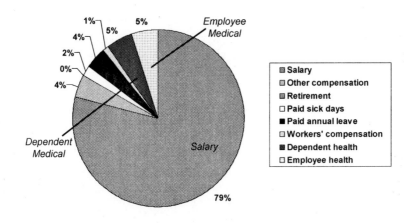

Health as Human Capital Research Group, 2006

Essentially, tracking presence is equivalent to tracking the activities for which 79% of compensation (salary) is intended.

One might assume that employers monitor those issues that are most important to their firm's viability. Our experience is that many employers invest significantly in tracking medical expenses. This suggests that for corporate America the amount of medical care an employee uses is more important than whether that employee is at work. From a human capital perspective, this is backwards. Applying the adage "you can't manage what you don't measure," we also see that employers have less consistent information about the patterns of performance and absence (which is the core of their business) than about what medical services employees use.

Our approach to an aligned incentive hierarchy for employers[3] would suggest tracking and rewarding performance first, presence second, health and safe practices third, and then thinking about other benefits utilization (including medical care). To make tracking more acceptable, consider providing cash-back for unused sick leave, or combining sick leave with vacation in a bank of days. We encourage organizations to think about their implicit and explicit measurement and management priorities.

December 17, 2006

References

1 Hewitt study shows companies underestimate cost of leaves of absence, July 29, 2004, http://www.hroaeurope.com/file/3294/hewitt-study-shows-companies-underestimate-cost-of-leaves-of-absence.html (accessed December 13, 2006).

2 Unscheduled absences rising at U.S. workplaces. CCH Absence Survey, October 25, 2006, http://hr.cch.com/news/hrm/102506a.asp (accessed December 13, 2006).

3 Lynch, W.D., Gardner, H.H., Health as Human Capital Research Group. A Hierarchy of aligned incentives: Health in the context of broader human capital enhancement. September 2006, http://www.hhcfoundation.org/hhcf/pdf/hierarchy_paper.pdf (accessed December 13, 2006).

Blog 8.2   Employee health problems are not the greatest threat to worker productivity

At a recent talk, I asked the audience a question: "True or false, employee health problems are the number one cause of lost productivity?" The vast majority answered "true." **Where did they get this impression? And is it correct?**

The past six years of productivity research have emphasized the impact of health problems (see references 3-12). Numerous studies have quantified the effects of health issues on worker productivity. Across most workforces, health problems produce significant decreases in productivity. Comparing the effects of different diseases, researchers find that chronic conditions—especially those that produce noticeable discomfort (pain, fatigue, trouble concentrating) and affect a significant number of people— tend to generate a significant amount of lost work time. We all know that any illness—even the common cold—will make a person less productive when they don't feel well.

What we rarely discuss is the relative importance of health problems among many issues facing a worker each day. Is it the primary issue affecting productivity? Is it even among the top three? Or is it a symptom of larger and in fact, more controllable organizational issues?

To answer these questions, we included a familiar productivity question in our recent health as human capital survey.[1] We asked over 1,800 workers with different jobs and different employers across the country about the factors interfering with their ability to be productive.

FIGURE 8.3   WHAT INTERFERES WITH PRODUCTIVITY?
PERSONAL HEALTH PROBLEMS

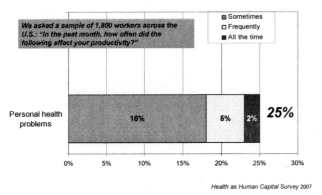

Consistent with other research, health interfered with productivity. Twenty-five percent of employees reported that personal health problems made them less productive sometimes, frequently, or all the time.

However, respondents reported that other factors affected productivity more often. Overall, respondents reported health problems affecting their productivity less frequently than most other work issues.

As seen in figure 8.4, the most frequent issues were low motivation, low morale among their co-workers, and poor communication. Inadequate training was reported more frequently than health problems as well.

*FIGURE 8.4   WHAT INTERFERES WITH PRODUCTIVITY?
LOW MOTIVATION*

Health as Human Capital Survey 2007

It's not that health is unimportant (as we all know from our own experiences of illness), but, when we look at health in isolation of other factors in the work environment, it often leaves us with the impression that health problems are the predominant problem for a workforce. *They are not.* One of my colleagues put it this way:

> *Think about your favorite sports team—or better yet, think back to a time when you may have played on a team. It goes without saying that it is best if all a team's players are healthy enough to compete, but as a goal, perfect health pales in comparison to having talented players who are well-coached, know how to play together and have a desire to win. In fact, nowhere is the impact of motivation and the desire to win/perform more visible than in sports, but this effect is also alive and well in business, as suggested by these survey results.*

In our special report, "Human Capital Motivation and Productivity,"[2] we discuss the factors that most strongly predicted motivation problems.

Among the strongest predictors of high motivation was the size of bonus a worker is eligible for (relative to a person's salary) as well as the perception that workers are recognized and rewarded for good work.

As decision makers think about workforce health, solutions must be addressed in the context of the overall work environment. Offering health management solutions in a context where employees do not feel rewarded may not be sufficient to overcome the dramatic effect of morale demonstrated here. In the big picture, business is about exchanging human capital for pay and rewards. If this exchange is poorly designed, so that workers do not have incentive to excel, health investments have little chance of being effective. People naturally seek value where it is available. If I am rewarded most for being at work and productive, I will respond to those incentives. If my compensation favors health benefits over bonuses, I will respond by seeking value in those benefits.

So in the end, if higher productivity is the goal, perhaps valuing the achievements of the person is the best medicine of all.

May 20, 2007

References

1 Lynch, W.D., Gardner, H.H., Melkonian, A., Kleinman, N.L. Understanding relationships between employee productivity, compensation, job satisfaction, and health: Results from the health as human capital survey 2007. Health as Human Capital Foundation; May 2007, (http://www.hhcfoundation.org/hhcf/pdf/SummaryReport.pdf (accessed May 18, 2007).

2 Lynch, W.D., Gardner, H.H., Melkonian, A., Kleinman, N.L. Human capital, motivation, and productivity: Brief report from the health as human capital survey 2007. Health as Human Capital Foundation, May 2007, http://www.hhcfoundation.org/hhcf/pdf/Brief1.pdf (accessed May 18, 2007).

3 Burton, W.N., Chen, C.Y., Conti, D.J., Schultz, A.B., Pransky, G., Edington, D.W The association of health risks with on-the-job productivity. *J Occup Environ Med* 2005;47(8):769-77.

4 Burton, W.N., Conti, D.J., Chen, C.Y., Schultz, A.B., Edington, D.W. The impact of allergies and allergy treatment on worker productivity. *J Occup Environ Med* 2001;43(1):64-71.

5 Burton, W.N., Conti, D.J., Chen, C.Y., Schultz, A.B., Edington, D.W. The economic burden of lost productivity due to migraine headache: a specific worksite analysis. *J Occup Environ Med* 2002;44(6):523-9.

6 Burton, W.N., Pransky, G., Conti, D.J., Chen, C.Y., Edington, D.W. The association of medical conditions and presenteeism. *J Occup Environ Med* 2004;46(6 Suppl):S38-45.

211

7 Goetzel, R.Z., Hawkins, K., Ozminkowski, R.J., Wang, S. The health and productivity cost burden of the "top 10" physical and mental health conditions affecting six large U.S employers in 1999 *J Occup Environ Med* 2003;45(1):5-14.

8 Goetzel, R.Z., Long, S.R., Ozminkowski, R.J., Hawkins, K., Wang, S., Lynch, W. Health, absence, disability, and presenteeism cost estimates of certain physical and mental health conditions affecting U.S employers. *J Occup Environ Med* 2004;46(4):398-412.

9 Kessler, R.C., Ames, M., Hymel, P.A., et al: Using the world health organization health and work performance questionnaire (hpq) to evaluate the indirect workplace costs of illness. *J Occup Environ Med* 2004;46(6 Suppl):S23-37.

10 Kessler, R.C., Greenberg, P.E., Mickelson, K.D., Meneades, L.M., Wang, P.S. The effects of chronic medical conditions on work loss and work cutback. *J Occup Environ Med* 2001;43(3):218-25.

11 Lerner, D., Adler, D.A., Chang, H., et al. The clinical and occupational correlates of work productivity loss among employed patients with depression. *J Occup Environ Med* 2004;46(6 Suppl):S46-55.

12 Wang, P.S., Beck, A.L., Berglund, P., et al. Effects of major depression on moment-in-time work performance. *Am J Psychiatry* 2004;161(10):1885-91.

Blog 8.3   PTO banks and health savings accounts—small steps toward shared economic incentives

Our health as human capital philosophy focuses on aligning economic incentives in ways that reward employees for high performance, good health, and attendance at work.

By implementing a balance of *shared economic rewards and responsibilities*, companies and employees have the same goals: be productive and stay healthy. This means an ideal work environment that offers meaningful, performance-based bonuses, as well as benefits that share economic responsibility for the positive and negative consequences of personal health.

What do we mean by *shared* rewards and responsibilities? It means that a person *gains* something by *not* using the benefit and *gives up* something when they use the benefit.

It is not surprising that employers report that the two most effective absence management strategies are: paid-time-off banks (where all days, sick leave and vacation, are in one pool to be used as the employee chooses), and absence buy-back programs (getting cash at the end of the year for unused sick days). As shown by figure 8.5 below, these approaches lead employers' perceptions of effectiveness.[1]

FIGURE 8.5 EFFECTIVENESS OF ABSENCE CONTROL PROGRAMS, 2006 RATINGS

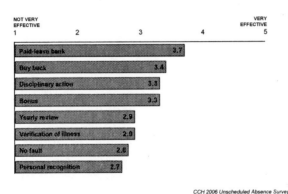

CCH 2006 Unscheduled Absence Survey

PTO banks share the "cost" of absence by asking employees to trade-in (give up) possible vacation time when they use a sick day. Sick-leave buy-back programs provide a small *gain* for those who stay healthy.

These policies align incentives with attendance and good health, instead of forcing employees to either leave value on the table (not using the allowed sick time) or to use it whether they need it or not. Too many of our policies have evolved in ways that create perverse incentives *to not work* in order to get full value of benefits.

The same effect applies to health savings accounts (HSAs)

The HSA is more than a cost-shifting fad that some believe.[2] It is a strong tool in aligning economic incentives. Like PTO banks and absence buy-back, an HSA is an employee-owned asset that rewards good health and shares responsibility for health issues. Over time, the individual *gains* significant financial equity by staying healthy. And he sacrifices some of that personal money when he uses care.

Like use-it-or-lose-it sick leave, in a traditional, employer-sponsored health plan the only way to get value is to *use* health services. Only the HSA offers a meaningful economic reward for remaining healthy. Even the health reimbursement arrangement (HRA, a similar account, but one that is only available while the employee remains at the same company), falls short of a meaningful reward for most employees who will switch jobs.

According to a new Mercer report, employers are offering consumer-directed health plans (CDHPs) at an increasing rate.[3] By the end of 2008, 43% of large employers will offer either an HSA or a HRA account. More impressive, 11% of small employers will offer one or both types of CDHP plans, up from only 5% in 2006. Other estimates indicate a rate of 10% overall.[4] This growth is accompanied by what Mercer describes as "evidence that these plans are cost effective." Seen here in figure 8.6, the cost for those in an HSA plan are the lowest.

FIGURE 8.6 HSAs vs. HRAs vs. high-deductible PPOs

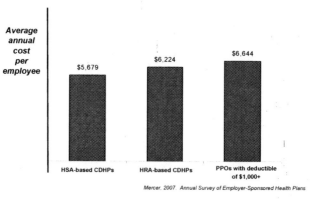

Mercer, 2007. Annual Survey of Employer-Sponsored Health Plans

The industry needs more concrete before-and-after evidence to understand the precise effects of HSAs, but economic theory would predict just what this graph shows: when consumers share in both gains and losses, they pay more attention to price and quality.

While growth in HSA accounts is dramatic (almost doubling in two years), the overall number of employers offering them remains small. However, almost 70% of large employers report that they believe CDHP plans are somewhat or very effective in containing costs.[5]

214

Why not quicker adoption?

Although anecdotal,[6] the Mercer report suggests that employers fear implementing HSA accounts because—since it represents a significant departure from the "norm"—it may harm their ability to attract and retain talent. Employees, especially those in large companies, have become accustomed to sharing little responsibility for healthcare and absence costs. Additionally, some employers maintain a paternal/maternal culture, insisting that the company must (over-) protect its "family" from the potential of (any) loss.

Our opinion is that an ideal employment contract is a mutually-beneficial business agreement. A team, perhaps, but not a pseudo-family. Unless individuals share at least some economic rewards and responsibilities for work performance and health, these outcomes hold less personal importance. The result does not harm employees; it simply requires them to make a personal tradeoff (vacation for sick time, additional savings for healthcare) when they spend "team" resources.

However, it is helpful for Americans to remember that our country did not determine that employers should provide paid time-off and health insurance because it was a proven, logical system. It all happened in the 1940s in response to wartime labor price and wage controls; employers decided to substitute benefits for wages temporarily during WWII. The move was intentional—but its purpose was to solve a labor problem, not to create a better system of healthcare. The trend continued after the 1940s because employees now expected insurance and paid time-off in their compensation packages. Now, such benefits are the norm, and their drain on companies and workers continues to grow. So much so that recent news suggests many American businesses support ending all employer-sponsorship of healthcare.[7]

While employees may not like the trend toward shared responsibility—who does?—it is a necessary step in taming healthcare and absence costs in a way that encourages good performance and good health. We believe that employees would prefer to share responsibility if it is in their best interest to do so, and that only occurs when they have proper incentives.

December 2, 2007

References

1 CCH. 2006 CCH unscheduled absence survey. Effectiveness of absence control programs. October 26, 2006, http://www.cch.com/absenteeism2006/Images/UseEffAbsControl.asp (accessed November 27, 2007).

2 Wojcik, J. Critics give grim prognosis for consumer-driven health plans. *Workforce Management,* October 24, 2007, http://www.workforce.com/section/00/article/25/18/53.html (accessed November 27, 2007).

3 Mercer. U.S. employers' health benefit cost continues to rise at twice inflation rate, Mercer survey finds. November 19, 2007, http://www.mercer.com/referencecontent.jhtml?idContent=1287790 (accessed November 27, 2007).

4 Henry J. Kaiser Family Foundation, Health Research and Education Trust. Survey of employer health benefits 2007. September 11, 2007, http://www.kff.org/insurance/7672/upload/7693.pdf (accessed November 27, 2007).

5 Kaiser Family Foundation.

6 Mercer.

7 Smerd, J. Business group seeks end to employer-based health coverage. *Workforce Management,* November 13, 2007, http://www.workforce.com/section/00/article/25/21/84.html (accessed November 27, 2007).

Blog 8.4   Job performance and voluntary turnover: who leaves, the best or the worst?

What does the performance of a population of workers look like? Which ones are more likely to stay? Which ones will leave? This entry is the first of two summarizing an interesting study from the *Journal of Applied Psychology.*[1] Researchers studied about 5,000 employees from a single company over a five-year period (starting on the date they were hired), looking at voluntary turnover rates, performance ratings, and other factors. In figure 8.7, we see average performance ratings during the employees' employment. As one would expect, most workers fall in the middle range of 2 to 3.5 out of 5. Very few employees performed poorly enough to consistently get a rating of one, or well enough to receive a perfect score of five.

FIGURE 8.7   JOB PERFORMANCE DISTRIBUTION

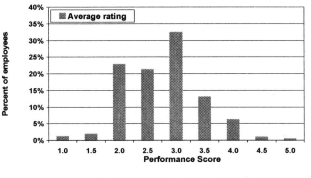

Trevor, C.O., Gerhart, B., Boudreau, J.W. *Journal of Applied Psychol* 1997;82(1) 44-61

In the health as human capital approach, we consider employment to be a voluntary contract entered in the job market. In this market, workers exchange their human capital services for compensation (including pay, benefits, training, and other opportunities). If the market is efficient,* we expect workers and employers to enter and leave employment relationships based on both parties' assessment of how well their arrangement is working. If workers think they are getting fair compensation for their efforts, they will be more likely to stay. If employers feel they are not receiving sufficient value for their investment, the employee is more likely to be terminated.

From the standpoint of voluntary turnover, one can imagine a variety of performance factors influencing a worker's decision to leave a job. Perhaps the worker knows he is not performing well and feels pressure to go elsewhere. Perhaps the worker feels he is being evaluated unfairly and seeks a better deal elsewhere. Traditional thinking has been that the lowest performers are more likely to leave. In fact, meta-analyses have found moderate, but significant, linear correlations showing that as performance increases, turnover rates decrease on average. And the study reviewed here found a linear correlation of -0.20 between performance and turnover.

---

* Markets are usually efficient when workers and firms are free to enter into contracts (mobility of labor and capital) and both sides are well-informed of the employment environment (employers identify people who can do the job and workers know what is expected of them).

Actually, however, the relationship is not strictly linear.

As we see in figure 8.8, the relationship is strongly curvilinear (which just means curved or U-shaped). While three-quarters of workers in the middle performance range remain employed after five years, only 24% of the lowest performers and 20% of the highest performers remain employed. Although the numbers are small in the tails, this company lost 80% of its best workers, but kept 75% of its average workers.

FIGURE 8.8   JOB PERFORMANCE AND VOLUNTARY TURNOVER

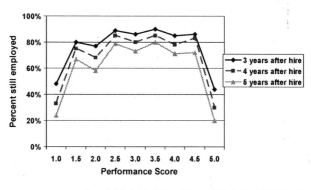

Trevor, C.O., Gerhart, B., Boudreau, J.W. *Journal of Applied Psychol* 1997;82(1) 44-61.

From a market perspective, both the worst and best performers took their human capital and decided to exchange it elsewhere—although probably for different reasons. Because salary guidelines often have inflexible rules (e.g., salary bands for certain jobs), we can expect that the extremes have the biggest discrepancy between their pay and the value they provide. The highest performers are underpaid and look for opportunities elsewhere. The lowest performers are overpaid—in the eyes of the employer—and get pressure to leave. In the middle, both worker and employer are more likely to think that the exchange of compensation for value is satisfactory. Who leaves? The best *and* the worst. Who stays? Those in the middle.

In the next blog entry[†] we will talk about how different types of rewards and incentives altered the patterns of voluntary turnover that this group experienced overall.

---

† See Blog 8.5 A study of what makes high performers stay.

May 1, 2006

References

    1 Trevor, C.O., Gerhart, B., Boudreau, J.W. Voluntary turnover and job performance: curvilinearity and the moderating influences of salary growth and promotions. *J Appl Psychol* 1997;82(1):44-61.

Blog 8.5   A study of what makes high performers stay

In the last entry,* we saw a study documenting that the highest and lowest performers were far more likely to leave a job than mid-level performers. In this entry, we ask the question, what might make high performers stay?

Employment studies remind us that turnover is a complex phenomenon that cannot be explained with one or two variables. For example, turnover decreases when job satisfaction is high. Job satisfaction results from many general and personal factors that include promotion opportunities, work environment, social connections, compensation, and others. Turnover also decreases when there is uncertainty or scarcity of other opportunities in the job market; workers having fewer (real or perceived) options do not leave as readily. In summary, from job to job, and person to person, different circumstances will contribute to the likelihood of leaving a job. One study does not provide the whole picture. However, some can be quite illuminating—like the one reviewed here.

We return to the study of 5,000 workers in the petroleum industry.[1] The authors documented salary increases and promotions to see how these events affected workers' likelihood of leaving. Although these events (promotions and salary growth) are correlated (0.66), they do not always happen in the same frequency and magnitude. Similarly (related to inflexible salary rules mentioned in the last blog), performance was only moderately related to salary growth (0.30) and hardly related to

---

*   See Blog 8.4 Job performance and voluntary turnover: Who leaves, the best or the worst?

promotions (0.06). By knowing all of these variables simultaneously, the research could examine the effects of one factor, while controlling for the others.

The authors hypothesized that promotions matter most to lowest performers (who need something on their resume for the next job) and salary matters most to the highest performers (whom they called franchise players), because there are more opportunities for them outside the firm. Considering the likelihood of inflexible and imperfect determinations of salary level in the system, this makes sense. If the highest performers are generally underpaid by a rigid system, then they will be most sensitive to adjustments in salary. If the lowest performers are generally overpaid, they will be less sensitive to salary and more sensitive to promotions.

Figure 8.9 shows how promotions affected turnover—comparing rates of turnover depending on the number of promotions employees received per year of employment. As we see, a high promotion rate[†] had the strongest effect on the worst performers (where those with most frequent promotions had a 90% departure rate compared to a departure rate of 45% for those having the least promotions). In essence, the promotions accelerated the departure of the poor performing workers. However, high performers did not respond to promotions.

FIGURE 8.9   EFFECTS OF PROMOTIONS ON TURNOVER

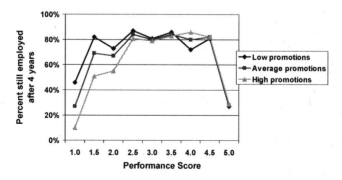

Trevor, C.O., Gerhart, B., Boudreau, J.W. *Journal of Applied Psychol* 1997;82(1) 44-61.

---

† See Blog 8.4 Job performance and voluntary turnover: Who leaves, the best or the worst?

In figure 8.10, we see the effect of salary increases (defined as the dollar difference from first to last salary divided by time employed)‡ on voluntary turnover. The effect on the highest performers is dramatic. Over 90% of the highest performers were still employed after four years if they experienced high salary growth. Only 40% of those experiencing average salary growth, and none of those experiencing low salary growth, were still employed after four years.

FIGURE 8.10 MITIGATING TURNOVER WITH SALARY GROWTH

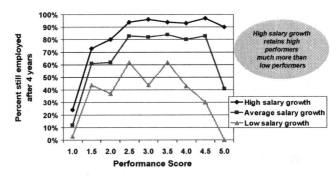

Trevor, C.O., Gerhart, B., Boudreau, J.W. *Journal of Applied Psychol* 1997;82(1) 44-61.

This is one of the more comprehensive illustrations of the employment contract as a dynamic exchange of human capital services for rewards. As a whole, the market behaves rationally. Workers expect fair compensation for their effort and, given opportunity to "sell" their human capital services in the market, will maximize opportunities to get a better price.

May 14, 2006

References
1 Trevor, C.O., Gerhart, B., Boudreau, J.W. Voluntary turnover and job performance: curvilinearity and the moderating influences of salary growth and promotions. *J Appl Psychol* 1997;82(1):44-61.

---

‡ For those interested in details, salary growth and promotion rates were defined as follows. Average annual salary growth while the person was employed was 9.8%, and high and low salary growth were set at one standard deviation above and below the mean. The average promotion rate was 0.41 promotions per year employed. A low promotion rate was defined as no promotions while employed and a high promotion rate was 0.96 promotions per year (one standard deviation above the mean), or more.

Implications

Incentives drive behavior. Aligned incentives lead to shared goals for success. Misaligned incentives lead to conflicting or incongruent efforts. The principles in this book describe many instances of misaligned incentives: paying doctors for transactions rather than results, paying workers as much for being absent as for being present, increasing the price of essential medications that reduce hospitalizations, and paying employees to show up rather than for what they accomplish.

Understanding these underlying incentives will help guide future policy and financing decisions. Wherever possible, effective human capital management results from sharing rewards and sharing consequences for performance and health status. The goal is to align rewards and consequences among employers, employees, and healthcare providers, so that there is mutual benefit from high achievement and good health.

Some implications revealed by this health as human capital paradigm conflict with traditional practices in healthcare and human resources management. Incentive alignment requires that organizations and individuals share the rewards of success. Yet, only about 50 percent of businesses award bonuses. Alignment also requires that organizations and individuals share (at least some) responsibility for loss and failure. Many modern social systems have evolved instead to provide near-full protection from negative events such as illness or poor corporate performance. Such extreme levels of protection, while well-intended, remove important shared incentives to excel in personal health and career success.

While general reactions to our blogs have been positive, we do hear criticisms from readers who believe that exposing individuals to any risk of loss is unfair and unkind. We respectfully disagree. Within an environment of aligned incentives, information, and choice, individuals are more likely to build and protect their own human capital assets (health, skills, and motivation). Furthermore, an environment of shared goals and rewards increases the potential for career growth and job satisfaction. When incentives are aligned between business goals and employee advancement, or between healthcare reimbursement and patient well-being, mutually beneficial results become more likely.

Index

The Health as Human Capital Foundation

www.hhcfoundation.org

Health as Human Capital is a concept, based on decades of research and evidence about what influences people to make specific choices about their livelihoods and lifestyles. The *health as human capital* approach relies heavily on economic principles that explain how and why people make choices regarding health and work. These economic principles guide the foundation's research and proposed solutions.

Our goal is to produce evidence and insights that lead to market solutions that apply to both the healthcare cost and quality problems in the U.S., and to employers' needs to efficiently recruit and retain valued employees.

The foundation conducts and disseminates research about the relationship of health to human capital. Foundation educators also deliver certified continuing education courses, available online at http://education. hhcfoundation.org.

Readers can find new blogs posted biweekly at www.hhcf.blogspot.com. Comments there are always welcomed.